The social logic of space

D1430495

The social logic
of space

BILL HILLIER

JULIENNE HANSON

Bartlett School of Architecture and Planning
University College London

CAMBRIDGE
UNIVERSITY PRESS

PUBLISHED BY THE PRESS SYNDICATE OF THE UNIVERSITY OF CAMBRIDGE
The Pitt Building, Trumpington Street, Cambridge, United Kingdom

CAMBRIDGE UNIVERSITY PRESS
The Edinburgh Building, Cambridge CB2 2RU, UK
40 West 20th Street, New York, NY 10011–4211, USA
477 Williamstown Road, Port Melbourne, VIC 3207, Australia
Ruiz de Alarcón 13, 28014 Madrid, Spain
Dock House, The Waterfront, Cape Town 8001, South Africa

http://www.cambridge.org

© Cambridge University Press 1984

First published 1984
First paperback edition 1988
Reprinted 1990, 1993, 1997, 2001, 2003

Printed in the United Kingdom at the University Press, Cambridge

Library of Congress catalogue card number: 83–15004

British Library Cataloguing in Publication data
Hillier, Bill
The social logic of space
1. Space (Architecture)-Social aspects
I. Title   II. Hanson, Julienne
729 NA2765

ISBN 0 521 23365 8 hard covers
ISBN 0 521 36784 0 paperback

Le fait humain par excellence est peut-être moins la création de l'outil que la domestication du temps et de l'espace, c'est-à-dire la création d'un temps et d'une espace humaine.

André Leroi-Gourhan: *La Geste et la Parole*

TO OUR STUDENTS

Contents

Preface

However much we may prefer to discuss architecture in terms of visual styles, its most far-reaching practical effects are not at the level of appearances at all, but at the level of *space*. By giving shape and form to our material world, architecture structures the system of space in which we live and move. In that it does so, it has a direct relation – rather than a merely symbolic one – to social life, since it provides the material preconditions for the patterns of movement, encounter and avoidance which are the material realisation – as well as sometimes the generator – of social relations. In this sense, architecture pervades our everyday experience far more than a preoccupation with its visual properties would suggest.

But however pervasive of everyday experience, the relation between space and social life is certainly very poorly understood. In fact for a long time it has been both a puzzle and a source of controversy in the social sciences. It seems as naive to believe that spatial organisation through architectural form can have a determinative effect on social relations as to believe that any such relation is entirely absent. Recent reviews of sociological research in the area (Michelson, 1976[1]) do not really resolve the matter. Some limited influences from such generalised spatial factors as density to social relations are conceded, subject to strong interaction with such sociological variables as family (p. 92), homogeneity (p. 192) and lifestyle (p. 94). But little is said about the ways in which strategic *architectural* decisions about built form and spatial organisation may have social consequences.

The puzzle is made more acute by the widespread belief that many modern environments are 'socially bad'. Again, there is a tendency to discuss these in terms of simple and general physical variables, such as building height. However, the inference that more fundamental spatial factors are involved is strongly supported by the failure of recent low-rise, high-density schemes to provide a convincing alternative following the débâcle of high-rise housing. Modern high- and low-rise housing have in common that they innovate fundamentally in spatial organisation, and both produce, in common it seems, lifeless and deserted environments.

It has become clear that a lack of understanding of the precise nature of the relation between spatial organisation and social life is the chief obstacle to better design.

The obvious place to seek such an understanding is in the disciplines that are concerned with the effect of social life on spatial organisation – how spatial organisation is in some sense a product of social structure. This has long been a central concern for geographers, but recently anthropologists (Lévi-Strauss, 1963; Bourdieu, 1973, 1977), theoretical sociologists (Giddens, 1981) and archeologists (Ucko et. al., 1972; Clarke, 1977; Renfrew, 1977; Hodder, 1978) have become aware of the spatial dimension in their subject, and its importance to questions of social morphology and structure.[2] This has created the early stages of a new interdisciplinary literature on the study of space and society.

The first result of this attention, however, has been to show how little effective theory and methodology there is in understanding the society–space relation, in spite of two decades or more of the 'quantitative revolution'. But while academic disciplines may simply deplore the lack of theory, for architects and planners the problem is a more pressing one, since as things stand there is no way that scientific theory of the society–space relation can either help to understand what has gone wrong with contemporary design or suggest new approaches.

The aim of this book is to reverse the assumption that knowledge must first be created in the academic disciplines before being used in the applied ones, by using architecture as a basis for building a new theory – and a new approach to theory – of the society–space relation. This is possible, we believe, because theories of the relation between society and its spatial form have encountered two fundamental difficulties. First, there is no consistent *descriptive* account of the morphological features of 'man-made' space that could be lawfully determined by social processes and structures. Second, there is no descriptive account of the morphological features of societies that could require one kind of spatial embodiment rather than another. The reason for this lack of progress is at root to do with the paradigm within which we conceptualise space which, even in its most progressive forms postulates a more or less abstract – certainly a-spatial – domain of society to be linked to another, purely physical domain of space. The paradigm in effect conceptualises space as being without social content and society without spatial content. Yet neither can be the case, if there are to be lawful relations between them.

The aim of *The Social Logic of Space* is to begin with architecture, and to outline a new theory and method for the investigation of the society–space relation which takes account of these underlying difficulties. First, it attempts to build a conceptual model within which the relation can be investigated on the basis of the social content of spatial patterning and the spatial content of social patterning. Second, it tries to establish, via a new definition of spatial order as restrictions on a random process, a method of analysis of spatial pattern, with emphasis on the relation between local morphological relations and global patterns. It establishes a fundamental descriptive theory of pattern types and then a method of analysis. These are applied first to settlements and then to building interiors in order to discover and quantify the presence of different local and global morphological features. On this basis, it establishes a descriptive theory of how spatial pattern can, and does, in itself carry social information and content.

The argument then turns to society, and extends the same morphological argument into the domain of social relations, by considering them as restrictions on random encounter patterns. From this naive spatial view of society, a theory is developed of how and why different forms of social reproduction require and find an embodiment in a different type of spatial order. This 'spatial logic of society' is applied first to some well-documented examples to establish the theory in outline, then is applied to try to give some account of the variability in spatial form in contemporary industrial societies.

The book is thus a statement of a new theory and sketch of new methods of spatial analysis. It should be emphasised, however, that a considerable number of studies have now been carried out at University College London using this framework, and it is intended that further volumes of case studies using the theory and method should follow *The Social Logic of Space* as soon as possible: these include the social logic of settlements, the social logic of housing, and the social logic of complex buildings.

Because it represents a new theoretical departure, however, *The Social Logic of Space* embeds itself only tangentially in the established frameworks and methods of the subject. Even fields of research that might appear, at first glance, to be close to our approach, turn out eventually to have limited relevance. For example, the 'pattern language' of Christopher Alexander and his colleagues at Berkeley (1977),[3] while appearing at first to be close to our notion of fundamental syntactic generators, is in fact quite remote, in intention as well as in its intrinsic nature. For our purposes, Alexander's notion of a pattern is too bound to the contingent properties of configurations to be useful for us; while at a more abstract level, his preoccupation with hierarchical forms of spatial arrangement (surprising in view of his earlier attack on hierarchical thinking in 'A city is not a tree' (1966)[4]) would hinder the formation of non-hierarchical, abstract notions of spatial relations which, in our view, are essential to giving a proper account of spatial organisation.

The more recent development of 'shape grammars' by Stiny and Gips (1978)[5] would again, at first sight, appear to be close to the notion of 'space syntax' as formulated in this book, the more so since 'shape grammars' are firmly concerned with the abstract generative principles of spatial patterns. But while conceding their superior mathematical refinement, we have found that shape grammars are in general too over-refined to model the untidy systems which are found in the real world of settlements and buildings. Our notion of 'syntactic generators' is insufficiently formalised for a full mathematical treatment, yet syntactic generators are right for the job that they are intended to do: capturing the formal dimensions of real-world spatial systems in terms of the social logic behind them. Syntactic generators are simpler than shape grammars. Moreover, they are shape free. We are convinced that it is unnecessary to specify shape in order to model real-world generative processes; indeed, that the concept of shape obscures the fundamental relational notions that underpin human spatial order. Moreover, with the limited role assigned to randomness in shape grammars – as opposed to the foundation of space syntax on the notion of randomness – we find that in their very foundations they tend to overdetermine the realities that we are trying to model.

At a more general level, we can properly be accused of ignoring the considerable development of mathematical methods of spatial analysis in quantitative geography. The reason for our lack of continuity with this work is more fundamental. To our way of thinking, two concepts underpin the geographic approach to formal spatial analysis (with the possible exception of the tradition from von Thunen (1826) to Christaller (1933) and Lösch (1954), which adds a geometric element into morphology): these are the notion of *distance*; and the notion of *location*.[6] It is crucial to our approach that neither of these concepts – in spite of their manifest usefulness for the purposes for which they have been applied – appears in the foundations of 'space syntax'. This is initially distance free, and for the concept of location is substituted the concept of morphology, by which we imply a concern with a whole set of simultaneously existing relations. It is in the analysis of the global properties of such complexes of relations that we believe that space syntax has a robust and demonstrable role, revealing aspects of structure which are obscured by conventional analyses.

We sincerely hope that in time this discontinuity between our work and more established lines will cease to exist as synthetic studies are carried out. But in the meantime the reader is asked to read the book as what it is intended to be: a statement of a wholly new theoretical approach, rather than a review of existing work – with all the weaknesses, as well as the advantages, that this can imply.

September 1982

Acknowledgements

This book was conceived in the mid-1970s in the later stages of my collaboration with Adrian Leaman. Some of the foundational concepts were elaborated first in a series of papers which we authored jointly in the early 1970s. The substantive theory set out in the book, and its associated methodologies, date, however, from my collaboration with my co-author, Julienne Hanson, which began in 1975. Since then, several people have made substantial and indispensable contributions to the development of both theory and method. The chief of these is Dr John Peponis, whose influence especially on the analytic chapters (3, 4 and 5) is too pervasive to be acknowledged in detail. The contribution of Paul Stansall during the early stages of the 'space syntax' research programme on which the book draws heavily, was also of key importance. The Science Research Council (now the Science and Engineering Research Council) must also be thanked for its sustained support of the 'space syntax' research programme over several years. This allowed us to turn abstract ideas into operational techniques of analysis.

Our debt must also be acknowledged to Paul Coates for his work in developing the computer software; to Mick Bedford, John Hudson and Richard Burdett for their contribution to the research programme; and to others who at various times worked in the research programme, especially Doug Smith, Justin de Syllas, Joss Boys and Chris Gill; to Janet Knight, Liz Jones, Nick Lee-Evans and David Thom for the graphic work; to William Davies, Pauline Leng, Carmen Mongillo and Jane Powles of Cambridge University Press; and to John Musgrove, Basil Bernstein, Phil Steadman. Tom Markus, Alan Beattie, Barrie Wilson, Dean Hawkes and Newton Watson, whose interest in and support of our work has been far more important than they realise.

Most of all, our thanks are due to the students of the MSc in Advanced Architectural Studies at the Bartlett and to MPhil and PhD students associated with its Unit for Architectural Studies, since without their prodigious and ingenious efforts, the constant testing of hypotheses on which progress in the research has depended, would not have been possible.

BILL HILLIER

Introduction

i

For the most part, the design of an artefact – whether it is a bridge, a cup or a surgical instrument – has a certain logic to it. First, *functional* objectives must be achieved: materials or elements must be assembled into a form which works for a well-defined purpose, or range of purposes. When this is done, a second dimension may be added: that of *style*. By this we mean that decoration, embellishments, or even modifications of shape, can give the artefact a significance over and above its practical uses, one belonging to the realm of cultural identity or 'meaning'. Sometimes, of course, it is difficult to tell which aspects of an artefact belong in which realm. But there is never any doubt that the artefact does belong to two realms. Invariably, artefacts are both functional and meaningful. Insofar as they are the first, they are of practical use; insofar as they are the second, they are of primarily *social* use, in that they become a means by which cultural identities are known and perpetuated.

At first sight, this simple scheme might seem to apply *par excellence* to that most omnipresent of artefacts, the building. Buildings are, after all, expected to function properly, and their appearance is often held to be such an important aspect of culture as to be a constant source of public controversy and debate. But it is not quite so simple. Buildings have a peculiar property that sets them apart from other artefacts and complicates the relation between usefulness and social meaning. It is this. Buildings may be comparable to other artefacts in that they assemble elements into a physical object with a certain form; but they are incomparable in that they also create and order the empty volumes of space resulting from that object into a pattern. It is this ordering of space that is the *purpose* of building, not the physical object itself. The physical object is the means to the end. In this sense, buildings are not what they seem. They appear to be physical artefacts, like any other, and to follow the same type of logic. But this is illusory. Insofar as they are purposeful, buildings are not just objects, but transformations of space through objects.

It is the fact of space that creates the special relation between

1

function and social meaning in buildings. The ordering of space in buildings is really about the ordering of relations between people. Because this is so, society enters into the very nature and form of buildings. They are social objects through their very form as objects. Architecture is not a 'social art' simply because buildings are important visual symbols of society, but also because, through the ways in which buildings, individually and collectively, create and order space, we are able to *recognise* society: that it exists and has a certain form.

These peculiarities of buildings as artefacts lead to a very special problem in trying to understand them, and even in trying to talk about them analytically. It is a fairly straightforward matter to talk about artefacts in general, because in so doing we are talking about objects, and the important properties of objects are visible and tangible. But in talking about buildings, we need not only to talk about objects, but also about systems of spatial relations.

Now it seems to be a characteristic of the human mind that it is extremely good at using relational systems – all languages and symbolic systems are at least complex relational systems – but rather bad at knowing how to talk about them. Relations, it seems, are what we think *with*, rather than what we think *of*. So it is with buildings. Their most fundamental properties – their ordering of space into relational systems embodying social purposes – are much easier to use and to take for granted than to talk about analytically. As a result, the discourse about architecture that is a necessary concomitant of the practice of architecture is afflicted with a kind of permanent disability: it is so difficult to talk about buildings in terms of what they really are socially, that it is eventually easier to talk about appearances and styles and to try to manufacture a socially relevant discourse out of these surface properties. This cannot be expected to succeed as a social discourse because it is not about the fundamental sociology of buildings.

At most times in the past, this disability might not have mattered. After all, if intuition reliably reads the social circumstances and reproduces them in desirable architectual form, then architecture can be a successful enterprise. But this is not the case today. Since the Second World War, our physical environment has probably been more radically altered than at any time since towns and cities began. By and large, this has been carried out on the basis of an architectural discourse which, for the first time, stresses explicit *social* objectives. Yet it is exactly in terms of its long-term social effects that the new urban environment has been most powerfully criticised. There is a widespread belief that we are faced with a problem of urban *pathology*, which results at least in part from the decisions of designers and the effects, for the most part unforeseen, of new building forms on the social organisation of space. In these circumstances an explicit discourse of architectural space and its social logic is an absolute requirement.

But in spite of its centrality in the act of creating architecture, and in its recent public pathology, the question of space has failed to become central in the academic and critical discourses that surround architecture. When space does feature in architectural criticism, it is usually at the level of the *surfaces* that define the space, rather than in terms of the space itself; when it is about space, it is usually at the level of the *individual* space rather than at the level of the system of spatial relations that constitute the building or settlement. As a result, a major disjunction has developed not only between the public pathology of architecture and the discourses internal to architecture, but also between the practical design and experience of buildings and these discourses. This disjunction is made worse by the persistence of an analytic practice conducted first through images, then through words; and neither images nor words responding to those images can go beyond the immediate and synchronous field of the observer into the asynchronous complex of relations, understood and experienced more than seen, which define the social nature of buildings and settlements. The rift has become complete as discourse tries to lead the way back into classicism – as though cosmetic artistry would cure the disease as well as beautify the corpse.

The architectural critic is, of course, handicapped by the representations of architecture with which he works. The only representative of spatial order in the armoury of the critic is the plan. But from the point of view of words and images, plans are both opaque and diffuse. They convey little to the image-seeking eye, are hard to analyse, and give little sense of the experiential reality of the building. They do not lend themselves easily to the art of reproducing in words the sentiments latent in images which so often seems the central skill of the architectural critic. Accordingly, the plan becomes secondary in architectural analysis. With its demise, those dimensions of the buildings that are not immediately co-present with the observer at the time that he formulates his comment are lost to discourse. In this way, architectural discourse conceals its central theme.

ii

In architecture space is a central *theoretical* discipline, and the problem is to find a way to study it. But the problem of space itself is not confined to architecture. In anthropology, for example, it exists as an *empirical* problem. The first-hand study of a large number of societies has left the anthropologist with a substantial body of evidence about architectural forms and spatial patterns,

which ought to be of considerable relevance to the development
of a theory of space. But the matter is far from simple. The body of
evidence displays a very puzzling distribution of similarities and
differences. If we take for example the six societies in Northern
Ghana whose architecture has been studied by Labelle Prussin, we
find that within a fairly restricted region with relatively small
variations in climate, topography and technology, there are very
wide variations in architectural and spatial form, from square-
celled buildings arranged in dense, almost town-like forms, to
circular-celled structures so dispersed as to scarcely form identifiable settlements at all.[1]

But no less puzzling than the differences within the same
ecological area are similarities which jump across time and space.
For example, villages composed of a concentrically arranged
collection of huts surrounding one or more central structures can
be found today as far apart as South America and Africa (see Figs.
30 and 133) and as far back in time as the fourth millennium BC in
the Ukraine.[2] Taking the body of evidence as a whole, therefore,
it seems impossible to follow the common practice when faced
with an individual case of assuming architectural and spatial form
to be only a *by-product* of some extraneous determinative factor,
such as climate, topography, technology or ecology. At the very
least, space seems to defy explanation in terms of simple external
causes.

Aware of these difficulties, certain 'structural' anthropologists
have suggested another approach. Lévi-Strauss for example, taking his lead from Durkheim and Mauss, saw in space the oppor-
tunity to 'study social and mental processes through objective and
crystallised external projections of them'.[3] A few anthropologists
have pursued this, and there now exists a small but growing
'anthropological' literature on space. However, as Lévi-Strauss
indicated in the same article, there are unexpected limitations to
this approach. Lévi-Strauss had already noted in reviewing the
evidence relating social structure to spatial configuration that
'among numerous peoples it would be extremely difficult to
discover any such relations . . . while among others (who must
therefore have something in common)the existence of relation is
evident, though unclear, and in a third group spatial configuration
seems to be almost a projective representation of the social
structure'.[4] A more extensive review can only serve to confirm this
profound difficulty and add another. Seen from a spatial point of
view, societies vary, it seems, not only in the *type* of physical
configuration, but also in the *degree* to which the ordering of space
appears as a conspicuous dimension of culture. Even these
difflerences can take two distinct forms. Some societies appear to
invest much more in the physical patterning of space than others,
while others have only seemingly informal and 'organic' patterns,
while others have clear global, even geometric forms; and some

societies built a good deal of social significance into spatial form by, for example, linking particular clans to particular locations, while others have recognisable spatial forms, but lack any obvious investment of social significance.

In studying space as an 'external projection' of 'social and mental processes' which by implication can be described prior to and independent of their spatial dimension, it is clear that structural anthropologists are therefore studying the problem of space neither as a whole nor in itself: the first because they are concerned chiefly with the limited number of cases where order in space can be identified as the imprint of the conceptual organisation of society within the spatial configuration; the second because they still see space as a by-product of something else whose existence is anterior to that of space and determinative of it. By clear implication this denies to space exactly that descriptive autonomy that structuralist anthropology has sought to impart to other pattern-forming dimensions of society – kinship systems, mythologies, and so on. Such studies can therefore contribute to the development of a theory of space, but they are too partisan to be its foundation.

The anthropological evidence does, however, allow us to specify certain requirements of a theory of space. First, it must establish for space a *descriptive autonomy*, in the sense that spatial patterns must be described and analysed in their own terms prior to any assumption of a determinative subservience to other variables. We cannot know before we begin what will determine one spatial pattern or another, and we must therefore take care not to reduce space to being only a by-product of external causative agencies. Second, it must account for wide and fundamental variations in morphological type, from very closed to very open patterns, from hierarchical to non-hierarchical, from dispersed to compressed, and so on. Third, it must account for basic differences in the ways in which space fits into the rest of the social system. In some cases there is a great deal of order, in others rather little; in some cases a great deal of social 'meaning' seems to be invested in space, in others rather little. This means that we need a theory that within its descriptive basis is able to describe not only systems with fundamental morphological divergencies, but also systems which vary from non-order to order, and from non-meaning to meaning.

iii

Several attempts have been made in recent years to develop theory and method directly concerned with the relation between society and its architectural and urban forms. Before going on to give a brief account of the theory and method set out in this book, some review of these is needed, if for no other reason than because

in our work we have not found it possible to build a great deal on
what has gone before. The general reason for this is that, although
these various lines of research approach the problem of space in a
way which allows research to be done and data to be gathered,
none defines the central problem in the way which we believe is
necessary if useful theories are to be developed. In spite of their
considerable divergencies from one another, all seem to fall into
certain underlying difficulties with the problem of space which
we can only describe as *paradigmatic*. The approach is defined
not out of the central problem of architecture itself, in the sense
that we have defined it, but out of a set of more philosophical
presuppositions about the nature of such problems in general.

By far the best known candidate for a theory which treats space
directly as a distinct kind of social reality, and the one that has
influenced architecture most, is the theory of 'territoriality'. This
theory exists in innumerable variants, but its central tenets are
clear: first, the organisation of space by human beings is said to
have originated in and can be accounted for by a universal,
biologically determined impulse in individuals to claim and
defend a clearly marked 'territory', from which others will be – at
least selectively – excluded; and, second, this principle can be
extended to all levels of human grouping (all significant human
collectives will claim and defend a territory in the same way that
an individual will). The theory proposes in effect that there will
always be a correspondence between socially identified groups
and spatial domains, and that the dynamics of spatial behaviour
will be concerned primarily with maintaining this correspondence. It asserts by implication that space can only have social
significance by virtue of being more or less unequivocally identified with a particular group of people. A whole approach to
urban pathology has grown up out of the alleged breakdown of
territorial principles in our towns and cities.[5]

An obvious trouble with territoriality theory is that, because its
assumption is of a universal drive, it cannot *in principle* account
for the evidence. If human beings behave in one spatial way
towards each other, then how can the theory be used to account
for the fundamental differences in physical configuration, let
alone the more difficult issues of the degree to which societies
order space and give significance to it? How, in brief, may we
explain a variable by a constant? But if we leave aside this logical
problem for a moment and consider the theory as a whole, then it
becomes a little more interesting. As we have said, the theory
leads us to expect that 'healthy' societies will have a hierarchically organised system of territories corresponding to socially defined groups. Now there are certainly cases where such a system
exists, and others where it exists alongside forms of group
organisation that lack a territorial dimension. But the extension of
this to the level of a general principle overlooks one of the most

fundamental distinctions made by anthropologists: the distinction between groups that have a spatial dimension through
co-residence or proximity, and groups whose very purpose
appears to be to cross-cut such spatial divisions and to integrate
individuals *across* space – 'sodalities' as some anthropologists call
them. It is in the latter, the non-spatial sodality, that many of the
common techniques for emphasising the identity of social
groups – insignia, ceremony, statuses, mythologies and so on –
find their strongest realisation, most probably for the obvious
reason that groups that lack spatial integration must use other,
more conceptual means if they are to cohere as groups. Now this
leads to a problematic yet interesting consequence for territoriality: social identification and spatial integration can often work in
contrary directions, not in correspondence as the theory requires.
It has even been suggested that sodality-like behaviour in social
groups varies inversely with spatial integration: the more dispersed the group, the more sodality-like the group becomes.[6] In
other words, territoriality appears to be not a universal group
behaviour but a limiting case, with the opposite type of case at
least as interesting and empirically important.

Territory theory, especially in its limitations, might be thought
of as an attempt to locate the origins of spatial order in the
individual biological subject. Other approaches might be seen as
trying to locate it in the individual cultural subject by developing
theories of a more cognitive kind. In such theories, what are at
issue are *models in individual minds* of what space is like:
models that condition and guide reaction to and behaviour in
space. If territoriality is a theory of fundamental similarity, these
cognitive theories tend to be theories of cultural, or even individual difference. The cognitive approach is less ambitious
theoretically, of course, because it does not aim to provide a
universal theory of space; rather it is concerned to provide a
methodology of investigating differences. Studies along these
lines are therefore extremely valuable in providing data on
differences in the ways in which individuals, and perhaps groups,
cognise their environment, but they do so on the whole in
response to an environment that is already given. The order that
is being sought lies in the mind and not in the physical environment itself, and certainly not in the social structuring of the
physical environment. Cognitive studies provide us, therefore,
with a useful method, but not with a theoretical starting point for
an enquiry into the *social logic of space* itself.

Other approaches to the problem are distinguishable as being
concerned initially with the environment as an object rather than
with the human subject, in the sense that the focus of research
shifts to the problem of describing the physical environment, and
its differences and similarities from one place or time to another,
as a prelude to an understanding of how this relates to patterns of

use and social activity. Of particular interest here is the work centred around the Massachusetts Institute of Technology and published in a recent volume, which brings together a range of studies with the central thematic aim of going beyond the more traditional classification approaches of geographers to urban morphology into an analysis of how differences in the organisation of architectural and urban space relate to and influence social life.[7] Once again this work has substantial relevance to the present work, but does not provide its starting point, since there is a fundamental difference in how the problem is conceptualised. The general aim of the MIT work is to describe environments and then relate them to use, whereas we conceive the problem as being that of first describing how environments acquire their form and order as a result of a social process. Our initial aim has been to show how order in space originates in social life, and therefore to pinpoint the ways in which society already pervades those patterns of space that need to be described and analysed. Only when this is understood is it possible to make a theoretical link to patterns of use.

Counterpointing the approach to an objective environment, in itself devoid of social content, is the approach of the architectural and urban semiologists who aim to describe the environment solely in terms of its power to operate as a system of signs and symbols. By developing models largely out of natural language studies, the object of these researches is to show how the physical environment can express social meanings by acting as a system of signs in much the same sort of way as natural language. In this sense, it is the study of the systematics of appearances. There is no doubt, of course, that buildings do express social meaning through their appearances, though no one has yet shown the degree to which we can expect this to be systematic. However, the reason that this line of work cannot provide our starting point is more fundamental: the semiologists for the most part are attempting to show how buildings represent society as signs and symbols, not how they help to constitute it through the way in which the configurations of buildings organise space. They are in effect dealing with social meaning as something which is added to the surface appearance of an object, rather than something that structures its very form; and in this sense the building is being treated as though it were no different from other artefacts. The semiologists do not in general try to deal with the special problems that buildings present in understanding their relation to society: they try to fit architecture into the general field of artefact semiotics.

In spite of considerable divergences, these approaches all seem to sidestep the central problem of buildings in the sense that we have described it: they do not first conceptualise buildings as carrying social determination through their very form as objects.

In fact, they characteristically proceed by separating out the problem in two ways: they separate out the problem of meaning from the intrinsic material nature of the artefact, that is, they treat it as an ordinary artefact rather than as a building; and they separate out a human subject from an environmental object and identify the problem as one of understanding a relation between human beings and their built environment. The effect of both shifts is the same. They move us from a problem definition in which a building is an object whose spatial form is a form of social ordering (with the implication that social ordering already has in itself a certain spatial logic to it), into one in which the physical environment has no social content and society has no spatial content, the former being reduced to mere inert material, the latter to mere abstraction. This we call the man–environment paradigm.[8]

An impossible problem is thus set up, one strongly reminiscent of the most ancient of the misconceived paradoxes of epistemology, that of finding a relation between abstract immaterial 'subjects' and a material world of 'objects'. By the assumption that what is to be sought is a relation between the 'social' subject (whether individual or group) and the 'spatial' object acting as distinct entities, space is desocialised at the same time as society is despatialised. This misrepresents the problem at a very deep level, since it makes unavailable the most fundamental fact of space: that through its ordering of space the man-made physical world is already a social behaviour. It constitutes (not merely represents) a form of order in itself: one which is created for social purposes, whether by design or accumulatively, and through which society is both constrained and recognisable. It must be the first task of theory to describe space as such a system.

iv

In view of the twin emphasis on spatial order and its social origins in defining the problem, it may come as a surprise that some early steps in formulating the present theoretical approach came from a purely formalistic consideration of randomness and its relation to form: or more precisely from some simple experiments in how restrictions on a random process of aggregating cells could lead to well-defined global patterns that bore some resemblance to patterns found in real buildings and settlements. For example, if an initial square cell is placed on a surface, then further squares of the same size are randomly aggregated by joining one full side of each onto a side already in the system, preserving one other side free (so that the cell could be entered from outside) and disallowing corner joins (as unrealistic – buildings are not joined by their corners), then the result will be the type of 'courtyard complex' shown in Fig. 2, with some courtyards larger than others. By varying the joining rules, other types of pattern would follow, in each case with a well-defined global form (that of a kind of net with unequal holes) following from the purely local rule (in the sense that the rule only specified how one object should join onto another) applied to the aggregation procedure. The differences between these patterns seemed to be architectually interesting in that some key differences between real spatial patterns appeared to be captured. More suprisingly, we discovered a settlement form that appeared to have exactly the global properties of the original experiment (Fig. 3).[9] This suggested to us that it might be interesting to try to see how far real global settlement forms might be generated from local rules. Having started on this path, we later realised that the courtyard complex form would not be tidily generated if one specified at the time of placing the cell which other side its entrance was to be on. It required this to be left open. In other words, our first experiment turned out to be unlifelike! Fortunately, by the time this was realised, we had some much more interesting results.

For a long time, we had been puzzled by the 'urban hamlets' of the Vaucluse region of France. Each hamlet seemed to have the same global form, in that each was organised around an irregular 'ring-street' (see Figs 6 and 8(a)–(d)) but at the same time the great variations in the way in which this was realized suggested that this had arisen not by conscious design but by some accumulative process. It turned out that these 'beady ring' forms – so-called because the wide and narrow spaces of the ring street seemed like beads on a string – could be generated from a process rather similar to the courtyard complex, by simply attaching a piece of open space to the entrance side of each cell, then aggregating with a rule that joined these open spaces one to another while randomising all other relations (see pp. 59–61 for a full description of this process). By varying the joining rules once again, other variations resulted, many of which appeared to duplicate variations found in this type of settlement form in different parts of the world.

There were several reasons why this seemed a promising development. First, it seemed that real problems in settlement generation might sometimes be solved through the notion of local rules leading to well-defined global forms. It raised the possibility that other settlement forms might be understood as the global product of different local rules. Second, and more important, it seemed that the nature of the process we had identified could be theoretically significant, in that structure had by implication been conceptualised in terms of restrictions on an otherwise random process. This meant that in principle it was possible to conceive of a model which included both non-order and order in its basic axioms. In effect, randomness was playing a part in the generation of form, and this seemed to capture an important aspect of how order in space can sometimes arise and be controlled in traditional settlement forms. Also by using the method of working out from an underlying random process, one could always keep a record of how much order had been put into the system to get a particular type of global pattern. This made possible a new question: given a real spatial pattern, say a settlement form, then in what ways and to what degree would it be necessary to restrict a random process in order to arrive at that form. If this proved a fertile approach to real settlement forms, then an even more interesting question could be asked: what was the nature of these restrictions, that is the 'rules', and how did they relate to each other? Were there a finite number, and did they in some sense form a system?

Of course, considering the range of cases available, it was clear that in many cases global forms could in no way be seen as the result of an aggregative process – for example where the global order resulted not from the local aggregation of individual cells, but by the superimposition on those cells of higher order, surrounding cells (see Fig. 16), in effect creating a hierarchy of boundaries. However, there was a fundamental difference when this occurred. If a single cell contained other cells, then the containing was accomplished through the inside of the superordinate cell; whereas the global patterns resulting from the beady ring type of process resulted from the cells defining space with their outsides. The difference is captured by the difference in the meaning of the words 'inside' and 'between'. Inside implies that one single cell is defining a space; between implies that more than one is defining space. This seemed a very general difference, relating to the different ways in which a random process could be restricted: in the one case cells were, as it were, 'glued' together by space which they defined between them; in the other cells were 'bound' together by having higher-order cells superimposed around them. Because the first always resulted in the global structure being defined only by virtue of the positioning of a collection of cells, we called it distributed, meaning that the 'design' of the global structure was distributed amongst all 'primary' cells; by the same token, we called the process of using the inside of a cell to define global patterns nondistributed, because this was always accomplished by means of a single cell rather than a collection.

Other important formal properties seemed to be implicit in the beady ring generative process. All that happened, formally speaking, in that process was that each cell (with its attached open space) had been made a continuous neighbour of one other cell. Now the relation of neighbour has the formal property that if A is a neighbour of B, then B is a neighbour of A – the property that mathematicians call symmetry. However, relations which involve cells containing other cells do not have this property. On the contrary, they are asymmetric, since if cell A contains cell B then cell *B* does not contain cell *A*. Now it was clearly possible for pluralities to contain space with their outsides as well as single cells with their insides. In a village green or a plaza, for example, a set of cells contained a space with their outsides. The generative relation of closed cells to open spaces was therefore asymmetric, in contrast to the beady ring case where the open spaces had only been symmetric neighbours of closed cells. By proceeding in this way, it was possible to conceive of an abstract model of the types of restriction on a random process that seemed to produce the kind of variations found in real cases.

These two pairs of relational ideas, together with the notion of open and closed cells, seemed to form the basis of a spatial language that had certain resemblances to natural language. The distinction between distributed and nondistributed was no more than a distinction between pattern elements defined by plural and singular entities; while the existence of asymmetric relations, in which one or more cells contained others, was like a sentence in which subjects had objects. These differences are in themselves simple, but of course give rise to a very rich system of possibilities. Chapter 2, 'The logic of space', sets out to show how these elementary ideas can be conceived of as restrictions on a random process to generate the principal types of global variation found in settlement forms, and through the construction of a consistent ideographic language to represent these ideas and their combinations as a system of transformations. This is not, of course, a mathematical system, and even more emphatically it is not a mathematical enumeration. It is an attempt to capture the fundamental similarities and differences of real space forms in as economical a way as possible. The axioms of the system are not mathematical axioms, but a theory of the fundamental differences stated as carefully as possible.

With the idea of a finite set of elementary generators applied as restrictions on a random process, it seemed that at least two methodological objectives could be formulated clearly. First, the problem of identifying morphological types becomes that of identifying the combination of elementary generators that yielded a particular form. This had the advantage that because one was talking about abstract rules underlying spatial forms, rather than spatial forms themselves – genotypes rather than phenotypes, in effect – then the comparative relations between different forms became easier to see. There were fewer genotypical variations than phenotypical variations.

Second, the problem of the degree to which societies invested order in space seemed restatable in terms of the degree to which it was necessary to restrict a random process in order to arrive at a form. A highly ordered form would require many restrictions applied to the process, while a less ordered form – such as the beady ring form – would require few. This would be reflected in the way in which rules were written down in the ideographic language: patterns with a good deal of randomness and few rules could in principle be written in a short ideographic sentence, whereas those with a great deal of order would require longer sentences. We could talk of 'short descriptions' and 'long descriptions' to express the distinction between a system with little order and much randomness, and one with much order and little randomness. It was a matter of how many of the potential relationships in the system had to be controlled to arrive at a particular pattern.

In this way, the model could easily express differences in the amount of order in the system. A simple extension of the argument then showed that it could also express differences in the amount of social 'meaning' invested in the pattern. In all cases we have described so far, the restrictions on the random process specify the necessary relations that have to hold among cells in the system, and omit the contingent ones, allowing them to be randomised. In this sense, a description, long or short, specifies the genotype of the pattern, rather than its phenotype in all detail. But although the genotype specifies necessary relations, it does not specify which cells should satisfy those relations in a particular position. In this respect, all the cells are interchangeable, in the sense that in a street considered simply as a spatial pattern, all the constituent houses could be interchanged without the pattern being in the least bit changed. Now there are many cases where this principle of interchangeability does not apply. In the village form shown in Fig. 30 for example, each hut and each group of huts has to be in a specific position in the ring: opposite some, next to others, and so on.

Now formally speaking, what is happening in these cases is that certain cells in the system are being made noninterchangeable with other cells. We are specifying not only that there has to be such and such a relation between cells in this part of the system, but that it has to be a relation between this particular cell and that particular cell. In effect, by requiring labels to have particular locations, we are including nonspatial factors in the necessary structure of the pattern, that is, in its genotype. In such cases, therefore, we cannot write down the necessary relations of the genotype simply by repeating the same restriction to the random process. We must at each stage specify which label we are adding where and in what relation to others, and this means that the sentence describing the genotype will be much longer. The limiting case, at the opposite pole to the random process itself, is the case where the relation of each cell to every other has to be specified. The addition of 'semantics' to the system then requires us only to extend the principles used to describe 'syntax'. Syntax and semantics are a continuum, rather than antithetical categories. This continuum, expressible in terms of longer and longer

models, in which more and more of the possible relations in the
system are specified as necessary rather than contingent, runs (as
required at the end of ii) both from non-order to order and from
non-meaning to meaning. All are unifiable in the same framework:
the conception of order in space as restrictions on an underlying
random process.

v

However, this model still did not amount to a proper theory of
space, and even less did it offer useful tools of analysis. At best it
permitted the problem of space to be re-described in such a way as
to bring together its various manifestations in a unified scheme,
and to make differences less puzzling. In order to move on, two
further steps had to be taken. First, a method had to be found for
using the model to analyse real situations; and second, the model
had to be embedded in a theory of how and why societies
generated different spatial patterns. As it turned out, the one led to
the other. Learning to analyse spatial patterns quantitatively in
terms of the model gradually revealed to us the outline of a
general sociology of these dimensions, and in the end led to a
social theory of space.

The first steps towards quantification came through turning our
attention to the interiors of buildings. Here the important pattern
property seemed to be the permeability of the system; that is, how
the arrangement of cells and entrances controlled access and
movement. It was not hard to discover that, in their abstract form,
the relational ideas that had been developed for settlements could
also be used for describing permeability patterns. It was no more
than a one-dimensional interpretation of what had previously
been two-dimensional spatial concepts. The distinction between
distributed and nondistributed relations became simply the distinction between spatial relations with more than one, or only one
locus of control with respect to some other space; while the
distinction between symmetry and asymmetry became the distinction between spaces that had direct access to other spaces
without having to pass through one or more intermediary spaces,
and spaces whose relations were only indirect. These properties
could, it turned out, be well represented by making a graph of the
spaces in a building, with circles representing spaces and linking
lines representing entrances, and 'justifying', it with respect to the
outside world, meaning that all spaces one step into the building
would be lined up on the same level, all those two deep at a level
above, and so on (see Figs. 93 and 94). This method of representation had an immediate advantage over the plan: it made the syntax
of the plan (its system of spatial relations) very clear, so that
comparisons could be made with other buildings according to the
degree that it possessed the properties of symmetry and asymmet-

ry, distributedness and nondistributedness. It was also possible to compare the relative position of differently labelled spaces in a sample of plans, thus identifying the syntactic relations characteristic of different labels. More important, it led on to the realisation that analysis could be deepened by learning to measure these properties.

For example, the degree to which a complex, seen from the outside, was based on direct or indirect relations could be calculated by using a formula that expressed how far a pattern approximated a unilinear sequence in which each space leads only to exactly one more – the maximally indirect, or 'deep' form – or a bush, in which every space is directly connected to the outside world – the maximally direct, or 'shallow' form (see Figs. 35 and 36). This could then be repeated, but from every point inside the building, giving in effect a picture of what the pattern looked like from all points in it, and from the outside. Once we did this, very surprising and systematic variations began to appear. For instance, in analysing examples of English houses, the 'relative asymmetry' – the degree to which the complex seen from a point possessed direct or indirect relations – from the room in which the best furniture was always kept always had a higher value than that from the space in which food was prepared. This space in turn always had a higher value than the space in which everyday living and eating took place (always provided, of course, that the three spaces were distinct). This turned out to be true across a range of cases, in spite of substantial variation in building geometry and room arrangement. Fig. 98(a) shows this difference in a typical case, and Fig. 99 shows a range of examples.

The distributed–nondistributed dimension could also be quantified. Since the existence of distributed relations in a system would result in the formation of rings of spaces, then quantification could be in terms of how any particular space related to the rings formed by the pattern. For example, in Fig. 98(a), the traditional example has the main everyday living space on the principal ring in the system, and this ring is only a ring by virtue of passing through the outside of the house. This location seemed important to the way in which the system was controlled, both internally and in the relation of inside to outside.

Investigation of a range of different types of buildings in this way eventually suggested certain general principles for the analysis of buildings as spatial patterns. First, space was intelligible if it was understood as being determined by two kinds of relations, rather than one: the relations among the occupants and the relations between occupants and outsiders. Both these factors were important determinants of spatial form, but even more so was the relation between these two points of view. However, it was exactly the difference between these points of view that could be investigated by analysing spatial relations both from points inside the system and from the outside. Quantitative analysis thus became, in a natural way, a means of investigating some fundamental aspects of the social relationships built into spatial form.

Second, there seemed to be certain consistencies in the way in which the dimensions of the syntax model related to social factors. The dimension of asymmetry was, it appeared, related to the importance of categories. For example, a front parlour was a space that traditionally was unimportant in everyday life, but of considerable importance as a social category of space, for very occasional use. As a result, it was relatively segregated from the principal areas of everyday living, and this had the effect of giving it a high relative asymmetry: it was, of all the major spaces in the house, the least integrated. The distributed-nondistributed properties of the pattern, on the other hand, seemed to refer to the kind of controls that were in the system. The everyday living space in the houses in Fig. 99, for example, has the least relative asymmetry, but often the most control of relations with other spaces. Seen this way, it seemed that the social meaning of spaces was actually best expressed in terms of the relationships in the physical configuration. Once again, the distinction between syntax and semantics became blurred. It seemed we were dealing with a unified phenomenon.

The measurement of relations had become possible because the spatial structure of a building could be reduced to a graph, and this in turn was possible because, by and large, a building consists of a set of well-defined spaces with well-defined links from one to another. In the case of settlements that is rarely the case. They are, it is true, always a set of primary cells (houses, etc), but there is also a continuous structure of open space, sometimes regular, sometimes irregular, sometimes forming rings, sometimes tree-like, which is not easily decomposable into elements for the purpose of analysis. The problem of analysing settlements is the problem of analysing this continuous space and how it is related to other elements.

This problem preoccupied us for a long time, but as had often happened, the eventual answer was lying in what had already been formulated, in the nature of 'beads' and 'strings'. The intuitive meaning of string was a space more marked by its linear extension than by its 'fatness'; in the case of beads, the space was fatter, rather than linear. Formally, this meant something quite simple: a string was extended in one dimension rather than in two; whereas a bead was as fully extended in the second dimension as the first. Once this was seen, then it became clear that it was not necessary to identify spaces in a definite way, but to look at the system in terms of both its two-dimensional organisation and its one-dimensional organisation, and then compare the two. Two-dimensional organisation could be identified by taking the convex spaces that have the best area–perimeter ratio, that is the 'fattest', then the next fattest, then the next, and continue until the surface is completely covered. The one-dimensional organisation can then be identified by proceeding in the same way, first drawing the longest straight– or axial – lines, then the next longest, and continuing until all convex spaces are passed through at least once and all axial links made. We thus arrive at both a convex or two-dimensional picture of the space structure, and an axial, or one-dimensional picture, both of which could be represented as graphs.

Once this was the case, then quantitative analysis could proceed on a richer basis than before, since not only could the settlement be looked at from the point of view of its constituent cells and from the outside, but each of these relations could be looked at in terms both of the convex and axial organisation of space. In effect, we were treating the public space of the settlement as a kind of interface between the dwelling and the world outside the settlement, the former being the domain of inhabitants and the latter being the domain of strangers. How this interface was handled seemed to be the most important difference between one type of settlement and another; and such differences were a function of the same two types of relation that had been so important in analysing interiors: the relations among inhabitants, and the relations between inhabitants and strangers. Not only were the forms of public space in settlements governed by the relationship between these two relations, but how differences arose was governed by fairly simple principles. Because strangers to a settlement, or part of a settlement, are likely to be moving through the space, and inhabitants are such because they collectively have also more static relations to the various parts of the local system, the axial extension of public space accesses strangers to the system, while the convex organisation creates more static zones, in which inhabitants are therefore potentially more in control of the interface. This made it perfectly clear why beady ring type settlements as they grew increased not only the size of their convex spaces, but also the axial extension of these spaces. The small town illustrated in Fig. 25, for example, is axially no deeper from the outside than a small beady ring hamlet. It was clear that the relation between inhabitants and strangers was a key determinant in how the settlement altered its principles of growth as it expanded. Important principles for the sociology of urban space in general followed from this. Urban market places in European countries, for example, wherever they are geometrically in the settlement, are nearly always axially shallow from the outside, and have the curious, though intelligible property that the axial lines in their vicinity are strong and lead to the square but never through it. Strangers are speeded on their way into the square, but once there are slowed down. The principle applies in a different way to a very large 'grown' town like London. In the original dense parts, in and near the City of London, there was always a main system of streets and a smaller system of back alleys and courts: yet at both levels the governing principle was that important foci or meeting points were usually no more than two axial steps apart, implying that there would always be a point from which both foci could be seen. Similar principles apply in the much talked-of 'villages' of London, which have been absorbed into the urban fabric. In general, they are local deformations, convex and axial, of a more regular grid which extends away from them, and links them together by few axial steps. A very common principle of urban safety is built into this principle of growth. The system works by accessing strangers everywhere, yet controlling them by immediate adjacency to the dwellings of inhabitants. As a result, the strangers police the space, while the inhabitants police the strangers. This is a more subtle, but also much more effective mechanism than that by which the grouping of inhabitants' dwellings alone is expected to produce a self-policing environment.

vi

It would seem clear then, that there is always a strong relation between the spatial form and the ways in which encounters are generated and controlled. But why should these patterns be so different in different societies? Could it be that different types of society required different kinds of control on encounters in order to be that type of society; because if this were so, we could reasonably expect it to be the deepest level at which society generated spatial form. Here we found the general sociology of Durkheim (though not his writings specifically about space) profoundly suggestive.[10] Durkheim had distinguished between two fundamentally different principles of social solidarity or cohesion: an 'organic' solidarity based on interdependence through differences, such as those resulting from the division of labour; and a 'mechanical' solidarity based on integration through similarities of belief and group structure. This theory was profoundly spatial: organic solidarity required an integrated and dense space, whereas mechanical solidarity preferred a segregated and dispersed space. Not only this, but Durkheim actually located the cause of the different solidarities in spatial variables, namely the size and density of populations. In the work of Durkheim, we found the missing component of a theory of space, in the form of the elements for a spatial analysis of social formations. But to develop these initial ideas into a social theory of space, we had to go back once again into the foundations, and consider the sociology of the simplest spatial structure we had found it useful to consider: the elementary cell.

Now the important thing about the elementary cell is that it is not just a cell. It has an outside as well as an inside, and of its outside space at least one part is unlike the remainder in that it is adjacent to the entrance to the cell: that is, it forms part of the threshold. The simplest building is, in effect, the structure shown in Fig. 10(c), consisting of a boundary, a space within the boundary, an entrance, and a space outside the boundary defined by the entrance, all of these spaces being part of a system which was placed in a larger space of some kind which 'carried' it. All these elements seemed to have some kind of sociological reference: the space within the boundary established a category associated with some kind of inhabitant; the boundary formed a control on that category, and maintained its discreteness as a category; the world outside the system was the domain of potential strangers, in contradistinction to the domain of inhabitants; the space outside the entrance constituted a potential interface between the inhabitant and the stranger; and the entrance was a means not only of establishing the identity of the inhabitant, but also a means of converting a stranger into a visitor.

Some of the consequences of the sociology of the elementary cell – the relations between inhabitants, and between inhabitants and others – have already been sketched. But the most important of all lies in the distinction between inside and outside itself; that is, in the distinction between building interiors and their collective exteriors. There are, in effect, two pathways of growth from the elementary cell: it can be by subdividing a cell, or accumulating cells, so that internal permeability is maintained; or by aggregating them independently, so that the continuous permeability is maintained externally. When the first occurs, we call it a building, and when the latter, a settlement. Now these two types of growth are sociologically as well as spatially distinct, in that one is an elaboration of the sociology of the inside of the elementary cell, and the other an elaboration of the sociology of the outside. Building interiors characteristically have more categoric differences between spaces, more well-defined differences in the relations of spaces, and in general more definition of what can happen and where, and who is related to whom else. Interior space organisation might, in short, have a rather well-defined relation to social categories and roles. The space outside buildings, in contrast, usually has far fewer categoric differences mapped into spaces, more equality of access from the cells that define the system, fewer categoric differences among those cells, and so on. At the same time, it has less control, in that while buildings tend to grow by accumulating boundaries, settlement space tends to grow by accumulating spaces into one continuous system. Settlement space is richer in its potential, in that more people have access to it, and there are fewer controls on it. We might say it is more probabilistic in its relation to encounters, while building interiors are rather more deterministic. The differences between inside and outside, therefore, are already differences in how societies generate and control encounters.

In their elementary forms, in effect, buildings participate in a larger system in two ways: first, in the obvious way they are spatially related to other buildings; and also, less obviously, by separating off systems of categories from the outside world – using spatial separation in order to define and control that system of social categories – they can define a relation to others by conceptual analogy, rather than spatial relation. The inhabitant of a house in a village, say, is related to his neighbours spatially, in that he occupies a location in relation to them, but also he relates to them conceptually, in that his interior system of spatialised categories is similar to or different from those of his neighbours. He relates, it might be said, transpatially as well as spatially. Now this distinction is very close to that between mechanical and organic solidarity. We might even say, without too much exaggeration, that interiors tend to define more of an ideological space, in the sense of a fixed system of categories and relations that is continually re-affirmed by use, whereas exteriors define a transactional or even a political space, in that it constructs a more fluid system of encounters and avoidances which is constantly re-negotiated by use. Alternatively, we might, without stretching things too far, define the exterior space as that in which the society is produced, in the sense that new relations are generated, and the interior space as that in which it is reproduced. The former has a higher degree of indeterminacy, the latter more structure.

Now while all societies use both possibilities to some degree, it is often clear that some social formations use one more than the other. In our own society, for example, a suburban lifestyle is characterised by values which are more strongly realised in maintaining a specific categoric order in the domestic interior, than in maintaining strong systems of local external spatial relations. We can at least distinguish a certain duality in the ways in which societies generate space, and this duality is a *function of different forms of social solidarity*. At the extremes, these differences are based on opposing principles; the one must exclude what the other requires. One requires a strong control on boundaries and a strong internal organisation in order to maintain an essentially transpatial form of solidarity. The other requires weak boundaries, and the generation rather than the control of events. The former works best when segments are small and isolated, the latter when the system is large and integrated.

But there is another dimension of difference, no less fundamental, and one which makes the whole relation of society to spatial form one degree more complex. The duality of inside mapping ideology and outside mapping transactional politics, is only the case *insofar as the system is considered as a local-to-global phenomenon* – that is, insofar as it constructs a global pattern from the inter-relations of the basic units. Insofar as a society is also a global-to-local phenomenon – that is, insofar as there is a distinct global structure over and above the level of everyday interaction – then the logic of the system reverses itself. One set of spaces is produced whose purpose is to define an ideological landscape through its exterior, and another set whose purpose is to produce and control a global politics through its interior; essentially, shrines of various kinds and meeting places of various kinds are the first specialised structures of the global formations of a society.

From this distinction, a second duality follows, as pervasive as the first: *the more the system is run from the global to the local, then the more the reversed logic prevails over the local-to-global logic.* The state can, for our purposes, be defined here as a global formation which projects both a unified ideology and a unified politics over a specific territory; and the more it acts to realise this aim, then the more the exterior is dominated by a system of ideologically defined structures, and the more the interiors are dominated by controlled transactions. The distinction between exterior and interior space becomes the distinction between power and control, that is, between an abstractly defined system of power categories which, prior to their projection into a unified symbolic landscape, have no form of spatial integration, and systems for the reproduction of social categories and relations which mould the organisation of interiors.[11]

The dimensions of indetermination and structure change place in the global-to-local logic: the exterior space is the space of structured and immutable categories; while the internal space is the space of personal negotiation, with the difference that the negotiation is always between people whose social identities form part of the global system and others whose identities do not. Fundamental to the global-to-local system is the existence of inequalities, realised everywhere in the internal and external relations of buildings: inequalities between teachers and taught, curers and patients and so on.

Urban form itself illustrates this duality. A town classically comprises two dissimilar spatial components: the space of the street system, which is always the theatre of everyday life and transactions, and the space of the major public buildings and functions. The former creates a dense system, in which public space is defined by the buildings and their entrances; the latter a sparse system, in which space surrounds buildings with few entrances. The more the global-to-local dimensions prevail, the more the town will be of the latter type, and vice versa. The fundamental differences between administrative capitals and business capitals is related to this shift in the social logic.

This is also the difference between ceremonial centres and centres of production as proto-urban forms. The ground-plan of Tikal, the Maya ceremonial centre shown in Fig. 14, is a good example of the ideological landscape created by the global-to-local logic. The primary cells in this system are inward facing and grouped at random in the vicinity of the ceremonial centre, seemingly ignoring its structure. In spite of their density, they define no global system of space. The global system is defined only by the relations between the major ceremonial buildings, linked as they are by 'causeways'. In both senses this is the opposite of the classical European idea of a medieval town, in which it is the primary cells that define the global structure of space, with main ceremonial buildings interspersed but not themselves defining the global order of the town. The ongoing deformation of the modern urban landscape into a landscape of strongly representational forms (for example, 'prestige' buildings) surrounded by a controlled landscape of zones and categories is, in the end, closely related to this conception.

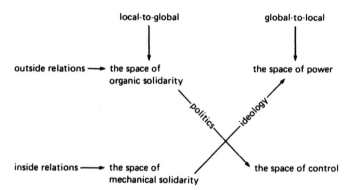

The simple diagram summarises how these basic social dynamics are articulated by the social potential of space. Space is, in short, everywhere a function of the forms of social solidarity, and these are in turn a product of the structure of society. The realisation of these differences in systematically different spatial forms is because, as Durkheim showed, society has a certain spatial logic and, as we hope we have shown, because space has a certain social logic to it.

vii

This schematic analysis summarises the argument presented in this book as to the fundamental dimensions of difference in how societies determine space. The question therefore arises in a new form: is there any sense in which space also determines society? This question is not the subject of the book. But since the text was completed, the continuing research programme at the Unit for

Architectural Studies in University College London has led us to an affirmative – if conditional – answer to that vexed question. Space does indeed have social consequences – but only if social is the right word for what we have discovered.

Briefly, what we have done is to take a number of urban areas – traditional areas of street pattern and a range of recent estates and groups of estates – and mapped and analysed them using the alpha-analysis technique set out in Chapter 3. Then we observed them repeatedly in terms of how many static and moving people were to be found in different parts of the system.

The first thing we found out was that such observations are much more reliable and predictable than ordinary experience would suggest. Observers were quickly able to anticipate with some accuracy how few or how many people they would be likely to encounter in different spaces. To test this, two observers would start from the same point and walk round a selected route in opposite directions and then compare observations. These were often remarkably similar, even though the two observers could rarely have observed the same people. The second finding was that there was remarkably little variation with the weather, and also remarkably little variation in the pattern of distribution with time of day. Relatively few observations, it seemed, would give a fairly reliable picture of the system.

Much more striking were the differences in the densities of people observed in the different types of area. This was not a function of the density of people living in the area. For example, we compared a rather quiet street area of North London with a famous low-rise, high-density estate nearby (both examples are used for analysis in Chapter 3) and discovered that in spite of the fact that the estate had three times the density of population of the street area, the observers encountered only one third of the number of people – and many of these the observers were only aware of for a much shorter time than in the street area. Taking into account all factors, there was a difference between the public space of the old and new in terms of awareness of people by a factor of about nine. These differences and general levels have since been verified in other cases, and seem fairly stable. Daytime in a new area (even where this has been established for several decades) is like the middle of the night in a traditionally organised area. From the point of view of awareness of others, living on even the most progessive and low-rise estate is like living in perpetual night.

Some understanding of why this might be the case came from correlating people densities with the syntactic measures of 'integration' and 'control' for each space. Every traditional system we have looked at, however piecemeal its historical development, showed a statistically significant (better than the 0.05 level) correlation between the patterns of integration values and the densities of people observed, with stronger correlations with moving people. There were always livelier and quieter areas, more or less along the lines of our integration and segregation maps (see Chapter 3) – but everywhere there were always at least some people to be seen.

In the new areas no such correlation has been found – with the single exception of one extraordinary design (the Alexandra Road estate at Swiss Cottage, London). The relation of people to space seems to approach randomness. Not only, it seemed, was the experience of others substantially diminished by the new spatial forms, but also it had lost its globally ordered pattern. Experience of people –other than a general lack of experience – is no longer inferable from the organisation of space and everyday movement in it.

What, then, was responsible for the strong correlation in one case and its absence in the other? In the present state of incomplete knowledge, two possibilities look promising. First, the correlation in traditional systems looks as though it is the result of the strong integrating cores that link the interior of the system with the outside, thus producing more journeys *through* the system – and therefore *longer* journeys which, because of their length, are more likely to select integrating spaces as part of a shortest route, since these by definition will be shallower to other spaces.

Second, computer experiments have shown that in traditional systems with the 'normal' degree of shallowness and ringiness the most powerful correlations between spatial pattern and movement densities (usually above 0.9) are produced by combining the global measure of integration with the local measure of control. Where the integration and the control system coincide the correlation is good, where they do not it breaks down. In other words, to the extent that the integration core is also a local control structure, then to that extent the density of potential encounters is inferable from the space pattern.

This is, of course, only hypothesis at this stage, and research is continuing. But if, as we expect, it turns out to be a key determinant, then it will substantiate our general argument that urban life is the product of the global order of the system, and of the presence of strangers as well as inhabitants, and is not a result of purely local patterns of spatial organisation. In fact the more localised, and the more segregated to create local identities, by and large the more lifeless the spaces will be.

Whatever the fate of this explanatory hypothesis, one thing seems already to be sure: that architecture determines to a substantial extent the degree to which we become automatically aware of others, both those who live near and strangers, as a result of living out everyday life in space. The differences between one system and another are substantial, and appear to correlate with ordinary verbal accounts of isolation and alienation, which are often vaguely said to be the products of architecture. The question is: are these effects *social* effects, in any important sense. According to present canons of sociological method it seems unlikely that they could be accepted as such. Society, it is said, begins with *interaction*, not with mere co-presence and awareness.

But we wonder if this is really so. The introduction of the concept of randomness into spatial order allowed us to build models that eventually led to an effective analysis of social order in space. We strongly suspect that the same may be true of society itself, both in the sense that the notion of randomness seems to play as important a structural role in society as it does in space — and in the sense that random encounters and awareness of others may be a vital motor of social systems at some, or even all levels. Whatever the case, there seems no doubt that this basic, unstructured awareness of others is powerfully influenced by architectural form, and that this must now be a major factor in design.

1

♦♦

The problem of space

SUMMARY

The aim of this chapter is to argue for, and to establish, a framework for the *redefinition* of the problem of space. The common 'natural'-seeming definition sees it as a matter of finding relations between 'social structure' and 'spatial structure'. However, few descriptions of either type of structure have succeeded in pointing towards lawful relations between the two. The absence of any general models relating spatial structure to social formations it is argued, has its roots in the fundamental way in which the problem is conceputalised (which in turn has its roots in the ways in which social theorists have conceptualised society), namely as a relation between a *material* realm of physical space, without social content in itself, and an *abstract* realm of social relations and institutions, without a spatial dimension. Not only it is impossible in principle to search for necessary relations between a material and an abstract entity, but also the programme is itself contradictory. Society can only have lawful relations to space if society already possesses its own intrinsic spatial dimension; and likewise space can only be lawfully related to society if it can carry those social dimensions in its very form. The problem definition as it stands has the effect of desocialising space and despatialising society. To remedy this, two problems of description must be solved. Society must be described in terms of its intrinsic spatiality; space must be described in terms of its intrinsic sociality. The overall aim of the chapter is to show how these two problems of description can be approached, in order to build a broad theory of the social logic of space and the spatial logic of society. The chapter ends with a sketch of how the problem may be set into a framework of scientific ideas adapted specifically for this purpose.

Society and space

In an obvious way, human societies are spatial phenomena: they occupy regions of the earth's surface, and within and between these regions material resources move, people encounter each other and information is transmitted. It is through its realisation in space that we can recognise that a society exists in the first place. But a society does more than simply exist in space. It also takes on a definite spatial form and it does so in two senses. First, it arranges people in space in that it locates them in relation to each other, with a greater or lesser degree of aggregation and

26

separation, engendering patterns of movement and encounter that may be dense or sparse within or between different groupings. Second, it arranges space itself by means of buildings, boundaries, paths, markers, zones, and so on, so that the physical milieu of that society also takes on a definite pattern. In both senses a society acquires a definite and recognisable spatial order.

Spatial order is one of the most striking means by which we recognise the existence of the *cultural* differences between one social formation and another, that is, differences in the ways in which members of those societies live out and reproduce their social existence. These might be differences between a society living in dispersed, highly subdivided compounds and another living in densely aggregated, relatively open villages; or differences between a city in which dwellings are directly related to the system of streets, as in London, and another in which closed courtyards interrupt this direct relation, as in Paris. In either case, spatial order appears as a part of culture, because it shows itself to be based on *generic principles* of some kind. Throughout the social grouping, a similar family of characteristic spatial themes is reproduced, and through this repetition we recognise *ethnicity* in space. At a general level, everyday language recognises this pervasive relation between spatial formations and lifestyles by using words like urban, suburban, village, and so on with both a spatial and a behavioural dimension to their meaning. In everyday life and language, it seems, the experience of spatial formations is an intrinsic, if unconscious dimension of the way in which we experience society itself. We read space, and anticipate a lifestyle.

But however pervasive, the link between society and space cannot be limited to questions of culture and lifestyle. Other evidence suggests that space is bound up even more deeply with the ways in which social formations acquire and change their very form. The most far-reaching changes in the evolution of societies have usually either involved or led to profound shifts in spatial form, and in the relation of society to its spatial milieu; these shifts appear to be not so much a by-product of the social changes, but an intrinsic part of them and even to some extent causative of them. The agricultural revolution, the formation of fixed settlements, urbanisation, the early development of the state, industrialisation, and even the growth of the modern interventionist state, have been associated with changes in the morphology of society in which social and spatial changes appear almost as necessary dimensions of each other. Different types of social formation, it would appear, require a characteristic spatial order, just as different types of spatial order require a particular social formation to sustain them.

Recently a new complication has been added to the relation between society and space in the form of a belief that, by careful forethought and conscious control, both the physical environment and the spatial form of society can be made more efficient, pleasurable, and supportive of the workings of society. As a result of this belief, we now have intervening in the relationship between society and space a kind of *moral science* of design – 'moral' in the sense that it must act on the basis of some consensus of what is agreed to be the good, and 'science' in the almost contradictory sense that its actions must be seen to be based on some kind of analytic objectivity. Because its institutional setting is normative and active rather than analytic and reflective, this moral science does not see it as a central concern to propose and develop better theories of the relationship between society and space. Rather it is forced to act as though this relation were well understood and not problematical.

But even if this moral science does not require an explicit theory of society and space, insofar as its actions are consistent it implies one. The existence of this consistency can hardly be doubted, since everywhere the effect of its intervention is to effect a transformation in the spatial order of society no less through-going and systematic than in any of the earlier phases of revolutionary change. The ideal of this transformation, and presumably its eventual point of aim, would seem to be a sparse landscape of free-standing buildings, or groups of buildings, arranged into relatively bounded and segregated regions, internally subdivided and hierarchically arranged, and linked together by a specialised and separate system of spaces for movement. The relationship of such a landscape to its predecessors can only be conjectural, since in its physical form it is virtually the opposite of the previous system in which densely and contiguously aggregated buildings defined, by virtue of their positioning alone, a more or less deformed grid of streets that unified the system into a uniformly accessible whole. The substitution of the notion of estate for that of street as the central organising concept encapsulates this transformation: a system of estates carries with it a high degree of segregation, a system of streets a high degree of integration.

It is now clear that the first outcome of this moral science and the transformation of space that it has sponsored is not environmental improvement but an environmental pathology of a totally new and unexpected kind. For the first time, we have the problem of a 'designed' environment that does not 'work' socially, or even one that generates social problems that in other circumstances might not exist: problems of isolation, physical danger, community decay and ghettoisation. The manifest existence of this pathology has called into question all the assumptions on which the new urban transformation was based: assumptions that separation was good for community, that hierarchisation of space was good for relations between groups, and that space could only be important to society by virtue of being identified with a particular, preferably small group, who would prefer to keep their domain free of strangers. However, although the entire conceptual structure of the moral science is in disarray, no clearly articulated alternative is proposed, other than a return to poorly understood traditional forms. Nothing is proposed because nothing is known of what the social consequences of alternatives would be, any more than anything is properly understood of the reason for the failure of the current transformation.

In this situation, the need for a proper theory of the relations between society and its spatial dimension is acute. A social theory of space would account first for the relations that are found in different circumstances between the two types of spatial order characteristic of societies – that is, the arrangement of people in space and the arrangement of space itself – and second it would show how both were a product of the ways in which a society worked and reproduced itself. Its usefulness would be that it would allow designers to speculate in a more informed way about the possible consequences of different design strategies, while at the same time adding a new creative dimension to those speculations. But more important, a theory would permit a systematic analysis of experiments that would enable us to learn from experience, a form of learning that until now has not been a serious possibility.

Unfortunately, because of the pervasive interconnections that seem to link the nature of society with its spatial forms, a social theory of space cannot avoid being rooted in a spatial theory of society. Such a theory does not exist. Although there are some preliminary attempts to link society with its spatial manifestations (reviewed briefly in the Introduction), there is no theory which purports to show how a society of its very nature gives itself one form of spatial order rather than another. Such a theory, if it existed, would probably also be a theory of the nature of society itself, and the fact that such a theory does not yet exist is a reflection of some very fundamental difficulties at the foundation of the subject matter of sociology itself, difficulties which on a close examination, as we shall see, turn out to be of a spatial nature.

The problem of space

'Nowhere', wrote Herman Weyl, 'do mathematics, natural sciences and philosophy permeate one another so intimately as in the problem of space.'[1] The reason is not difficult to find. Experience of space is the foundation and framework of all our knowledge of the spatio-temporal world. Abstract thought by its very nature is an attempt to transcend this framework and create planes of experience, which are at once less directly dependent on the immediacy of spatio-temporal experience and more organised. Abstract thought is concerned with the principles of order underlying the spatio-temporal world and these, by definition, are not given to immediate experience. In the problem of space, abstract thought addresses itself again to the foundations of its experience of the immediate world. It returns, as it were, to its original spatio-temporal prison, and re-appraises it with all its developed power of abstraction.

The consequences of this re-appraisal have been far-reaching. The origins of what we today call science lie in the development of a mathematical system capable of representing and analysing the abstract properties of space in a comprehensive way: Euclidean geometry. Geometry provided the first means of interrogating the spatio-temporal world in a language whose own structure was consistent and fully explicit. In the understanding of space the advance of knowledge – science – and the analysis of knowledge – philosophy – became inextricably intertwined. Speculation about the nature of space inevitably becomes speculation about how the mind constructs its knowledge of space and, by implication, how the mind acquires any knowledge of the spatio-temporal world.

It is not only in the higher regions of mathematics, science and philosophy that the problem of space appears. It appears wherever abstract thought appears, and not all abstract thought is scientific or philosophical. 'Magical' thought, for example, is not less abstract than science, and on occasions, in astrology for example, it is no less systematic in its use of a consistent logic. Magical thought differs from what we might loosely term rational thought not by its preference for consistency and logic, but by the assumption that it makes about the relation between abstract thought and the spatio-temporal world. Rational thought, for example, assumes that immaterial entities may be imagined, but cannot exist; everything real must have location, even if (as with the case of the 'ether') it is everywhere.

Likewise, rational thought insists that immaterial relations between entities cannot occur. Every relation of determination or influence must arise from the transmission of material forces of some kind from one location to another. Magical thought asserts the two contrary propositions: that immaterial entities can exist, and that immaterial relations of determination or influence may hold between entities. Belief that it is possible to harm or cure a distant person by performing actions on an effigy, or to affect a distant event by the power of thought, is a specific denial of the two basic postulates of rationality; and these two postulates concern the legitimate forms that abstract thought about the spatio-temporal world can take. In essence, rational thought insists on a continuity between our everyday practical experience of how the world works and the more abstract principles that may inhere in it. It holds that common sense intuitions, founded on physical contact with the world, are reliable guides to all levels of abstract thought about the world. Magic denies this and posits a form of thought and a form of action in the world that transcend the spatio-temporal reality that we experience.

But just as not all abstract thought is rational, so not all rational thought is scientific. In fact in the history of science, the more science has progressed, the more it has been necessary to make a distinction between scientific thought and – at the very least – a strong version of rational thought that we might call *dogmatic rationality*. Dogmatic rationality may be defined as rational thought that insists on the two basic spatio-temporal postulates of rational thought to the point that no speculation about the world is to be allowed unless the principle of continuity between common sense intuition and underlying order in nature is obeyed to the letter. This distinction became necessary as soon as science, in order to give a satisfactory account of underlying order in nature in mathematical terms, had to posit the existence both of entities and relations whose spatio-temporal form could not be imagined, and perhaps even entailed contradictions.

The tension between scientific and rational thought is shown for example in the objections to Newton's cosmological theories at the time of their appearance. As Koyré shows, Leibniz objected to Newton's theories on the grounds that, while they appeared to give a satisfactory mathematical description of how bodies moved in relation to each other, in so doing they did violence to common sense conceptions of how the system could actually work:

His philosophy appears to me rather strange and I cannot believe it can be justified. If every body is heavy, it follows (whatever his supporters may say, and however passionately they deny it) that Gravity will be a scholastic occult quality or else the effect of a miracle ... It is not sufficient to say that God has made such a law of nature, therefore the thing is natural. *It is necessary that the law should be capable of being fulfilled by the nature of created things.* If, for example, God were to give a free body the law of revolving round a common centre, he would either have to join it to other bodies which by their impulsion would make it always stay in a circular orbit, or put an Angel at its heel.[2]

And elsewhere:

Thus we can assert that matter will not naturally have [the faculty of] attraction ... and will not by itself move in a curved line because it is not possible to conceive how this could take place there, that is to explain it mechanically: whereas *that which is natural must be able to become distinctly conceivable.* [our emphasis][3]

The assumptions about the given world which are made in order to rescue common sense from magic are not therefore necessarily carried through into the more abstract realms of science. In a sense the advance of science revives problems – of action at a distance, of apparently immaterial entities and forces, of patterns whose existence cannot be doubted but whose reasons for existing appear inexplicable – which seemed to have been

buried along with magical thought. And these problems are often
centred about one fundamental issue: that of the nature and order
of space and, in particular, how systems can work as systems
without apparently possessing the kind of spatial continuity that
would satisfy dogmatic rationalism.

In sociology the problem reappears in another, exacerbated
form. The most striking property of a society is that, although it
may occupy a continuous territory, it cannot be regarded as a
spatially continuous system. On the contrary, it is a system
composed of large numbers of autonomous, freely mobile, spatially discrete entities called individuals. We do not have available in
rational thought the concept of a system composed of discrete
individuals. On the contrary, that such a collection can be a
system at all runs counter to the most deeply held prejudices of
rationality about what a system – any system – is: that is, a
spatially continuous whole. Society, it appears, if it is a system at
all, is in some sense a discontinuous or *discrete system*, trans-
cending space; that is, the type of system that was disqualified
from the domain of rational thought with the elimination of
magic. It works – at least in some important respects – without
connections, without material influence, without physical
embodiment at the level of the system.

This presents sociological theory with a difficult problem, with
philosophical as well as scientific implications: it cannot take for
granted that it knows what kind of an entity a society is, or even if
society exists at all in any objective sense, before it can begin to
speculate as to the nature of its laws. It has to formulate a solution
to the problem of conceptualising how a discrete system can be a
real system at all, before it can begin to speculate about its
possible lawfulness. The question hinges around the reality of the
system, since it is here that the most paradoxical difficulties are
found. Is the discrete system real or does it only exist in the
imaginations of individuals? If it is real, then in what sense is it
real? Is it real in the sense that an object or an organism is real?
And if it is not real in this sense, then in what sense can we
legitimately use the word real? If, on the other hand, the discrete
system is not actually real, but somehow simply a product of the
minds of individuals, then in what ways may we expect it to be
governed by laws? It seems we cannot have it both ways. Either
the system is real, in which case it is overdetermined by being
reduced to a mere physical system of some kind; or it is imaginary
in which case it is underdetermined, since it is hard to conceive
how there could be laws governing an imaginary entity.

For most practical purposes, including that of conducting
research, the sociologist is well advised to avoid these philosophical problems and shelter behind convenient fictions. The
problem is avoided, for example, if it is resolved to treat society as
though it were no more than a collection of individuals, with all

that is distinctively social residing in the mental states, subjective experiences and behaviour of those individuals. In such a resolution, 'structures' above the level of the individual will tend to be of a purely conceptual nature, or constitute a communications system of some kind. Such entities may be mental constructs, but at least they can be discussed. Alternatively, the problem can be avoided in principle by introducing some kind of spatial metaphor at the level of society itself, usually that of some kind of quasi-biological organism. No one need believe that society really is a kind of organism in order for the metaphor to make it possible to discuss society as though it were such a system. Neither tactic is a philosophical solution to the problem of how a discrete system can exist and have its own laws, but both save rationality and permit sociology to proceed as though it were not on the brink of this vast epistemological chasm.[4]

Unfortunately, from the point of view of a social theory of space neither stance is workable. The reason is simple. From the point of view of space, the spatial problem of the discrete system is not a philosophical problem but a scientific one. It is intrinsic to the problem to be solved. If we wish to build a theory of how society, through its internal dynamics, produces order in space, then we must have some conception of what kind of spatial entity a society is in the first place. We cannot deal with the spatial form of an imaginary object, nor can we deal with the spatial dimension of an entity that is already an object, as would be the case if the organism theory were true. The spatial theorist is therefore trapped in the same impasse as has prevented sociology from developing a spatial sociology. He cannot use an existing spatial theory of society, because none exists. Nor can he hope to solve the philosophical problems of social theory before beginning on his own enterprise. In effect, he is forced to improvise. He cannot do without some conception of how a discrete system could be real and produce, through its lawful internal working, an output in the form of a realised spatial order. He must therefore try to skirt around the problem by giving some attention to the elementary dynamics of discrete systems.

The logic of discrete systems

If we attend first to very simple examples and gradually explore slightly more complex cases, there need be nothing at all mysterious about discrete systems or about their acquisition of a real spatial form. Discrete systems, composed of nothing but mobile individuals, can quite easily form themselves into global systems whose existence as objective realities need not be doubted. By examining simple cases we can begin to build a picture of how such systems may arise, be lawful and have different types of structure. To begin, consider an example given by René Thom: the cloud of midges.[5] The global form, the 'cloud', is made up only of a collection of individual midges who manage to constitute a recognisable cloud that remains stationary for considerable periods of time. This global form retains a certain 'structural stability' (to use Thom's phrase) so that we can see it and point to it in much the same way as we would see or point to an object, even though the constitutents of that global form appear to be nothing but randomly moving, discrete individual midges. How can such a situation arise? The answer could be quite simple. If each midge moves randomly until half its field of vision is clear of midges, then moves in the direction of midges, the result will be a stable cloud. We have, in effect, put a *restriction on the randomness* of individual movement, and the global form has arisen as a consequence of this. Now in this case, saying that the global form can *arise* from individual behaviour is not the same as saying that it is *reducible* to individual behaviour, since the model shows how the cloud comes to exist as an objective reality. The global form is real, even though composed only of discrete individuals. It arises from something like a relation of implication between the local and global properties of collections of midges.

Of course, a cloud of midges is nothing like a society, but it does have a number of formal properties which may be of interest. First, although the global form is undoubtedly real, no individual midge need have a conception of a cloud in order to realise it. The cloud is the global, collective product of a system in which discrete organisms follow a purely local rule, that is, a rule relating each midge only to whatever other individuals happen to be in the vicinity at the time. The design of the global object, as it were, is not located in a particular spatio-temporal region: it is *distributed* throughout the collection. Yet it is not enough to say that the restriction on randomness – that is, the local rule followed by individual midges – is what constitutes the system. The existence of the rule does not by itself produce the global result. The cloud results from the rule being realised in spatio-temporal reality in a process where random movement is assumed in the first place as a background to the operation of the rule. Given this, global order emerges of its own accord from a purely locally ordered system. The system in effect requires both a spatio-temporal embodiment, and a randomly operating background process in order to produce its order.

Seen in this way, discrete systems can both be objectively real and have definite structure, even though that structure is neither determinative nor at the level of the global system itself. Moreover, the system is fully external to individuals, while at the same time being entirely dependent on individuals for its existence and composition. The system depends on abstract rules; but it also depends on the embodiment of these rules in a dynamic spatio-temporal process. These rules do not simply prescribe what is to occur in the manner of a ritual. This would be only a limiting case of such a system: one from which the random background process had been entirely removed. The operation of the rules within a spatio-temporal process which is otherwise operating only randomly gives rise to new levels of order in the system *because* there is a random background process. If there is no random background, then there is no gain in global order. In such a system the new levels of order are not necessarily conceived of at any stage by any individual participating in the system. At the same time both the rules and the higher-level emergent orders are objective realities independent of subjects.

In the light of this example, we may next consider a case where what is being arranged is not individuals, but space itself, namely a simple process by which a complex composite object can be generated from a collection of simple single objects, rather as a settlement can be generated by aggregating together a collection of houses. The elementary objects are square cells; the rule of addition of cells is a full facewise join (Fig. 1(a)), with all other joins, such as the vertex join (Fig. 1(b)), excluded; and the aggregation process is one in which objects are added randomly to whatever is already aggregated subject to only one restriction: each cell must retain at least óne of its four 'walls' free from other cells. By the time a hundred cells have been aggregated, this generative process (which the reader may try for himself with paper and pencil) will look something like Fig. 2.

(a)   (b)

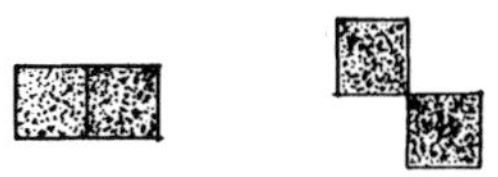

Fig. 1

Whatever the actual sequence of placing of objects, provided the process is properly randomised, the same generic global form will result: a dense and continuous aggregate of cells containing a number of void spaces – rather like courtyards – some of which are the same size as the cells, some twice the size, and some even larger. As the object grows larger 'holes' will appear.

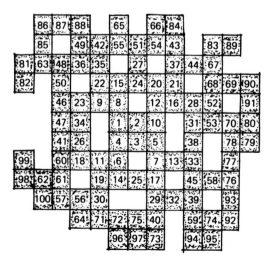

Fig. 2 A random full-face aggregation of square cells with one face per cell kept free, numbered in order of generation.

Once again, a well-defined *global* object has arisen from a purely *local* rule, in this case a rule requiring only that each cell should be joined facewise onto at least one other. In this sense the process is analogous to the cloud of midges: the global form has not been conceived of or designed by any individual: it has arisen from the independent dynamics of a process that is distributed among a collection of individuals. But it is a stronger case than the midges, in that the global object is not simply a random aggregation with only the fact of aggregation giving the global coherence of the object: in this case the global object has a definite *structure*.

Some important principles may be drawn from this simple but instructive example. First, in spite of appearances, space can work analogously to a discrete system, in that the fact and the form of the composite object are not a product of spatio-temporal causality, but a rule followed by spatially discrete entities. In this sense, contiguity is a logical fact, as well as a physical one. To be precise, in that it is a physical fact it is also a logical one. The global object is, as it were, welded into a whole by abstract as well as material facts. Second, although the global structure of the object has arisen through the agency of those who constructed the object, the form the object has taken is not the product of that agency, but of *spatial* laws which are quite independent of that agency. Indeed, they appear more like natural laws than like the products of human agency.

Now this has the effect of making the customary demarcations we draw between the natural and the artificial extremely tenuous. If we come across a real case of an object that appears to have precisely this form – see Fig. 3 – it is far from obvious that the

Fig. 3 The village of Seripe, after Mumtaz.

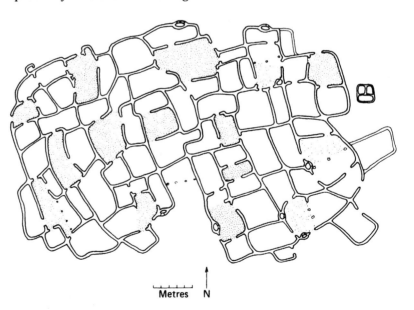

Metres   N

normal type of explanation of such forms in terms of human
puposes is complete. Of course the process by which the form was
actually manufactured was purposeful, but the global form must
in some sense also be the product of spatial laws that prescribe the
possibility, even the necessity of such a form, given the initial
conditions and an aggregative process. Third, and perhaps most
important, the global object that has resulted from the 'locally
ruled' process has a *describable* structure. We know this must be
the case, because we have described it to the reader, and the
reader has, we hope, recognised it. As a result, we could each
make another such form without going through the aggregative
process. We have retrieved *a* description of the global object
resulting from a spatial process, and we can reproduce it at will.
The importance of such descriptions is shown in the third
example, which will once again add new dimensions to the
system.

If the first example referred to an arrangement of individuals
and the second to an arrangement of space, the third brings both
together: the children's game of hide-and-seek. Imagine that a
group of children come across a disused factory and, after a period
of initial exploration, begin to play hide-and-seek. Like many
children's games, hide-and-seek is very spatial. In fact it depends
on a fairly complex global description being available in the
spatial milieu in which the game is played. There must be a focal
home base linked to a sufficiently rich set of invisible hiding
places, though not too many, or confusion will result. Connecting
the hiding places to the home base there must be a sufficiently rich
variety of paths, but again not too many. These paths must also
have among themselves a sufficient number of interconnections,
but again not too many. There must be enough children to make
the game interesting, but again not too many. The required global
description is partly topological, in that it deals with very general
spatial relations in a network of points and lines, and partly
numerical, in that while precise numbers are not given, there has
to be sufficient, but not too much of everything, if the game is to be
playable. We can call this global description, complete with its
topological and numerical parameters, the model of the game of
hide-and-seek.

Now clearly a very large class of possible environments will
more or less satisfy the model, but equally clearly another large
class would fail to satisfy them. One might be too poor in some
respect; another too rich. Too much structure, as well as too little,
it would seem, can make the game difficult to play. The factory,
with its finite size, its disused machines and occasional stores and
offices might create just the right mix to make the game playable,
without repetition, for a reasonably long time.

A number of further principles can be derived from this
example. It is clear that the factory, in some perfectly objective

sense, satisfies the topological and numerical requirements of the hide-and-seek model. The abstract model of the game is actually embodied in the physical circumstances of the factory. But equally, for the game to be playable at all, the abstract model of the game must be carried around by each participant child in its head. It would not be sufficient if each child had in their head simply a mental picture of places where he or she had previously played the game. In all likelihood the factory would not resemble any of them. In fact, the model in the child's head could not in any sense be tied to the previous places where he or she had played the game, since if this were the basis on which the model of hide-and-seek were held, it would lead the child to seek similar-looking places to play the game next time. Only one form of mental model is consistent with the way in which children discover the game in totally unfamiliar environments: an abstract model of the basic topological and statistical invariants of the game; that is a purely relational model, of some complexity, and with probabilities attached to relations.

Thus the abstract model of the game is in some sense present objectively in the spatial organisation of the factory; but it is equally objectively present in each child's mental apparatus. In these circumstances it is clearly a serious reduction to talk about a child's subjective response to the factory environment. The child's mental model is as objective as the reality. Given that the child is the active part of the system, it seems at least as accurate – though still incomplete – to talk of how the environment responds to the child's imposition of its mental model of hide-and-seek upon it, as to talk about how the child responds to the environment. But neither is an adequate formulation. The embodiment of the model appears to involve both mental processes and physical reality. It does not unambiguously belong in either domain. The distinction between subjective minds and the objective spatio-temporal world does not seem to hold. Reality has logical properties, the mind, physical models, or at least models of relations holding in the physical world.

But in spite of the difficulty in assigning it a unique location, there is nevertheless a definite structure to the game. This structure will be modified to a greater or lesser extent in different physical circumstances, but always within limits which can themselves be specified. There is, in effect, a *genotype* to the game of hide-and-seek, one whose presence can always be described as the underlying organising principle of the *phenotypes* of the game, that is, the actual realisation of the game in different physical milieux.

A fourth example can add a further dimension. An army marches all day. At nightfall, a halt is called beside a river and unpacking begins. Tents of various sizes and kinds are placed in certain definite relations; kitchens, sentry posts, flags, fences and other paraphernalia are erected. A complete environment is, as it were, unfolded. The next day the same procedure is followed, but this time camp is made on a hilltop; the next day in a narrow gulley; and so on. Once again, as locations change, the phenotypes of the camp change, but the genotype, of course, remains the same.

The army experiences this as a simple, repetitive procedure, but the situation is a good deal more complex. As in the case of hide-and-seek, there is an abstract relational model governing the arrangement of the camp. But this time, it is not simply a tacit, unconsciously learned structure, but a clear set of instructions inscribed somewhere in an army manual. Moreover, it carries a great deal more information than the hide-and-seek model. The hide-and-seek model has nothing more to it than its structure. The army camp model carries information about such matters as social structures and relationships, patterns of organised activity, and even ideological beliefs. If the hide-and-seek model means nothing but itself, the army camp model means a highly structured organisation which will be re-duplicated in other army camps.

But the members of the army do not really carry this much more complex model about with them in their heads, using it creatively in new situations and experimentally improvising new versions. On the contrary, the contribution of the indivdual brains of soliders is deliberately minimised. The abstract model is carried and transmitted much more through the material and equipment that the group carries in order to construct its environment: its 'instrumental set', so to speak.[6] There is, it seems, something of a reversal when we compare hide-and-seek with the army camp. In the former, the model in the head predominates over the physical structure of the environment, which it uses actively and creatively. In the latter, the physical structure of the environment dominates the thought patterns of individuals, and to a considerable extent provides the organising model for behaviour. It is able to do this because the abstract model on which it is based contains far more structure than the hide-and-seek model. Yet each involves a similar dialectic between mental model and spatiotemporal reality.

The army camp example raises a crucial question for the understanding of discrete systems and their spatial realisations: what is the nature of this extra information which appears to be programmed into the spatial structure. Is it simply nonspatial information? It clearly is social information, since it is predominantly about statuses and their relations. But does this mean that it is therefore simply extraneous to the discrete system, or is there some sense in which it is an intrinsic and even a necessary part of the discrete system? The answer can be made clear by considering for a moment another system where the issue of space makes a –

perhaps somewhat unexpected – appearance: the foundations of
natural language.

Space makes its appearance in natural language in the form of
the distinction between particular and universal terms, that is, in
the difference between words which refer to a particular instance
of an object and those which refer to a class of such objects. When
a particular is named the act of naming implies that some entity is
distinguished in the spatio-temporal flux of potential experience
by being identified with a particular, more or less unified region of
space. A particular can be, if not actually pointed to, then at least
indicated in some way. Its location and its organisation permit it
to be indicated as a particular. It need not be spatially continuous.
A cloud of midges, as well as a midge, can be indicated as a
particular. All that is required is that some set of – to borrow
Quine's term – 'ostensions', that is observable items of some kind,
should be integrated into a single object and summarised by a
name, such that the name then refers not only to all the various
individual ostentions, but also the single, spatially integrated
objects that they constitute globally.[7] The naming of a particular
follows from a procedure of identifying stable entities in the flux
by summing ostensions capable of what might be called *spatial
integration* into unified objects.

A universal term is also formed by a procedure involving
summation and identification, but in this case the entity identified
is conspicuously not characterised by existing in a single, more or
less unified region of space. On the contrary, what is summarised
is a collection of entities without regard for their location or
indicability. A universal names a class of entities which is
nothing more than an imaginary assemblage formed in the brain.
The objects integrated are not indicated, and in fact their existence may even be purely hypothetical. Because the naming of
universals is as importantly independent of spatial integration as
the naming of particulars was dependent on it, for our purposes a
term is needed that reflects this distinction. Universal terms will
therefore be said to result from a procedure of *transpatial integration*, that is, the summation of objects into composite entities
without regard for spatio-temporal indicability or location. A
midge, or a cloud of midges, is therefore an example of spatial
integration by which particulars are named, and midges an
example of transpatial integration, by which categories are
named.

The introduction of categories into the discrete system and its
spatial realisation is not therefore simply the introduction of
nonspatial elements, but the introduction of specifically *transpatial* elements. It means in effect the introduction of elements
and relations into the system whose reference points are not
simply within the system in question, but outside it in other
comparable systems *across space*. We may define a transpatial

relation as one which is realised in one local discrete system in the same form as it is realised in others. Now the existence of a transpatial relation has a very precise effect on the way in which this relation is realised in the local spatial system – that is, the particular army camp. It renders certain elements and their relations *noninterchangeable* with others. In the hide-and-seek model, which it will be recalled 'meant' only its own structure, all spaces except the focal space, were interchangeable with each other. The introduction of the transpatial dimension into the system means that particular spaces are required to be in specific relations to other spaces. This is the formal correlate of what we mean intuitively when we say that one system has more structure than another. It means that more necessary relations between elements have been introduced.

Once the transpatial has been defined in this way as forming a conceptual relation between local systems, then we can immediately see that it can also be found within the locally realised discrete system itself. It is to be found in the concept of a *rule*. If a rule is followed by a set of discrete individuals, it follows that the rule exists as a transpatial entity as well as a spatial entity. It follows from the very nature of the system. The concept of the transpatial does not therefore add a totally new dimension to the discrete system. It simply extends its structure in a particular direction.

The discrete system may therefore quite easily acquire a series of morphologically interesting properties to restrict its random base: essentially spatial rules, transpatial rules, and the retrieval of global descriptions. Even with such a simplified system we can already begin to analyse its potential dynamics. For example, if we have a collection of random individuals and provide them with a spatial rule by which at least two spatially distinct aggregates are formed, and a transpatial rule by which at least two categories of individuals are formed (*A*s and *B*s) with description retrieval applicable to both, then we have created a system with two entirely different pathways of development. In case 1 all the individuals of category *A* will be in one spatial group and all the *B*s in the other:

$$
\begin{array}{ccc\ ccc}
A & A & A & B & B & B \\
A & A & A & B & B & B \\
A & A & A & B & B & B \\
\end{array}
$$

in which case we have a *correspondence* between those relations defined spatially and those defined transpatially; in case 2 each category is distributed between the two spatial groups:

$$
\begin{array}{ccc\ ccc}
A & B & B & B & A & A \\
B & A & B & A & B & A \\
A & B & A & B & B & A \\
\end{array}
$$

in which case we have a *noncorrespondence* between the two types of relation.

Now let us suppose that description retrieval happens equally with respect to both spatial and transpatial groupings, and that these descriptions are then embodied in future behaviour. In the correspondence case, the long-term effect of description retrieval will be to reinforce the local group at the expense of the global system comprising both (or all) of the spatial groups. In the noncorrespondence case, description retrieval will be split between reinforcing the local spatial group and reinforcing relations across space with members of other spatial groups. The latter will therefore tend to reinforce the global system as much as the local system, and the more noncorrespondence there is, the more it will do so.

All human social formations appear to exhibit this duality of spatial and transpatial, of local group and category. A member of a university for example is a member of two fundamentally different kinds of group, the one spatial the other transpatial, by virtue of his position. On the one hand he is a member of a particular university, which is more or less spatially defined; on the other he is a member of an academic discipline, which is transpatially defined. Different aspects of his total behaviour will be concerned with reinforcing the descriptions of both groups. The dialectic between the two types of grouping is one of the principal generators of local spatial patterning. Chapter 7 of this book is concerned largely with exploring some of these dimensions of difference. At this stage we must concern ourselves with an anterior question: given these properties of a discrete system, then how can we define the discrete system in *principle* as a system capable of scientific investigation and analysis.

The inverted genotype

In describing the last two illustrative examples, hide-and-seek and the army camp, we found ourselves making use of the biological distinction between phenotypes and genotypes. This is interesting not least because phenotype is a spatial concept and genotype a transpatial concept. Does this mean that we can treat discrete systems as being in principle comparable to biological systems? The answer is that in a very important sense we cannot, but by clarifying the reason why we cannot we arrive at a suitable general characterisation of the discrete system.

The biological concept of a genotype is essentially an informational concept. It describes something like a total informational environment within which the phenotypes exist, in the sense that individual phenotypes are linked into a continuously transmitted information structure governing their form. Through the genotype, the phenotype has transtemporal links with his ancestors and

descendents as well as transpatial links with other contemporane-
ous organisms of the same kind. The genotype is at least partially
realised in each individual organism through what might be
called a *description centre*. A description centre guarantees the
continuity of the class of organisms in time and their similarity in
space. The description centre holds instructions locally on how
some initial material is to adapt local energy sources in order to
unfold into a phenotype. The description centre does not have to
be a particular organ; it may be spread throughout the organism. It
is a description centre because it contains a local embodiment of
genetic instructions.

It is very tempting to import this powerful and simple concept
direct into the analysis of discrete systems. After all, both human
societies and their spatial formations vary from each other, yet are
recognisably members of the same 'species' of entity, sharing
many features in common as well as having differences. Unfortunately the idea collapses as soon as it is applied for a very obvious
reason: there is no description centre. Of course, we may try to
escape from this by arguing that the specialised institutional
structure of a society is its description centre; but this leads
nowhere, since the more elementary a society is, the less likely it
is to have specialised institutions. Or we may instead try to extend
the concept of the biological genotype governing the social
behaviour of individuals and argue that society is accounted for in
terms of genetically transmitted instructions for behaviour between species members. This is equally unconvincing. How could
such a model account even in principle for the global morphological variation of social formations, or indeed for their extraordinary complexity? Either kind of reduction seems unrealistic. A
model of a society must deal with society in its own terms, as an
entity in its own right. It seems the concept of genotype has led us
on only to fail the critical test.

However, a simple adaptation of the concept of genotype can
provide what is needed: a model that characterises the structure
and continuity as well as the variety and differences of discrete
systems without recourse to biologism, but saves the continuity of
social and biological mechanisms and allows for both evolution
and stability in social forms. The first adaptation is the *substitution of a local description retrieval mechanism for a description
centre*. The components of a discrete system do not carry within
them, jointly or severally, a genetically transmissable description
of the system. Instead they have a mechanism which permits them
to retrieve a description of the system from the system itself at any
point in it.[8] This would make no difference to the stability of the
system under normal circumstances since, if the system were
stable, the same description would always be retrieved. Thus the
system would behave as though it had the kind of stability that
comes from the genotype. But if such a system were to be changed

by an outside agency – say a natural disaster of some kind, or a conquest – then a new system could quickly stabilise that would have no necessary similarity to the previous one. The system is highly susceptible to external perturbation through the natural operation of the description retrieval mechanism.

The second adaptation is almost implied by the first. *The structured information on which the system runs is not carried in the description mechanism but in reality itself in the spatio-temporal world.* The programme does not generate reality. Reality generates a programme, one whose description is retrievable, leading to the self-reproduction of the system under reasonably stable conditions. Thus in effect reality is its own programme. The abstract description is built into the material organisation of reality, which as a result has some degree of intelligibility.

Description retrieval enables us to conceive of a discrete system, and even perhaps of a society as a special kind of 'artefact': one whose embodiment is its output. Whereas in a biological system the phenotype, insofar as it is an example of the genotype, exists in the spatio-temporal informational environment, and is preceded and followed by a series of comparable phenotypes who have passed on the form from one to the next, a discrete system runs on an *inverted genotype*, which exists as a transpatial or informational structure within an environment of human spatio-temporal reality and activity.[9] What genetic instructions are to a biological system, spatio-temporal reality and activity are to a discrete system. Thus in this sense also the genotype–phenotype mechanism is inverted. The consistency in human activity at the social level is not the product of a biological genotype but of an artefactual genotype: one that is retrieved as a description from reality itself which has already been constructed by the activity of man.

The inverted genotype of the discrete system is able to operate in many comparable ways to the biological genotype. For example it can permit that mixture of structural stability and evolutionary morphogenesis which has been widely noted as a property of both biological and social systems. On the other hand, there are critical differences. The discrete system, while being generally stable, can undergo revolutionary rather than evolutionary changes and establish radical discontinuities in its history. It is a system without genetic memory. It tends to conserve the present and have no regard for the past. Its inertia lies in the fact that its genetic structure is transmitted through an enormous number and variety of real spatio-temporal behaviours by its individual members, including those ordering space itself. On the other hand, it can also be changed by deliberate and conscious action. Reflective action could operate on the system's description of itself in much the same way as an external perturbation or catastrophe. It could probably succeed in wiping out the past.

An even more radical difference between the biological genotype and the inverted genotype is that discrete systems, governed
by inverted genotypes, can be a great deal untidier than biological
systems. As has been seen, it is a property of a discrete system that
because of its random background it generates a good deal more
than is already contained in its genotype, both in the sense of the
production of more global patterns of order and in the production
of disorder. An inverted genotype is much more precarious than a
biological genotype. It must be constantly re-embodied in social
action if it is not to vanish or mutate. In other words, the
self-reproduction of a discrete system will require a good deal of
work. But this social reproduction, it is clear, is the most fundamental feature of human societies. Every society invests a
certain proportion of its material resources not in the biological
perpetuation of individuals, but in the reproduction of the global
society by means of special biologically irrelevant behaviours
which are aimed purely at the enactment of descriptions of the
society as a whole. This is why, as Durkheim knew, the social is
founded in the behaviours that we now call religious – that is, a
set of biologically pointless, intensified behaviours whose value
lies purely in their description potential for the larger society.[10]
The apparently absurd act of sacrifice, biologically unaccount-
able, but a universal feature of religious observances, is simply a
shift of resources from the local to the global, from the spatial to
the transpatial, and from everyday life to the perpetuation of
descriptions.

Morphic languages

The whole notion of a discrete system as we have defined it
depends on the *retrievability* of descriptions. This leads to a
straightforward methodological requirement if we are to understand the working of such systems: we must learn to characterise
discrete systems in such a way as to clarify how their descriptions
are retrievable in abstract form. We will in effect be trying to
describe an order that is already present in the system, in that the
minds of individuals have already been able to grasp that such an
order exists and can be duplicated and built on. We must try to
characterise what is to be known in terms of how it can be known.
But it does not quite end there. As we have already seen,
something like the laws of constructibility of patterns have
already played a role in producing global order out of local rules.
Any characterisation of descriptions should also take into account
this aspect. Methodologically there is a problem of *morphology* –
what can be constructed so as to be knowable – and a problem of
knowability – how it is that descriptions can be known. Ultimately the crucial question will be how these two are related to each
other, and even how far they can be regarded as the same thing.

In view of the primacy accorded to abstract descriptions, it might be expected that the methodology of research would therefore be a mathematical one. However, this is not strictly the case. Mathematics may be too strong a language for characterising the structures on which discrete systems are run, although these structures will always include elements of both a topological and numerical nature. In our view, a less delicate, more robust strategy is called for in trying to identify the essentials of these descriptions than any branch of mathematics currently provides. Moreoever, we believe there are strong grounds for adopting a methodology that is less than fully mathematical, in present circumstances at least. The reasons for this belief centre around the problem of representing knowability in complex systems generally, and perhaps we can best explain our case by reference to various comments in another field where the problem of knowability has been paramount: that of artificial intelligence.

The problem in artificial intelligence study seems to be something like this. A computer program is essentially a procedure, and the skill in simulating intelligent behaviours – playing chess, recognising complex patterns, having an intelligent conversation – lies essentially in showing how the necessary mental operations can be set out as a procedure. Success in reducing cognitive processes to procedures has led to machines that can translate a good proportion of texts, play chess tolerably well, and analyse patterns with no small degree of success. But in the long run, this success has been at the expense of rather unlifelike simulation, since human beings do not appear to act intelligently on the basis of extremely complex procedures, but on the basis of something much more difficult to analyse and represent: knowledge. As Michie says: 'Machine intelligence is fast attaining self-definition and we have as a touchstone the realisation that the central operations of intelligence are (logical and procedural) transactions on a knowledge base.'[11] And later, talking of chess playing machines: 'As with other sectors of machine intelligence, rich rewards await even partial solutions of the representation problem. To capture in a formal descriptive scheme the game's delicate structure; it is here that future progress lies, rather in nano-second access times, parallel processing, or mega-megabit memories.'[12]

What seems to be in doubt is whether or not the delicate formal structure of these 'knowables' is actually made out of the apparatus of mathematics. On this issue, the comments of several of the pioneers of artificial intelligence are illuminating. Von Neuman, in *The Computer and the Brain*, wrote shortly before he died:

Thus logic and mathematics in the central nervous system, when viewed as languages must structurally be essentially different from those languages to which our common experience refers ... when we talk of mathematics, we may be discussing a *secondary* language built on the *primary* language truly used by the central nervous system. Thus the outward forms of *our* mathematics are not absolutely relevant from the point of view of evaluating what the mathematical of logical language *truly* used by the central nervous system is. However ... it cannot fail to differ considerably from that which we consciously and explicitly consider as mathematics.[13]

A similar comment is made by McCulloch:

Tautologies, which are the very stuff of mathematics and logic, are the ideas of no neuron.[14]

Likewise Kac and Ulam, discussing the logic of biochemical processes:

The exact mechanics, logic, and combinatorics ... are not yet fully understood. New logical schemes that are established and analysed mathematically doubtless will be found to involve patterns somewhat different from those now used in the formal apparatus of mathematics.[15]

A possible guide for our recent purposes comes from the work of Piaget on the development of intellective functions in children, including spatial concepts.[16] Piaget has an intriguing general conclusion. Whereas the mathematical analysis of space began with geometry, then became generalised to projective geometry, and only recently acquired its most general form, that of topology, children appear to learn about the formal properties of space the other way round. The first spatial ideas that children learn by manipulating the world and its objects are in the main what Piaget calls topological, though without requiring this term to be used in its strictest mathematical sense. Piaget's observation appears in principle to be sound and interesting. Children first develop concepts of proximity, separation, spatial succession, enclosure and contiguity, and these concepts lie within the purview of topology rather than geometry or projective geometry.

If it is the case that some of the deepest and most generalised mathematical concepts are close to intuition then we may hazard a guess as to how von Neuman's challenge might be taken up with the representation of knowables in view. It may be that certain very abstract and general mathematical ideas are learnt from our elementary transactions with the world. Might it not be the case that, as von Neuman suggests, there may be two types of development from this basis? First, there is the secondary language of mathematics proper, which we have to learn consciously; and second, a primary language, which sets up combinatorial systems founded on fundamental mathematical ideas, whose object is not to evolve rigorous, self-contained mathematical systems, but to give the formal structures by which we encode and structure our knowledge of the world. In other words, the formal structure of knowables in the man-made world may be constructed on the basis of elementary concepts that are also found in mathematics, but are not themselves mathematical.

If this is the case (and it can only be put forward at this stage as a long-term hypothesis), it would explain why little progress has been made with the problem of the formal representation of knowables. Mathematics as we have it is not the family of structures that we need. They are too pure and they have another purpose. The proper name for such formal, presumably combinatorial systems ought to distinguish them clearly from mathematics proper. We therefore propose to call them *syntaxes*. Syntaxes are combinatorial structures which, starting from ideas that may be mathematical, unfold into families of pattern types that provide the artificial world of the discrete system with its internal order as knowables, and the brain with its means of retrieving description of them. Syntax is the imperfect mathematics of the artificial.

Any set of artificial entities which uses syntax in this way can be called a *morphic language*. A morphic language is any set of entities that are ordered into different arrangements by a syntax so as to constitute social knowables. For example, space is a morphic language. Each society constructs an 'ethnic domain' by arranging space according to certain principles.[17] By retrieving the abstract description of these principles, we intuitively grasp an aspect of the social for that society. The description is retrievable because the arrangement is generated from syntactic principles. But social relationships also are a morphic language. For example, each society will construct characteristic encounter patterns for its members, varying from the most structured to the most random. The formal principles of these patterns will be the descriptions we retrieve, and in which we therefore recognise an aspect of the social for that society. Viewed this way, modes of production and co-operation can be seen as morphic languages. In each society we learn the principles and create behaviours accordingly, even those that negate the accepted principles of order.

The concept of a morphic language links together the problem of knowability, defined as that of understanding how characteristic patterns in a set of phenomena can be recognised by reference to abstract principles of arrangement, with that of morphology, defined as that of understanding the objective similarities and differences that classes of artificial phenomena exhibit, by proposing that both are problems of understanding syntax. To explain a set of spatio-temporal events we first describe the combinatorial principles that gave rise to it. This reduction of a morphology to combinatorial principles is its reduction to its principles of knowability. The set of combinatorial principles is the syntax. Syntax is the most important property of a morphic language. What is knowable about the spatio-temporal output of a morphic language is its syntax. Conversely, syntax permits spatio-temporal arrangements to exhibit systematic similarities and differences.

The nature of morphic languages can be clarified by comparing them to two other types of language: the natural and the mathematical. The primary purpose of a natural language (irrespective of particular linguistic functions) is to represent the world as it appears, that is, to convey a meaning that in no way resembles the language itself. To accomplish the task of representation in an infinitely rich universe, a natural language possesses two defining characteristics. First, it has a set of primary morphic units which are strongly individuated, that is, each word is different from all other words and represents different things; and second, a formal or syntactic structure which is parsimonious and permissive, in that it permits infinitely many sentences to be syntactically well-formed that are semantically nonsense (that is, effectively nonsense from the point of view of linguistic form as a whole). Conversely, meaning can be transmitted (that is represented) without well-formed syntactic structure. The defining characteristics of a natural language are a relatively short, possibly conventional syntax and a large lexicon.

By contrast, mathematical languages have very small lexicons (as small as possible) and very large syntaxes, in the sense of all the structure that may be elaborated from the initial minimal lexicon. Such languages are virtually useless for representing the world as it appears because the primary morphic units are not individuated at all, but rendered as homogeneous as possible – the members of a set, units of measurement, and so on. Mathematical symbols strip the morphic unit of all its particular properties, leaving only the most abstract and universal properties – being a member of a set, existing, and so on. To be interested in the particular properties of particular numbers is for a mathematician the equivalent of a voyage in mysticism. Mathematical languages do not represent or mean anything except their own structure. If they are useful for representing the most abstract forms of order in the real world it is because, in its preoccupation with its own structure, mathematics arrives at general principles of structure, which, because they are deep and general, hold also at some level in the real world.

Morphic languages differ from both, yet borrow certain properties from each. From mathematical languages, morphic languages take the small lexicon (that is, the homogeneity of its primary morphic units), the primacy of syntactic structure over semantic representation, the property of being built up from a minimal initial system, and the property of not meaning anything except its own structure (that is to say, they do not exist to represent other things, but to constitute patterns which are their own meaning). From natural languages, morphic languages take the property of being realised in the experiential world, of being creatively used for social purposes, and of permitting a rule-governed creativity.

Thus in a morphic language syntax has a far more important

role than in natural language. In natural language the existence of
a syntactically well-formed sentence permits a meaning to exist,
but neither specifies it nor guarantees it. In a morphic language
the existence of a syntactically well-formed sentence itself
guarantees and indeed specifies a meaning, because the meaning
is only the abstract structure of the pattern. Morphic languages are
the realisation of abstract structure in the real world. They convey
meaning not in the sense of representing something else, but only
in the sense of constituting a pattern. Thus if, as we believe, both
space organisation and social encounter patterns are morphic
languages, the construction of a social theory of space organisation becomes a question of understanding the relations between
the principles of pattern generation in both.

This does not mean that architectural and urban forms are not
used to represent particular meanings, but it does argue that such
representation is secondary. To achieve representation of meaning in the linguistic sense, the morphic language of space does so
by behaving as a natural language. It *individuates* its morphic
units. Hence buildings which are intended to convey particular
meanings do so by the addition of idiosyncratic elaboration and
detail: decoration, bell-towers, and so on. In so doing, the morphic
units come to behave more like particular words in natural
language. Conversely, when natural language is useful to convey
abstract structure as, for example in academic monographs, it
does so by increasing the importance of syntax over the word.[18]

Morphic languages are also like mathematics and unlike natural
language in that they pose the problem of the description, in
addition to that of the *generation* of structure. Current linguistic
theory assumes that a theoretical description of a sentence would
be given by a formula expressing generative and transformation
rules. This would hold even if current efforts to build semantically (as opposed to syntactically) based theories were successful. In
mathematics, however, structure is only reducible to generation if
one takes a strong philosophical line opposing reification or
Platonisation of structure and argues that all mathematical structure is self-evidently reducible to an ordering activity of mathematicians, not to be thought of as existing in its own right. In fact,
the dialectic of generation and description appears to be of
fundamental importance in the real-world behaviour of morphic
languages. Any ordered collective activity that is not fully pre-
programmed gives rise to the problem of retrieving a description
of the collective pattern. Meaning can be seen as a stably retrievable description.

We now have a definition in principle of what the discrete
system and its spatial realisation is like, and how, again in
principle, it acquires and perpetuates its order. We might call a
discrete system, together with its reproducible order, an *arrangement*. An arrangement can be defined as some set of initial

randomly distributed discrete entities, which enter into different kinds of relations in space–time and, by retrieving descriptions of the ordering principles of these relations, are able to reproduce them. An arrangement is essentially the extension of spatial integration into the realm of transpatial integration: that is, it creates the appearance – and in a more limited sense, the reality – of spatially integrated complexes which, properly speaking, retain their discrete identity as individual objects. A class, or transpatial integration of objects is an *unarranged* set. Arrangement of these sets gives each object a new *relational* identity; and out of the accumulation of these relational identities in space–time global patterns can arise which, by description retrieval, can also become built into the system.

The basic forms of order in arrangements are these relational systems considered abstractly, that is, considered as syntaxes of morphic languages. The next stage of our argument must, therefore, be the presentation of a syntax for the morphic language of human spatial organisation, such that the syntax is both a theory of the constructibility of spatial order and a theory of how abstract descriptions may be retrieved from it: that is, a theory of morphology, and at the same time a theory of abstract knowability.

2

The logic of space

SUMMARY

This chapter does three things. First, it introduces a new concept of order in space, as restrictions on an otherwise random process. It does this by showing experimentally that certain kinds of spatial order in settlements can be captured by manual or computer simulation. Second, it extends the argument to show that more complex restrictions on the random process can give rise to more complex and quite different forms of order, permitting an analytic approach to space through the concept of a fundamental set of elementary generators. Third, some conclusions are drawn from this approach to order from the point of view of scientific strategy. However, the chapter ends by showing the severe limitations of this approach, other than in establishing the fundamental dimensions of analysis. The reader is warned that this chapter is the most tortuous and perhaps the least rewarding in the book. Those who do not manage to work their way through it can, however, easily proceed to the next chapter, provided they have grasped the basic syntactic notions of symmetry–asymmetry and distributed–nondistributed.

Introduction

Even allowing for its purely descriptive and non-mathematical intentions, a syntax model must nevertheless aim to do certain things:
- to find the irreducible objects and relations, or 'elementary structures' of the system of interest – in this case, human spatial organisation in all its variability;
- to represent these elementary structures in some kind of notation or ideography, in order to escape from the difficulty of always having to use cumbersome verbal constructs for sets of ideas which are used repeatedly;
- to show how elementary structures are related to each other to make a coherent system; and
- to show how they may be combined together to form more complex structures.

In view of the acknowledged scale and complexity of human spatial organisation this is a tall order. Even so, there is an additional difficulty which cannot be avoided. Leaving aside the

question of meaning (and the different ways in which different
societies assign meanings to similar spatial configurations), there
is also the fundamental dimension of difference noted in the
Introduction: some societies seem to invest much less in spatial
order than others, being content with random, or near-random
arrangements, while others require complex, even geometric
forms.[1] Clearly it would not be possible to build a social account
of spatial organisation in general if our initial descriptive model
was unable to characterise an important class of cases.

What follows must therefore be seen as having philosophical
and methodological aims, rather than mathematical. The philosophical aim is to show that it is possible in principle to construct
a syntax model which, while describing fundamental variations
in structure, also incorporates the passage from non-order to
order. This will turn out to be of major importance in the later
stages of this book, where attention is turned to a more far-
reaching consideration of the kinds of order that are possible in
spatial and social arrangements, including those where meaning
is introduced. The methodological aim is to discover the
elementary relational concepts of space that are required for the
development of the methods of spatial analysis set out in Chapters
3, 4 and 5.

These aims are more modest than they may appear at first sight,
for a simple reason. At the most elementary levels there are
relatively few ways in which space *can* be adapted for human
purposes, and at more complex levels, severe constraints on how
they may unfold and remain useful. For example, at some level all
settlement structure must retain a continuous system of permeability outside its constituent buildings, while what we mean
by a building implies a continuous boundary (however permeable) as well as continuous internal permeability. These limitations and constraints make the *effective* morphology of space
much less complex than it would appear to a mathematician
attempting an enumeration of possibilities without taking these
limitations into account.

Compressed descriptions

Every science has for its object a morphology: that is, some set of
observable forms, which present such similarities and differences
to observation that there is reason to believe these to be in some
way interconnected. A theory describes this interconnectedness
by setting up a family of organising principles from which each
difference can be derived. A theory, in effect, shows a morphology
to be a *system of transformations*.

The principle that theories should be as economical as possible
follows. A good theory is one which with few principles accounts
for much variability in the morphology; a bad theory one which

with many principles accounts for little. The least economical
description of a morphology would be a list of principles and a list
of phenomena, each as long as the other. A good theory is the
opposite of a list. It is as compressed a description of the
morphology as possible in terms of its organising principles.

Belief in the economy of theories is not therefore a matter for
aesthetic preference. It reflects a deeper belief in the economy of
nature. If nature unfolded under the scope of arbitrarily many
principles, then sciences would not be possible. Lists of phenomena and lists of principles would be almost as long as each
other. These we would not recognise as scientific in any useful
sense. Belief in the well-ordering of nature *implies* the compressibility of descriptions.

In decoding artificial systems like spatial arrangements or social
structures, a parallel belief in the economy of principles and the
consequent compressibility of descriptions is not unreasonable.
Although it is often objected that the methods of natural science
cannot apply to the man-made, since man creates as he chooses,
the evidence suggests this is only partly true. Artificial phenomena, such as settlement forms (or languages for that matter),
seem to manifest to observers about the same level of similarities
and differences as nature. No two cases are alike, yet comparisons
suggest variations on underlying common principles. On reflection, this is a very probable state of affairs. There must be some
compromise with complete indeterminacy in man-made systems.
This compromise comes from the recognition that even the most
arbitrary creation of man cannot be independent of objective
morphological laws which are not of his own making. Man
manipulates morphological laws to his own ends, but he does not
create those laws. It is this necessary compromise that admits the
artificial to the realm of science, and makes it accessible to the
method of compressed descriptions.

The subject of Chapter 2 is the compressed description of the
physical patterns of space arranged for human purposes. It is a
description of space not in terms of these purposes (as is more
customary in architecture), but in terms of the underlying morphological constraints of pattern formation within which human
purposes must work themselves out. It is based on two premises:
first, that human spatial organisation, whether in the form of
settlements or buildings, is the establishment of patterns of
relationships composed essentially of boundaries and permeabilities of various kinds; and second, that although there are infinitely
many different complexes of spatial relations possible in the real
world, there are not infinitely many underlying sets of organising
principles for these patterns. There is on the contrary a finite
family of generators of complexity in human space organisation,
and it is within the constraints imposed by this family of
generators that spatial complexity is manipulated and adapted

for social purposes. It is conjectured that this basic family of generators is small, and is expressible as a set of inter-related structures. The objective of this section is to describe this basic set of generators as a syntactic system.

The rudiments of the methodology have already been presented to the reader in Chapter 1 (see pp. 35–6); Given a random process of assigning objects of some kind – say, single cells – to a surface, then what kind of spatial patterns emerge when this random process is subject to restrictions of various kinds? In the example given in Fig. 2 the restrictions were two: that each cell should be joined facewise to at least one other; and at least one face on each cell should be free of a facewise join. This, as we saw, produced a pattern of the same general type as a certain settlement form. The object is to find out what kinds of restriction on randomness will generate the family of patterns that we actually find in human settlement forms. In other words, we are trying to build a syntax for the morphic language, space, based on some system of restrictions on an underlying random process.

In what follows the notion of the random background process is of the utmost importance. It is the foundation the argument starts from, and it will return to play a significant role even in the most complex, semantic stages of the theory. The assumption of a random background process seems as liberating to the student of pattern in artificial phenomena as the assumption of inertia was to the physicist. In certain ways it is conceptually comparable. Instead of trying to found the systematic analysis of human spatial patterns in individual motivations – making individuals the unmotivated motivators of the system – it is assumed that human beings will deploy themselves in space in some way, perhaps without interconnection from one individual to the next, in which case the process is random. The question then is how far individuals have to relate their spatial actions to those of others in order to give rise to pattern and form in space.

The first stage of the argument is formal but not strictly mathematical. The aim is to represent certain basic rules of spatial combination and relation in an ideographic language, such that when these rules are coupled to a random background process, they become propositions expressing generative principles for spatial order. The advantage of this procedure is that it makes it possible to be entirely rigorous about what we mean by pattern in space, so that questions about the social origins and consequences of these patterns can at least be formulated in an unambiguous way. Some examples can introduce the argument.

Some examples

In the region of the Vaucluse in Southern France, west of the town of Apt and north of the Route N.100, the landscape has a striking

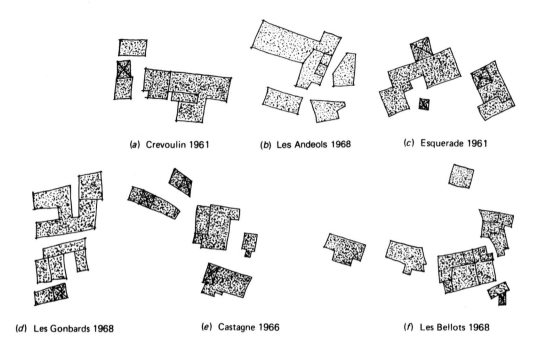

(a) Crevoulin 1961   (b) Les Andeols 1968   (c) Esquerade 1961

(d) Les Gonbards 1968   (e) Castagne 1966   (f) Les Bellots 1968

Fig. 4 Six clumps of building from the Vaucluse region of France.

feature; everywhere there are small, dense groups of buildings, collected together in such a way that from a distance they appear as disordered clumps, lacking in any kind of planning or design. The clumps are as inconsistent in size as they are in layout. A selection of the smallest clumps displays, it seems, total heterogeneity of plan (Fig. 4(a)–(f)). At first sight, even the largest, where we might expect to find more conscious attempts at planning, appear no less varied (Fig 5). However, all is not quite as it seems. The smallest undoubtedly appear heterogeneous, but as they approach a certain size a certain global regularity begins to appear. Perrotet, for example, is a hamlet of about forty buildings in the Commune of Gargas. About half of the buildings are currently in ruins, although the decline has been arrested in

Fig. 5 Hamlet of Les Petits Clements, 1968.

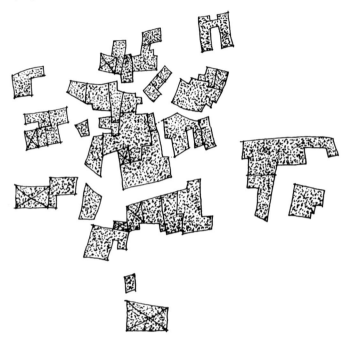

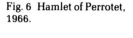

Fig. 6 Hamlet of Perrotet, 1966.

recent years by the arrival of *estivants* from the major towns, who rebuild and renovate the old dwellings as holiday villas. The layout of the hamlet may show little sign of order or planning (Fig. 6), but the impression the settlement makes on the casual observer is far from one of disorder (Fig. 7).

In plan the settlement appears irregular because it lacks the formal, geometric properties we normally associate with spatial order. Yet as a place to walk about and experience, it seems to possess order of another, more subtle, more intricate kind. The very irregularity of the ways in which the buildings aggregate appears somehow to give the hamlet a certain recognisability and suggests a certain underlying order.

This impression is reinforced when an attempt is made to enumerate some of the spatial properties of the complex. For example:

- each individual building fronts directly onto the open space structure of the hamlet without intervening boundaries;
- the open space structure is not in the form, for example, of a single central space with buildings grouped around it, but is rather like beads on a string: there are wider parts, and narrower parts, but all are linked together direct;
- the open space is eventually joined to itself to form one major ring and other sub-rings, the main beady ring of space being the strongest global characteristic of the complex;

- the beady ring is everywhere defined by an inner clump of buildings, and a set of outer clumps, the beady ring being defined between the two;
- the outer set of clumps has the effect of defining a kind of boundary to the settlement, giving it the appearance of being a finite, even finished object;
- the beady ring structure coupled to the immediate adjacency of the building entrances gives the complex a high degree of permeability and mutual accessibility of dwellings: there are by definition at least two ways from any building to any other building.

The sense of underlying order is reinforced dramatically when we compare Perrotet first to a number of other settlements of comparable size in the vicinity (Fig. 8(a)–(d)), and then to a selection of the same settlements, including Perrotet, as they were nearly two hundred years ago (Fig. 9(a)–(d)).

In all cases the beady ring structure is invariant, although in some cases the locus of the principal beady ring has shifted over the years, and in others the structure is somehow incomplete. In spite of the great differences between the hamlets, and in spite of their changes over time, it seems reasonable to describe the beady

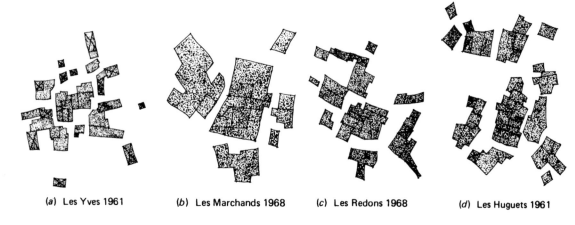

(a) Les Yves 1961   (b) Les Marchands 1968   (c) Les Redons 1968   (d) Les Huguets 1961

Fig. 8 Four 'beady ring' hamlets from the Vaucluse region.

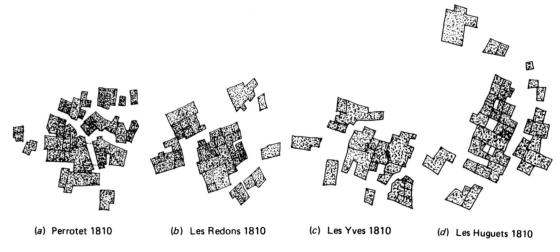

(a) Perrotet 1810   (b) Les Redons 1810   (c) Les Yves 1810   (d) Les Huguets 1810

ring structure, together with all the arrangemental properties that define the beady ring, such as direct access to dwellings, as a genotype for hamlets in that region, with particular hamlets as individual phenotypes.

Fig. 9 A selection of 'beady ring' hamlets from the same region, as they were in the early nineteenth century.

The question is how could such a genotype arise in the first place and be reproduced so regularly. A paradigm problem is, in effect, presented for the morphic language approach: what restrictions on a random process of assigning objects to a surface would give rise to the observable pattern that we see, in this case the beady ring genotype? The answer turns out to be remarkably straightforward. The following model, simplified to allow computer simulation, shows the essentials of the generative process.

Let there be two kinds of objects, closed cells with an entrance (Fig. 10(a)), and open cells (Fig. 10(b)). Join the two together by a

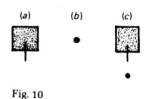

Fig. 10

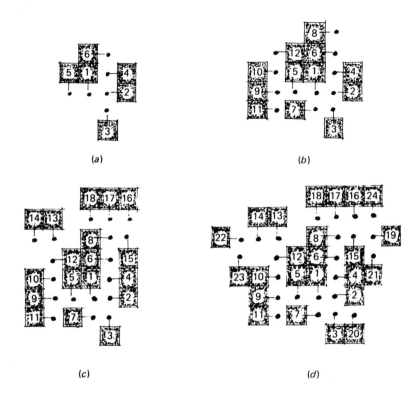

(a)   (b)

(c)   (d)

Fig. 11 Four stages of a
computer-generated 'beady
ring' structure.

full facewise join on the entrance face to form a doublet (Fig.
10(c)). Allow these doublets to aggregate randomly, requiring
only that each new object added to the surface joins its open cell
full facewise onto at least one other open cell. The location of the
closed cell is randomised, one closed cell joining another full
facewise, but not vertex to vertex. Fig. 11(a)–(d) illustrates a
typical local process defined by these restrictions on randomness,
with the closed cells numbered in order of their placing on the
surface.

The global beady ring effect results from the local rules in the
process in the same way as the global cloud effect followed from
the spatio-temporal unfolding of the local rule followed by the
midges. This process is robust, and can survive a great deal of
distortion. For example, it will work almost regardless of the
shape of the initial objects, provided the open-closed relation is
maintained. Interestingly, variation in the precise size and number of the beady rings will follow from changing the probability of
closed cells being joined to each other, or even allowing the open
cells not to be joined provided the closed cells are. This means
that not only will global forms arise from restrictions on the
background random process, but also that variations on these
forms will follow from changing the value of probabilities
assigned to these restrictions.

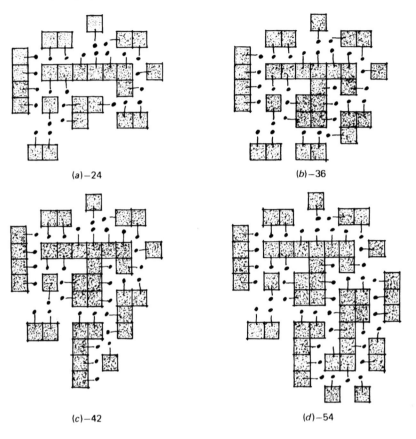

(a) – 24

(b) – 36

(c) – 42

(d) – 54

Fig. 12 An extended 'beady ring' process.

Once this process is understood, the heterogeneous set of very small aggregations (Fig. 4(a)–(f)) suddenly makes sense as settlements in the process of growth towards beady ring status, with a fairly high closed-cell join probability – that is, as a process governed by a model with topological and numerical properties, as suggested by the hide-and-seek case. But what of the larger example? This has a small beady ring, and a very much larger one, so that the beady ring form still holds for the global structure of a considerably larger settlement. Can this occur, for example by extending the same generative process, or will it be necessary to introduce more structure into the machine? The unfolding is suggestive (Fig. 12(a)–(d)). In other words, the process *can* produce the beady ring structure at more global levels. But of course, in the real case, one suspects that a certain perception by individuals of the emerging global structure would play its part, and that this would become more accentuated as the aggregation becomes larger. Exactly how this can occur without violating the principles of the model is taken up in Chapter 3, where the numerical dimensions of the model are explored. At this stage, we are concerned with basic spatial relations, and, in particular, with isolating their formal properties.[2]

The generative process that forms the beady ring has a number of formal properties of interest. First, the generative relation is *symmetric*, in the sense that the restriction on randomness required only that cell A and cell B become contiguous neighbours of each other. The relation of neighbour always has the property that the relation of A to B is the same as the relation of B to A. The process also has the distributed property, discussed in relation to the examples in the Introduction, (pp. 11–12) in that the global structure is created purely by the arrangement of a number of equal, individual cells rather than, for example, by the superimposition of a single superordinate cell on those cells.

The two contrary properties can also be defined. The property of *asymmetry* would exist when the relation of cell A to cell B was not the same as the relation of cell B to cell A, for example, if cell A contained cell B. If a single cell A did contain a single cell B, then that relationship of containing could be said to be also *nondistributed*, since the global structure is governed by a single cell rather than a plurality of cells. A composite object of the form (Fig. 13) could therefore be said to be both asymmetric and nondistributed.

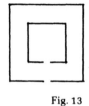

Fig. 13

However, the property of asymmetry can also co-exist with the property of distributedness. Consider another example of an apparently highly randomised arrangement (Fig. 14). If we set out

Fig. 14 The proto-urban
agglomeration of Tikal,
after Hardoy, central area.

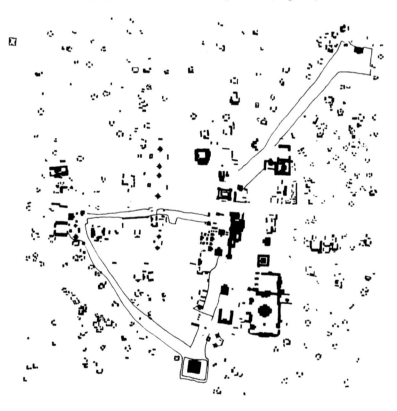

a selection of local complexes in order of size (Fig. 15), we find an evolutionary process governed by a restriction on randomness which associates not, as before, a single closed cell with a single open cell in a neighbour relation, but a plurality (i.e. at least two) of closed cells in a relation of containing a single open cell – using the term containing in a rather broad way to include the case where one object is between two others. Every cell added to the original aggregate complex is defined in relation to the same initial open cell. When all the available space is taken up, these higher order courtyard complexes form the primary cells of a higher order complex of the same kind.

The inverse case can also occur, where a nondistributed complex (one whose global form is governed by a single cell) co-exists with symmetric cells, for example in the case where a single cell contains a plurality of otherwise unarranged cells. An instance of this scheme occurs in Fig. 16.

We may complicate the argument a little further by looking at a reconstruction of what may be one of the world's earliest real examples of a street system, defining this as a continuous system of space at ground level accessible equally to all primary cells in the system (following on from earlier continuous aggregates of cells with roof entrances, with the roofs acting as the 'public' space) (Fig. 17). This is of course a beady ring structure, but it looks rather too regular to have been generated by the usual process. It seems that in some way the global form has been the generator. We therefore need to describe this global structure

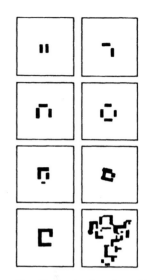

Fig. 15 A selection of small aggregates from Tikal showing the 'many contains one' principle.

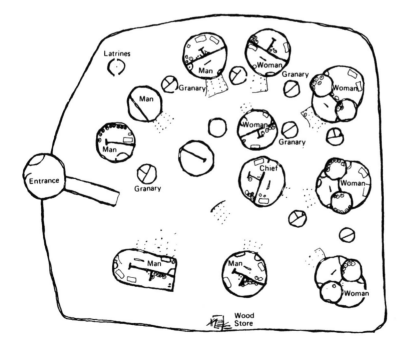

Fig. 16 Moundang compound in Cameroun showing the 'one contains many' principle, after Beguin.

Fig. 17 Reconstruction of
sixth level of Hacilar, 6th
millenium BC, after
Mellaart.

Hacilar 6

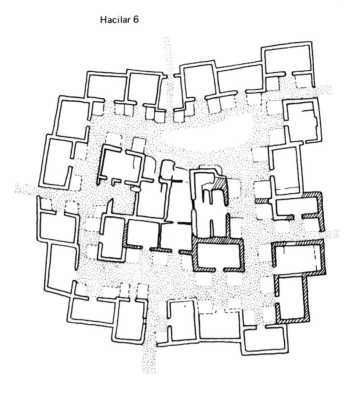

syntactically, since it can itself be the restriction on a random
process giving rise to yet more ordered complexes. The global
structure is clearly distributed, but the open space is more
complex. The notions of both symmetry and asymmetry are
necessary to describe it. Both the inner block and the outer blocks
have cells in a symmetric relation to each other; but the relation of
the outer blocks to the inner block is asymmetric. These properties are combined with that of having the space structure
between the outer and inner blocks, in spite of the fact that one
contains the other. In fact this structure combines all the distributed properties so far enumerated, and we can therefore think of
it as a symmetric–asymmetric distributed generator. Because it
typically generates *rings* of open space, we will see in due course
that it is required to characterise the structure of the various types
of street system (see pp. 71, 78–9).

Just as the distributed asymmetric generator was inverted to
find a nondistributed asymmetrical generator, so the street system
generator has a nondistributed inverse (Fig. 18). In this case, a
single outer cell contains a single inner cell, and these two
symmetrically define between them the space in which all the
smallest cells are placed. In effect, the outer and inner plural
aggregates of the previous example have been replaced by a pair of
singletons, and the single structure of space of the previous one
has been converted into a collection of symmetric cells.

This family of generators and, more importantly, the model that governs them, has several properties that are strongly reminiscent of certain basic syntactic distinctions in natural language. For example the distinction between singular and plural entities seems very fundamental: once there are two, then there can be as many as we please without changing the essential nature of the generator. But also the relation of asymmetry introduced a dimension which brings to mind the subjects and objects of sentences. An asymmetric generator will be one in which the subjects – say the containing cells – have objects – the contained cells; and there can be singular subjects and plural objects and vice versa.

In other words, some of the most pervasive configurational properties distinguishing one spatial arrangement from another seem to be based on a small number of underlying relational ideas, which have a strongly abstract form as well as a concrete manifestation. Some cases are more complex than others, but complex cases seem to be using compounds of the simpler relations applied simultaneously. From the point of view of the objects co-ordinated by these relations the system seems even simpler: nothing has been invoked that is not one or other of the two primitive objects called upon to generate the beady ring: that is, the closed cell, or the cell with its own boundary; and the open cell, or the cell without its boundary. All that happened is that these primitive objects have been brought into different relations in different numbers.

This suggests an intriguing possibility: that not only can real-life spatial arrangements be understood as the products of generative rules, acting as restrictions on an otherwise random process, but also that these rules might themselves be well ordered, in the sense of being themselves the product of an underlying com-

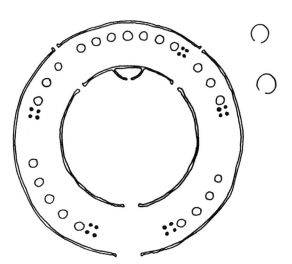

Fig. 18 Zulu Kraal homestead, after Krige.

binatorial system governing the possibilities of forming rules. It is this possibility that justifies the next stage of the argument: the construction of an ideographic language for representing the construction of spatial arrangements – a syntax for the morphic language of space. If it is possible to isolate and represent symbolically a small number of elementary concepts, such that sequences of these symbols first encapsulate the relational concepts necessary to produce patterns by restricting a random process, and second capture the structure of more complex combinations, then rules for forming sequences of symbols will offer a way of writing down a formal descriptive theory of spatial arrangements. This is what the ideographic language is: a descriptive theory of spatial organisation seen as a system of transformations. It follows that it is also an attempt to represent spatial arrangements as *a field of knowables*, that is, as a system of possibilities governed by a simple and abstract underlying system of concepts. If human beings are able to learn these concepts then it is reasonable to expect that more complex cases are understood through the recursive and combinatorial application of these concepts. It all depends on the rules for forming rules: the rule–rules.

Elementary generators: an ideographic language

The concepts required to construct the ideographic language are in fact so elementary as to be found in the concept of an object itself, or more precisely in what might be called the *elementary relations of the object*. By object we mean only that an entity satisfies the minimal conditions for spatial integration (see p. 40), namely that it occupies, however temporarily, a *finite and continuous region of space*. By elementary relations we mean only those relational properties that must hold for any object, regardless of any additional properties that it may have. Over and above the elementary relations of the object, one further notion is required: that of a randomly distributed set or class of such objects. This is, of course, the concept of transpatial integration (see p. 40), or the set of objects without any unified location in space–time. Thus it is intended to construct the ideographic language only from the postulates of an object and a class of objects, objects being entities that have a specific location, classes of objects being entities that do not.

Let us define object to mean the simple open or closed planar cells used in the previous section – although the basic arguments would work equally well for any reasonable three-dimensional object.[3] To say that an object has location means that it is to be found in some finite and continuous region of space. Since the object is finite, then it exists as some kind of discontinuity in a larger space. This larger space, which can be termed the 'carrier' space, has a definite relation to the object: the larger space 'contains' or surrounds the object. If the carrier space is represented by Y, the relation of containing by o, and the property of being a finite and continuous region of space by $(\ )$ (allowing us to make some further description of the object within the brackets if we wish), the left–right formula

$$Y o (\ )$$

expresses the proposition that a carrier space contains an object.

Given these conventions, a number of more complex types of spatial discontinuity in a carrier space can immediately be represented. For example, if we take two pairs of brackets and superimpose on them a pair of brackets that encompasses both:

$$Y o ((\ )(\ ))$$

the formula expresses the proposition that two objects are combined together so as to form, from the point of view of the carrier, a single continuous region of space. If the overall bracket is omitted:

$$Y o (\ )(\ )$$

the formula expresses the proposition that a carrier contains two independent finite objects, which, from the point of view of the carrier, are not continuous. The latter thus expresses spatial *disjunction*, while the former expresses spatial *conjunction*.

This immediately leads to the formula for the random array of objects in a carrier:

$$Y o (\ )(\ )(\ ) \ldots (\ )$$

(for as many objects as we please), meaning that each object is located in Y independently, without reference to the location of any other object. In other words, the least-ordered sequence of symbols corresponds in an intuitively obvious way to the least-ordered array of objects: the one in which each location is assigned without taking into account the location of any other. If we then add numbers from left to right, that is, in the order in which the formula is written:

$$Y o (\ )_1 (\ )_2 (\ )_3 \ldots (\ )_k$$

we have a representation of a *process* of randomly assigning objects to a carrier.

The combination of randomness with contiguity that characterised the beady ring process can also be captured in a very simple way. If a third object is added to a pair which already forms a contiguous composite:

$$Y o (((\ )_1 (\ )_2)(\ )_3)$$

then the formula expresses the proposition that the third object is joined to the composite, without specifying which of the sub-

objects of the composite it is joined to. If the formula is consistently extended using the same bracketing principle:

$$Y \ o \ ((\ )_1 (\ )_2)$$
$$(((\ )_1 (\ )_2)(\ )_3)$$
$$((((\ )_1 (\ )_2)(\ )_3)(\ )_4)$$
$$(((((\ )_1 (\ )_2)(\ )_3)(\ )_4) \ldots (\ )_k)$$

then the array will be one in which the location of each object is
random subject only to being attached to some part of the
composite. This formula precisely expresses the degree and type
of relational structure present in the beady ring type of process
(though nothing has yet been specified about the objects inside the
brackets).

The first of these processes, the random process, specifies no
relations among objects other than being assigned to the same
region of space – a region which we might in fact identify as that
Y which is sufficient to carry all the assigned objects. So long as this
region is not unbounded – that is, in effect, so long as it is not
infinite nor the surface of a sphere – then the product of the
process will always appear as some kind of planar *cluster*,
however randomly dispersed, in much the same way as the cloud
of midges forms a definite though indeterminate three-dimensional cluster. In terms of its product, therefore, we might call the
process the *cluster syntax*, noting that while it is the least ordered
process in our system of interest, it nevertheless has a minimum
structure. The second process has more structure, but only
enough to guarantee that the product will be a dense and
continuous composite object. We might therefore call it the *clump
syntax*. Neither process specifies any relations among objects
other than those necessary to *constitute* a composite object. The
first specifies no relations; the second only symmetric relations,
those of being a contiguous neighbour.

Suppose we then specify only asymmetric relations (meaning
that in the ideographic formula describing the process, the symbol
for containing, *o*, will be written between every pair of objects – or
more precisely between the composite object so far constituted by
the process and the new object added), we then have the formula:

$$Y \ o \ ((\ )_1 \ o \ (\ )_2)$$
$$(((\ )_1 \ o \ (\ )_2) \ o \ (\ )_3)$$
$$((((\ )_1 \ o \ (\ )_2) \ o \ (\ )_3) \ o \ (\ )_4)$$
$$(((((\ )_1 \ o \ (\ )_2) \ o \ (\ )_3) \ o \ (\ )_4) \ldots (\ )_k)$$

This formula, of course, specifies initially the concentric pair of
objects, one inside the other, illustrated in Fig. 13, and then an
expansion of this by the addition of further cells, each in the same
relation of concentric containment. In terms of its product we
might then call this process the *concentric syntax*, noting that the
substitution of an asymmetric relation for a symmetric relation at

every stage of the process has resulted in a composite object as different as it is possible for it to be.

However, the differences in the product are not the only differences. There is another formal difference between the two processes which is no less important. It is this. When the third object is added to the growing composite object, not only is it added as before to the composite object already specified by the relations of the first two objects in the formula, but it also has specific relations to each of those objects: it is immediately inside the second object, but it is not immediately inside the first object. The fact that the first contains the second, means that if the second contains the third, then the second must intervene between the first and the third. In other words, specific relations are required among all the objects of the composite: it is no longer enough to say that the new object is added randomly to any part of the composite. All these relations have become *noninterchangeable*, where in the previous case they were all *interchangeable*. This important property is the by-product of the *transitive* nature of the relation of containment – that is, A contains B and B contains C implies A contains C – compared to the *intransitive* nature of the neighbour relation – A being a neighbour of B and B of C does not imply that A is a neighbour of C.

A key difference between the clump and concentric processes is that in the clump, relations are defined between the outsides of objects, whereas in the concentric process one object is nested inside another. In fact, the matter is more complicated because, as we shall see, in all but the simplest cases, most objects will be inside one and outside another. However, the concentric process depends on this relation of 'insideness' which is not present in the structure of the clump process. Now the concept of inside has a very precise syntactic form, one reflected in the formula: it means 'one contains'. The word implies that the containing entity is single. This is interesting because language also offers us the concept of between, which implies something like a containing relation, but referring specifically to two objects, and two objects which act with their outsides to contain something else rather than with their insides. In this, natural language reflects a simple fact of nature: two objects cannot contain the same object with their insides unless there are also relations of containing between those two, as in the concentric process. The notion between in effect expresses *distributed containment*, that is a form of containment carried out by more than one object, whereas the notion of inside expresses *nondistributed containment*. The analogy between the two forms of containment – outside with more than one, inside with one – can easily be shown by allowing the two in the between relation to become many. The effect can only be that the objects group themselves around the object originally between the first pair, until they very obviously contain it.

Outside containment thus allows us to define a new process, one whose 'germ' is the idea of betweenness and whose defining rule is that many objects contain one. We might call it the *central space syntax* and note that it has the properties being both distributed and asymmetric. This can be expressed in the ideography quite simply by adding further objects to the left of the *o*-symbol:

$$Y \, o \, ((\;)_1 (\;)_2 \, o(\;))$$
$$((\;)_1 (\;)_2 (\;)_3 \, o \, (\;))$$
$$((\;)_1 (\;)_2 (\;)_3 (\;)_4 \, o \, (\;))$$
$$((\;)_1 (\;)_2 (\;)_3 (\;)_4 \ldots (\;)_k \, o \, (\;))$$

implying that all cells to the left of the *o*-symbol that are not yet subject to higher order brackets equally govern that symbol and contain the object on the right side of the *o*-symbol. We may clarify this and at the same time show through the ideography that the concept of many is an extension of the idea of 'twoness', by introducing a diamond bracket around each pair, which implies that each object within the diamond brackets equally relates to whatever is on the right of the *o*-symbol:

$$Y \, o \, (\langle (\;)_1 (\;)_2 \rangle \, o \, (\;))$$
$$(\langle \langle (\;)_1 (\;)_2 \rangle (\;)_3 \rangle \, o \, (\;))$$

meaning that each time an object is added, it forms a pair with the pair, or pairs, already in the formula. Since this could lead to rather long and unnecessarily complicated formulae we can also introduce a piece of notation for a concept that we introduced at the beginning, that of a *set* of objects, without specifying the number of objects in the set. Thus:

$$Y \, o \, (\{ \; \} \, o(\;))$$

can be taken to mean that a set of cells contains a single cell. However, neither of these two items of notation is strictly necessary to the structure of formulae. They are really a device to clarify the concepts that are present in formulae and to permit simplification.[4]

The structure of formulae for the remaining forms described in the previous section can now be written without too much difficulty. The relation of a single cell containing a plurality of cells can be written:

$$Y \, o \, ((\;) \, o \, (\;)(\;))$$

with the same rules for turning the right side pair into many as applied to the left side pair in the central cell case, allowing:

$$Y \, o \, ((\;) \, o \, \{ \; \})$$

This – the asymmetric nondistributed generator – could be called the *estate syntax*, since an outer boundary with internal blocks is the modern estate's most characteristic global form. The case where an outer plurality of cells – i.e. at least a pair – contained an inner plurality, and the two then contained a single space between them, can then be expressed:

$$Y o (( )( ) o ( )( ) o ( ))$$

or clarifying more of its structure:

$$Y o ((\langle( )( )\rangle o \langle( )( )\rangle) o ( ))$$

or more simply

$$Y o (\{ \} o \{ \} o ( ))$$

implying that both the inner and outer set of cells act conjointly to contain the space between them. This is then the symmetric–asymmetric distributed generator and could be referred to as the *ring–street syntax*. The nondistributed version of the same kind of relation can then be written:

$$Y o (( ) o ( ) o ( )( ))$$

or again clarifying its internal structure:

$$Y o ((\langle( ) o ( )\rangle o \langle( )\{)\rangle))$$

or most simply:

$$Y o (( ) o ( ) o \{ \})$$

implying that two cells, one inside the other, have between them many cells. This could be called the *kraal syntax*, after one of its most familar products.

Now these simple formulae do two things. First, they show exactly what we mean by the degree of order that is introduced into the random process in order to arrive at certain forms. The degree is given by the number of necessary co-ordinations that are introduced among objects, and these are expressed in the number of brackets and relation signs that are introduced into the formula describing the process. In this sense, it is perfectly clear that some processes are more structured than others, precisely because they require more necessary relations among objects to realise them. The corollary of this is that relations that are not necessary are contingent. For example, if many cells contain a single cell, then provided that relation is satisfied, any other relations holding among the containing cells – some might be contiguous, others not – can be randomised. The formula only specifies what must occur, not what can occur as a by-product of the structure of the process. This is very important, since it preserves at every stage of the argument the link with the underlying random process, which may at any stage produce relations not written into the formula. This has the very important consequences that we can in some cases describe the addition of further objects to a formula simply by substituting the set brackets for more complex structures. In other words, in these cases descriptions can be maintained more or less at their initial level of compression. The formula simply says add more objects, provided only that they satisfy the relation described – that of making a composite object, or surrounding a single cell, or being contained by a single cell. Such cases will be quite different from those where the addition of further cells requires the introduction of further structure. The extreme case is the concentric syntax, where each added cell requires an added containing relation.

Secondly, the formulae show that by permuting and combining a few elementary relations, a family of fundamentally different forms can be generated from the random process; and these relations are nothing more than the basic linguistic concepts of singulars and plurals, subjects and objects, giving rise to distributed and nondistributed, symmetric and asymmetric relations. We have as it were kept track of the kinds of relational order we need to introduce into the system in order to give rise to different families of forms, considered as spatial structures, and we have done so until the possibilities of combination of these elementary relations come up against the limitations of what is possible in real space.

But we have not used all possible combinations of the terms and concepts we have introduced, and the reason for this is that we have not yet considered which types of cell – open or closed – belong in which locations in formulae – or indeed, whether there are any limitations on where they may occur. Such limitations exist, and they are strong limitations. They arise from very fundamental properties of space that have to do with its practical usability for human purposes. These limitations are one of the principal reasons why we are not concerned here with a purely mathematical enumeration of combinatorial structures, but with the mapping and inter-relating of the real strategies that human beings have found useful in organising effective space. However, even though they are more in the nature of real world constraints than purely mathematical limitations, they can still be formally stated, and stated within the formalism that we have established.

Closed and open cells are made up of two kinds of raw material: continuous space, which we have already introduced in its initial state and called Y; and the stuff of which boundaries are made, which has the property of creating discontinuities in space. We do not have to know what kind of stuff this is in order to give it a label. It can, if we like, have a purely notional nature – markings on the ground even. Provided it leads to discontinuities in space, then whatever it is and wherever it is we will call it X. Space organised for human purposes is neither Y nor X. It is 'raw' Y converted into *effective space* by means of X. In order to be effective it has to maintain the property of being continuous in spite of being transformed by the presence of X. The imperfection of the logic of space results largely from this paradoxical need to maintain continuity in a system of space in which it is actually constructed by erecting discontinuities.

Now the notion of 'boundary' can be very easily defined. It is some X that has the property of containing some part of Y: $(X o Y)$. The Y inside X is now transformed in the sense that its relation to the rest of Y has been changed by the intervention of X. It now forms part of a small local system with a definite discontinuity in respect to the large system. Let us agree to call this contained segment of Y: y' (y-prime – the reason for the prime will be clear in a moment). Now y' *will not be fully discontinuous with Y* because, to make y' part of an effective system of space, the boundary must have an entrance. Outside this entrance there will be another region of space also distinguishable from Y, but this time distinguishable not by virtue of being discontinuous with the rest of Y, but by virtue of being continuous with y' – in the sense that a region of space that is only adjacent to a part of the boundary without an entrance will not be so distinguishable. We may label this space y, and note that it is created by the conversion of Y by X, even though it does not itself have a boundary or indeed definite limits. However, we do not need to know its limits in order to know that such a region as y exists. We only need to know the change in local conditions that leads to its identification (Fig. 19). Just as y' can be defined in terms of its local syntactic conditions, so can y: y is an open cell contiguous with the global $(X o y')$ and also contiguous with y'. This can be expressed by slightly complicating the bracketing system:

Fig. 19

$$Y o ((X o [y']y])$$

with the square brackets expressing the contiguous neighbour relation of y' and y, but for simplicity we can write

$$Y o ((X o y') y)$$

and assume that where they are adjacent, then the two ys will be continuous.

A whole series of axiomatic statements about Y and its relation to X can now be made: $(YY) = Y$ and $(Y o Y) = Y$ (i.e. continuous spaces added contiguously to each other or put one inside the other will remain one continuous space), and in general Y is Y unless either $(X o y')$ or $((X o y')y)$; that is Y, the carrier, remains Y until it is converted into effective space either by being contained by a boundary – the insideness rule – or by being adjacent to such a space – the outsideness rule. Then we can add $(yy) = y$, meaning that effective outside spaces joined to each other are a continuous space. Alternatively, the rule for the creation of y implies that larger systems of y can only exist by virtue of being everywhere constructed by $((X \, o \, y')y)$. The relations of y' with each other are a little more complex since, on the basis of what we have so far said, they do not come into direct contact with each other. However, by clarifying the way in which y' is structured by nondistributed systems, we can then clarify some simple axioms for the whole system by which effective space is created by the intervention of X.

Consider first the concentric syntax. Here, even in the minimum form where two cells are nested one inside the other, we have two different conditions for y'. The space within the interior cell is simply y' by usual definition; but the space inside the outer cell also has the property of being between the outer and inner cell. However, we already know in principle how to represent this property, and it can serve our purposes here:

$$Y \, o \, (\langle X_1 \, o \, (X_2 \, o \, y_2')\rangle \, o \, y_1')$$

meaning that X_1 the outer boundary contains X_2 the inner boundary (which contains y_2' on its own) and y_1' is between X_1 and X_2 (the diamond brackets can of course be eliminated). This principle can then be extended to as many concentric cells as we like:

$$Y \, o \, (X_1 \, o \, (X_2 \, o \, (X_3 \, o \, y_3') \, o \, y_2') \, o \, y_1')$$

and so on. However far we extend this process, the y' spaces will always appear side by side in the formula. However, because X intervenes between each pair (other than at the entrance), it will not in general be true to say that $(y' \, o \, y') = y'$. On the contrary, each y' maintains a discrete identity except at the entrance. However, since y' is anterior to y in the sense that it is by virtue of y' that y is defined, then we can say that a space adjacent to an entrance ceases to be y and becomes y' as soon as it is contained by a superordinate boundary.

If we then take the estate syntax, in which in the minimal form one cell contains more than one, then

$$Y \, o \, (\langle X_1 \, o \, \langle (X_2 \, o \, y_2')(X_3 \, o \, y_3')\rangle\rangle \, o \, y_1')$$

expresses the fact (again diamond brackets can be omitted) that both x_2 and x_3 together, and the pair formed by those two and x_1 all define y_1. We can then allow the inner pair to become contiguous:

$$Y \, o \, (\langle X_1 \, o \, ((X_2 \, o \, y_2')(X_3 \, o \, y_3'))\rangle \, o \, y_1')$$

or to define a distributed region of space between them:

$$Y \, o \, (\langle X_1 \, o \, (\langle (X_2 \, o \, y_2')(X_3 \, o \, y_3')\rangle \, o \, y)\rangle \, o \, y_1')$$

and in such cases the formula will describe the relational structure of the space as well as of the boundaries. Or we can eliminate the space between the inner and outer boundaries completely, creating the form of the 'block' in which the outer boundary is, as it were, pressed tightly onto the inner cells at all points (although in practice there must always be some additional structure of internal space to allow access):

$$Y \ o \ (X_1 \ o(X_2 \ o \ y_2')(X_3 \ o \ y_3'))$$

In the more complex case of the kraal form we can still see that the formula

$$Y \ o \ (\langle\langle X_1 \ o \ (X_2 \ o \ y_2')\rangle \ o \ \langle(X_3 \ o \ y_3')(X_4 \ o \ y_4')\rangle\rangle \ o \ y_1')$$

specifies all the different relations of space as well as those of boundaries – though once again the diamond brackets are really only needed to clarify all the pair relations that between them define y'.

Finally, we can consider the case of the simplest nondistributed structure, the closed cell itself; this is the form that results from the conversion of X into a boundary. This conversion, it turns out, can be described in terms of the basic concepts of the language. Consider for example a convex piece of X, one that contains no segment of Y (Fig. 20). Now if we wish to deform this X so that it does in some sense contain some Y, we must introduce a concavity into it (Fig. 21). This concavity will always have a very definite form in the region where it does the containing. It will appear that the X somehow bifurcates in that region forming two arms, and it is these arms that do the containing. A boundary is simply an X that is bifurcated and then co-ordinated with itself – the two bifurcated arms are in some sense brought together again to form a complete ring. Since all the boundaries in which we are interested will be permeable, we know that the 'co-ordination with itself' will be by virtue of the fact that these two bifurcated arms will have between them a piece of Y, and it is this Y that will complete the circle. This in effect defines another type of 'converted' Y, one that we might call the 'threshold' and label it y''. This co-ordination of X with itself can then be expressed quite simply by applying the pair brackets to the single object – this is what bifurcation means – and then using the between relation to define the threshold (Fig. 22):

$$Y \ o \ (\langle X\rangle \ o \ y'')$$

This most basic of all transformations uses, appropriately, all the basic concepts in the language exactly once. This is the internal structure of the object we know as X.

This rather complicated diversion has shown that, in all the types of case we have specified, it is possible to describe the configuration of inside space that results from the arrangement of boundaries. We already know that outside space can be described through the continuity rule – space joined to space in space. In other words, the ideography can describe the structure of space, even though we complicate the local relational conditions that

Fig. 20

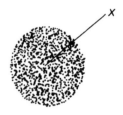

Fig. 21

Fig. 22

define that space as either y' or y. If we can now take this for granted, we can immediately clarify the structure of formulae and embark on the rules for forming them by agreeing only to deal with open and closed cells and their relations, calling the closed cell – with all its internal structure – X and the open cell y.

Once this is done, one rule is sufficient to specify where X and y occur in formulae. If we define a *place* in a formula as a position where cell-symbols occur without intervening o – implying that if an o-relation does exist, there are two places, one either side of o – then all we need say is: all formulae end with y except those with single X in the first place; all other cells are X. In other words, distributed formulae end with y but are otherwise X, while nondistributed formulae are X all the way through.

Thus, leaving aside the random process and the cell co-ordinated with itself, $(( )( ))$ becomes (Xy), $(( )( ) o ( ))$ becomes $(XX o y)$ and $(( )( ) o ( )( ) o ( ))$ becomes $(XX o XX o y)$ in the distributed cases; while $(( ) o ( ))$ becomes $(X o X)$, $(( ) o ( )( ))$ becomes $(X o XX)$ and $(( ) o ( ) ( ))$ becomes $(X o X o XX)$ in the nondistributed cases. Intuitively we can think of distributedness as using y to *glue* cells together – that is, to join each cell to others by virtue of what they have between them, and of nondistributedness as using X to *bind* cells together – that is, to join each cell to others by virtue of what is added around both. Thus beady ring forms based on clump generators, plaza-type forms based on central cell generators, and street systems based on ring-street generators all have in common that the closed cells are glued together by a system of space with which they maintain direct relations as they grow; while concentric forms, estate forms and kraal forms are all bound together by some form of hierarchial superimposition of further boundaries which add discontinuities to the system.

The rule for X and y specifies what particular configurations of space described relationally in the formula will be like in reality. It is not so much an abstract axiom as an empirical postulate: these are the ways in which human beings have found it possible to organise effective space such that it possesses relational properties that enable it to satisfy different types of human purpose. Through it we can arrive at a compressed description of the underlying principles of real types of pattern found in human spatial organisation. But to achieve our original objective – to show that these compressed descriptions themselves form a system, and that the forms they describe can be understood as a system of transformations – we have to proceed in a slightly more careful way. Having shown that the ideographic formulae can give descriptions of spatial relations underlying forms so that the complexities of X and y can always be represented by complicating the formula, showing the patterns themselves to be a system of transformations then becomes a matter of showing that the formulae themselves are constructed according to rules. The argument must proceed in three stages. First, we must show the rules for constructing any formula. Second we must show how formulae form types by following rules of construction. Third, we must show what additions may be made to formulae without changing type, and by implication what will bring about a transformation from one type to another.

A *formula* is a left-right sequence of symbols with at least an initial cell symbol to the right of Y o, or with a sequence of cell symbols, with or without intervening o, in which each cell is bracketed either ⟨⟩ or () with at least one other already in the formula. A place (as we have already seen) is a position in a formula where cell symbols occur without intervening o. An *object place* is a place which follows but does not precede o. All other places are *subject places*.

Syntactic nonequivalence (and by implication equivalence) can be defined by the following: a subject place followed by o is not equivalent to one not followed by o and subject places are not equivalent to object places; singular places are not equivalent to plural places; and closed cells are not equivalent to open cells (the last really follows from the first rule, given the internal structure of the formula for a closed cell). Formulae are nonequivalent if they contain one or more nonequivalent cell or place.

The set of *elementary nonequivalent formulae* can then be defined as those with at least one and no more than two subject places; at least one and no more than two cell symbols per place (two being the least realisation of plurality); no repetition of relations and places; and no round brackets other than the pair that surround every formula.

Elementary formulae are therefore the least realisations of the basic family of linguistic differences between patterns: that is, different ways of arranging subjects and objects, singular and plurals, within the constraints of the system of open and closed cells. The family of possible elementary formulae can be set out first in the form of a list, in which formulae are called Z and numbered $Z_{1...8}$ (see list on p. 78) then in the form of a table governed by the basic dimensions of the model: distributed–nondistributed, realising relations governed by plural and singular subjects; and symmetric–asymmetric, realising the differences between relations with and without o (Fig. 23).

Any formula which repeats the same objects in the same relations can therefore be reasonably thought of as a member of the same family type – for the simple reason that a formula establishes a set of principles of organisation, and any more complex patterns based on the same principles can be thought of as belonging to the same family type. *Recursive* (that is repetitive) processes can therefore be thought of as applying a certain set of ordering principles to an indefinite number of cells added one at a

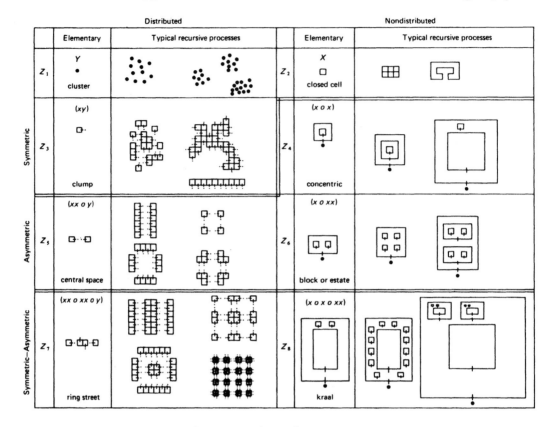

Fig. 23 Elementary
formulae and recursions.

List of elementary formulae

$Z_1 : y$
$Z_2 : X$
$Z_3 : (Xy)$
$Z_4 : (X \, o \, X)$
$Z_5 : (X \, X \, o \, y)$
$Z_6 : (X \, o \, XX)$
$Z_7 : (XX \, o \, XX \, o \, y)$
$Z_8 : (X \, o \, X \, o \, XX)$

time. Some of these processes have therefore already been described. The cluster, or random process, is a process of adding
unco-ordinated cells to the elementary generator, the unco-ordinated cell. The clump process is the process of adding neighbours
to the elementary generator, the open and closed neighbour pair.
The central space process is the process of adding cells to a central
space defined between the initial pair of the elementary generator.
The ring-street process is that of adding cells to the initial ring of
the elementary generator.

All of these distributed processes can also repeat in more
complex ways. For example, by the same means as the cluster is
generated a series of clusters can be re-bracketed to give a cluster

of clusters. The same would apply to a clump of clumps. In the clump process also, if we introduce more bracketing of closed cells with each other, then we will generate a form in which the islands that define the beady rings become increasingly irregular and increasingly penetrated with deep, wandering courtyards – a simple product of requiring more closed cells to join randomly to each other. With the central cell process, if we introduce bracketing so that each initial closed cell becomes itself a continuous grouping of cells, while still requiring each to relate directly to the central space, then we may generate forms which have a central space between expanding lines of closed cells – long street rather than village green forms. Alternatively we can replace each closed cell in the elementary generator with an elementary generator of the same type – still requiring all closed cells to relate directly to whatever y-space is defined by their arrangement – and then we have the seed of a 'crossroads' form, which can add objects down each of its constituent 'roads'.

Again in the ring-street generator we can introduce more groups of subject cells with o-relations, in which case we define a ring-street system expanding concentrically; this may be extended as far as we like, provided we introduce round brackets wherever necessary to specify between which existing rings of cells a new ring will be located. Alternatively we can add further groups of cells by bracketing, but without new o-relations, in which case we specify a ring-street process that expands symmetrically in the sense of adding new rings which are intersecting neighbours of rings already in the system. For example, if the second group of closed cells in the formula becomes a pair of groups, the effect will be that the outer group with the pair of discrete inner groups will define a pair of intersecting rings, rather than a single ring. Evidently this may be extended for as many such symmetric rings as we like. Both the symmetric and asymmetric ways of expanding the ring-street generator offer useful insights into the essential structure of street systems. The essence of such a system is the ring – not, for example, the single linear space – and in any reasonably large system each street will be the unique intersection of a pair of rings and each square or market-place the unique intersection of several rings. This seems exactly to capture the property of a street: that it is a unique and distinguishable entity, yet at the same time is only such by virtue of its membership of a much larger system of spatial relations.

Repetition of relations in nondistributed forms will also vary with the relations to be repeated. If the transformation that creates the boundary – the cell co-ordinated with itself – is repeated on the the same object, the result will be a multicellular object with as many cells as the number of times the transformation is repeated. We have already seen that the repetition of the concentric relation will make further concentric relations, although there is also the case where the new cells and the o-relation are added to the elementary form without round brackets – that is, implicitly with diamond brackets – which means that the third cell will be between the inner and outer boundaries. The estate or block syntax can both repeat closed cells or it can repeat the boundaries that contain them, in the first case giving a less hierarchical, in the second a more hierarchical form. Similarly with the kraal syntax. The simplest form of repetition is adding new object cells in the final place in the formula; but it is also possible to add more complex relations including, of course, the whole structure. In each of these cases, as in the distributed cases, the syntactic form of repetition depends on the structural relations that prevail for the cells in the places where new cells are added.

At this stage, however, the limitations of this exercise are already becoming clear. The more complex the situation to which we apply these simple generative notions, the more general the relational structures seem to be and the more tenuous their description. At most we may say that is is usually possible to give an approximate and imperfect sketch of the global form of a spatial pattern by reference to the elementary generators and their recursions. The next section will adapt the elementary generators to a somewhat different approach to the analysis of the complexity of real cases.

The aim in this section has been more limited: to show that however complex spatial order becomes, it still seems to be created out of certain elementary relational ideas, applied singly or in combination, as restrictions on an underlying random process. Essentially it says that if we add a cell to a growing collection, then either the new cell is outside others, in which case it can be in no relation, in a contiguous neighbour relation, in a relation of jointly defining space, or jointly defining a ring; or if it is inside it is concentrically inside as a singleton, plurally within an outer boundary parallel to others, or is between an outer and an inner boundary. Practically speaking, these seem to be the possibilities that exist. It is to be expected therefore that logic of human spatial organisation will both explore and be constricted by these possibilities.

The aim of the ideography was to show that these structures and their internal complexity could be represented rigorously without going beyond the initial objects and relations: the open and closed cells and the basic syntactic relations of distributed–nondistributed and symmetric–asymmetric.

It is only these elementary concepts of object and relation that are carried forward into the analytic methodologies that are to be set out in the next three chapters. The generative structures, together with their ideography, are, as it were, thrown away and will not reappear. Their object was to show that certain fundamental kinds of complexity in the elementary gestuary of space could be shown to be a system of transformations built on these elementary concepts. But for analytic purposes these structures are already too complex to form a reliable basis for an objective, observation-based procedure of analysis. For such an analysis we can only depend on observing the elementary objects and relations themselves. The conjecture that these also unfold into a generative syntax is of interest, but the next stages of the argument do not depend on this being true. Spatial analysis is an independent structure of ideas, although built on the same foundations as the generative syntax.

The argument of the book in effect bifurcates at this point. The next three chapters take the elementary spatial concepts of object and relation and build them into a set of analytic techniques for spatial patterns, techniques from which we hope it is possible to infer the social content of patterns. The three following chapters then take the general model of restrictions on a random process as an epistemological scheme for considering the whole issue of the spatial dimension of social structures. Neither of the bifurcating paths therefore fully uses the generative model we have set out, but both are founded in it. Although generative syntax may in itself be a 'dead end', the spatial and epistemological notions that it establishes are the means by which the next key – analytic – stages of the argument can be attempted.

3

••

The analysis of settlement layouts

SUMMARY

The basic family of generative concepts is taken and made the basis of a method of analysis of settlement forms, using the generative syntax to establish the description of spatial order, and concepts dealing with the type and quantity of space invested in those relations are introduced. The model of analysis sees a settlement as a bi-polar system arranged between the primary cells or buildings (houses, etc.) and the carrier (world outside the settlement). The structure of space between these two domains is seen as a means of interfacing two kinds of relations: those among the inhabitants of the system; and those between inhabitants and strangers. The essence of the method of analysis is that it first establishes a way of dealing with the global physical structure of a settlement without losing sight of its local structure; and second – a function of the first – it establishes a method of describing space in such a way as to make its social origins and consequences a part of that description – although it must be admitted the links are at present axiomatic rather than demonstrated.

Individuals and classes

At this point the reader could be forgiven for expecting the eventual product of the syntactic method to be some kind of classificatory index of idealised settlement forms, such that any real example could be typed and labelled by comparing it visually with the ideal types and selecting the one that gave the closest approximation. This expectation may have been inadvertently reinforced by the form in which the syntactic argument has been presented: examples have been used to illustrate the relation between syntactic formulae and spatial pattern in such a way as to make this relation as obvious as possible. Unfortunately this will have biased selection in the direction of small, simple and consistent examples, and this may well have given the reader the impression that in general settlement forms could be analysed by a simple procedure of visual comparison.

This is not the case, and nor was it ever to be expected. The fundamental proposition of the syntax theory is not that there is a relation between settlement forms and social forces, but that there is a relation between the *generators* of settlement forms and social forces. Only in the simplest cases can we expect these forces and generators to be few enough and uniform enough to permit instant recognition. Most real cases will tend to be individuals, in the very important sense that the differences between one example and another are likely to be as significant for analysis as the similarities, even when the examples are members of the same broad equivalence class.

Take for example the three pairs of settlements, graded in order of size, from nineteenth-century maps of the North of England (Fig. 24(a)–(f)). The two smallest, Muker and Middlesmoor, are both variants on the beady ring form, but differ from the French examples in having several small clumps rather than a single large clump, in having larger and less well-defined spaces, and in

Fig. 24 ((a)–(f)) Six settlements of various sizes in the North of England, with similarities and differences.

(a) Muker

Fig. 24 *(cont.)*

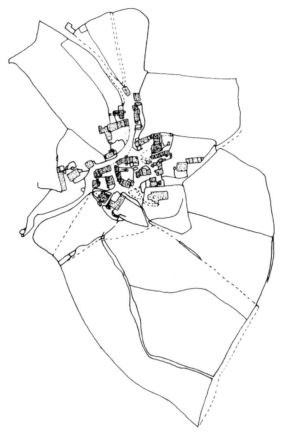

(b) Middlesmoor

general appearing more loosely constructed than their French counterparts. The two middle-sized examples, Heptonstall and Kirkoswald, both have beady ring components coupled to a strong linear development away from the beady rings, all linear components taking the form of strings of beads but with strong variations in the degree of beadiness. The largest pair, Grassington and Hawes, again both have the beady ring property, but for the most part on a larger scale. Both also have a global property that characterises a very high proportion of English towns: an overall linear form even when there is substantial 'ringy' development locally. In effect, syntax seems to confirm what intuition might in any case tell the visitor: that there is a certain family resemblance within the group, but nonetheless each is strongly recognisable as a unique individual.

However, syntax can suggest one possibility that is not obvious to intuition: that the pathway from similarity to difference, from equivalence class to individuality, is also the pathway from local generators to global forms. It is not simply the existence of certain generators that gives the global configurational properties of each

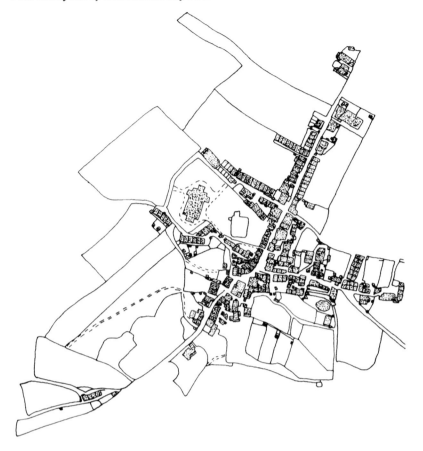

Fig. 24 (*cont.*)

(c) Heptonstall

individual. It is the way in which variations in the application of the generators govern the growth of an expanding aggregation. What is required to move the syntax theory from the status of abstract principles to that of operational techniques is not therefore a recognition procedure, but a methodology of analysis that captures and expresses not only common generators in the pathways from local to global forms but also significant individual differences. Some way must be found to approach individuality without sacrificing generality.

Elsasser offers a useful starting point by defining individuality from the point of view of the theoretical biologist. Any combinatorial system, he argues – say black and white squares arranged on a grid – will generate a certain number of different possible configurations or individuals.[1] As the number of possible configurations increases beyond the actual number of instances that are ever likely to occur in the real world, the probability of each real case being unique increases. The more this is so then the more the property, and the theoretical problem of individuality exists.

Fig. 24 (*cont.*)

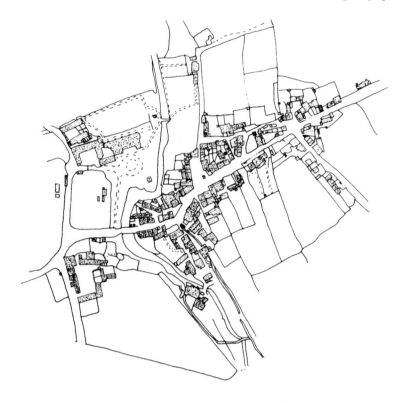

(*d*) Kirkoswald

Elsasser graphically illustrates the pervasiveness of the problem of individuality by comparing the number of possible configurations generated by a simple 10×10 grid, namely 10^{200}, with the number of seconds that have elapsed since the beginning of the universe, approximately 10^{18}.

Another name for the problem of individuality is of course the problem of the 'combinatorial explosion' as encountered by most attempts to model some set of 'similarly different' phenomena by using combinatorial methods. Because any combinatorial system tends to generate far too many different individuals, the chief problem tends to become that of defining equivalence classes of the individuals generated by the system. The syntax theory had hoped to avoid this problem from the outset by defining equivalence classes as all patterns produced by the same restrictions on the underlying random process. It was therefore a theory of what to ignore, as well as what to attend to, in examining spatial patterns in the real world. A fundamental question therefore poses itself: does the re-admission of the notion of individuality to the syntax theory also re-admit the combinatorial explosion with all the restrictions this would impose on the possibility of making general statements – even general descriptive statements – about spatial patterns.

Fig. 24 (cont.)

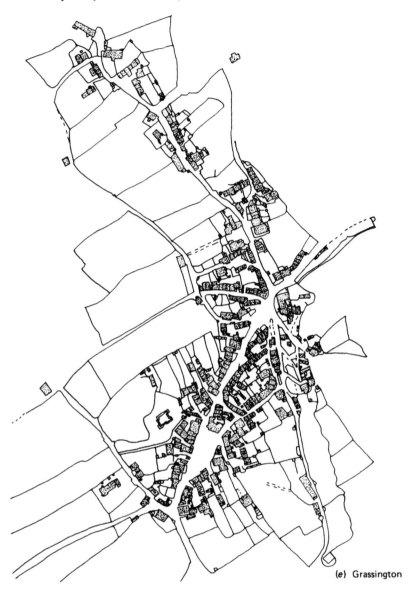

(e) Grassington

The answer is that it does not, and the reason is that we have not yet taken numbers into account. The reader may recall that in the analysis of the game of hide-and-seek used to discuss the notion of a spatial structure it was shown that the abstract spatial model on which the game depended had both a topological and a numerical component, in that certain spatial relations had to exist in sufficient numbers (but not too many) for the game to be playable in a particular place. The syntax theory as so far set out has virtually ignored the numerical dimension, distinguishing only singular from plural and allowing all recursions to be repeated an arbitrary number of times. But numbers control the degree to

Fig. 24 (cont.)

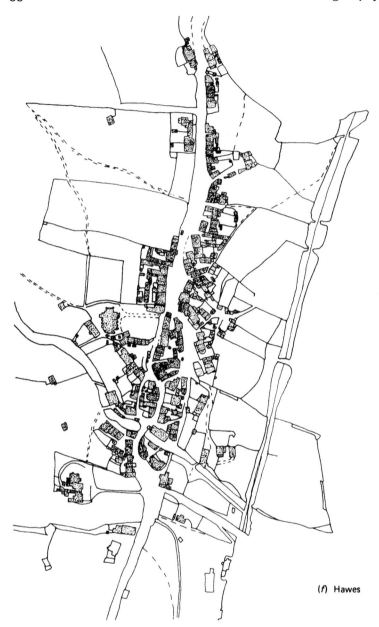

(f) Hawes

which particular syntactic relations are realised in a complex, and
clearly no real example will be properly described without some
indication of the degree to which particular types of relation are
present. The analytic method will in effect be principally concerned with quantifying the degree to which different generators
underlie a particular settlement form. It is through this that the
problem of individuality will be tractable. In general, it will be
argued, *structures generate equivalence classes of forms, but
numbers generate individuals.*

Numbers, however, can be introduced into syntax in two different ways. First, we can talk about the numbers of syntactic relations of this or that type that bear on a particular space or object. Second, we can talk about the quantity of space (or size of objects) invested in those relations. The latter may become numerically more complicated if we introduce questions of shape. Seen planarly as part of the layout, shape is likely to involve variations in the extension of a space or object in one dimension or the other; the area–perimeter ratio of the space, and so on.

But what is it that can be counted so as to reveal the differences between one settlement structure and another? From this point of view, the plan of the settlement is singularly uninformative. Most settlements seem to be made up of the same kinds of 'elements': 'closed' elements like dwellings, shops, public buildings, and so on, which by their aggregation define an 'open' system of more or less public space – streets, alleys, squares, and the like – which knit the whole settlement together into a continuous system. What is it that gives a particular settlement its spatial individuality, as well as its possible membership of a generic class of similar settlements?

Everyday experience, as well as commonsense, tells us that it can only lie in the relations between the two: buildings, by the way in which they are collected together, create a system of open space – and it is the form and shape of the open space system as everywhere defined by the buildings that constitute our experience of the settlement. But if a syntactic and quantitative analysis is to focus on this relation by which the arrangement of closed elements defines the shape of the open element, then a substantial difficulty is encountered. In an important sense (and unlike the closed elements which are clearly identifiable, both as individuals and as blocks) the open space structure of a settlement is one continuous space. How is it then to be analysed without contradicting its essentially continuous nature?

Here we find a great difficulty. If we follow the planning practice of representing the system as a topological network, much of the idiosyncrasy of the system is lost. The equivalence class is much too large and we have failed to analyse either the individuality or the generic nature of the system. If, on the other hand, we follow the architectural method of calling some parts of the system 'spaces' and others 'paths'[2] – derived, probably, from an underlying belief that all traditional settlements are made up of 'streets and squares' – then we will be faced in most real cases with unavoidable difficulties in deciding which is which – difficulties that are usually solved arbitrarily and subjectively, thus destroying any usefulness the analysis might have had.[3]

Settlement analysis therefore raises a problem which is anterior to analysis: that of the representation, preferably the objective representation, of the open space system of a settlement, both in

terms of itself, and in terms of its interface with the closed
elements (buildings), and in such a way as to make syntactic
relations identifiable and countable. The section that follows is an
attempt to solve this problem by building a basic model for the
representation, analysis, and interpretation of settlements seen in
this way. It is followed by an outline of a step by step analytic
procedure, carried out on some illuminating examples. The whole
methodology, model and procedure, we call alpha-analysis, in
order to differentiate it from the analysis of building interiors
(gamma-analysis) introduced in the next chapter.[4]

A model for syntactic representation, analysis, and interpretation: alpha-analysis

The central problem of alpha-analysis (the syntactic analysis of
settlements) – which is that of the continuous open space – can be
represented graphically. Fig. 25 is the ground plan of the small
French town of G, represented in the usual way. Fig. 26 is a kind
of negative of the same system, with the open space hatched in
and the buildings omitted. The problem of analysis is to describe
in a structured and quantitative way how Fig. 26 is constructed.

On the face of it, the negative diagram appears to be a set of
irregular intersecting rings forming a kind of *deformed grid*.
However, a closer look, in the light of the previous chapter, can
suggest a little more. Seen locally, the space system seems
everywhere to be like a beady ring system, in that everywhere
space widens to form irregular beads, and narrows to form strings,
at the same time joining back to itself so that there are always
choices of routes from any space to any other space.

But the answer to the representation problem lies *not* in
identifying what is a bead and what is a string, but in looking at
the *whole* system in terms of *both* properties, or rather in terms of

Fig. 25 The small town of G
in the Var region of France.

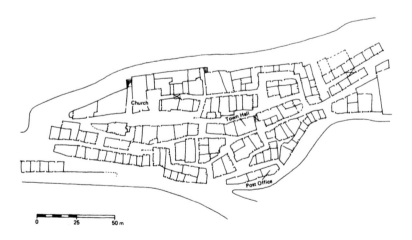

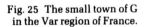

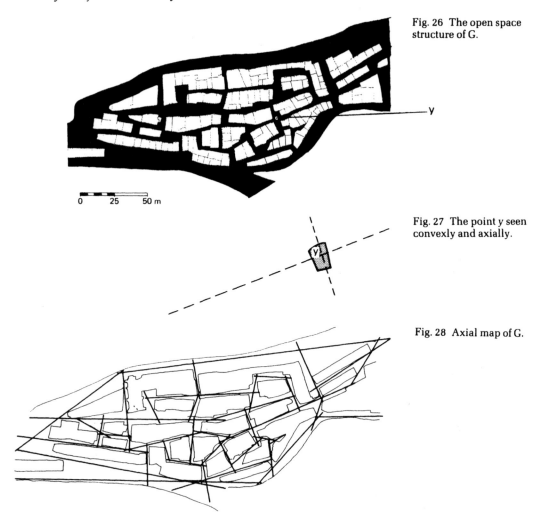

Fig. 26 The open space structure of G.

0   25   50 m

Fig. 27 The point y seen convexly and axially.

Fig. 28 Axial map of G.

each in turn. We can define 'stringiness' as being to do with the extension of space in one dimension, whereas 'beadiness' is to do with the extension of space in two dimensions. Any point in the structure of space – say the point marked y – can be seen to be a part of a linearly extended space, indicated by the dotted lines passing through the point, which represents the maximum global or *axial* extension of that point in a straight line. But the point marked y is also part of a *fully convex fat space*, indicated by the shaded area; that is, part of a space which represents the maximum extension of the point in the second dimension, given the first dimension. Differences between one system of space and another can it will be shown be represented in the first instance as differences in the one- and two-dimensional extension of their space and in the relation between the two.

Both kinds of extension can be objectively represented. An *axial map* (Fig. 28) of the open space structure of the settlement

Fig. 29 Convex map of G.

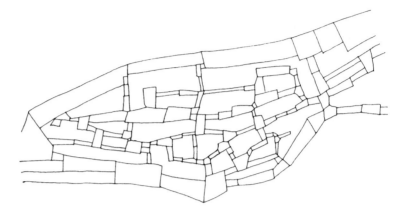

will be the least set of such straight lines which passes through
each convex space and makes all axial links (see below for details
of procedure, section 1.03): and a *convex map* (Fig. 29) will be the
least set of fattest spaces that covers the system (see below for
details of procedure, section 1.01). From these maps it is easy to
see that urban space structures will differ from one another
according to the degree of axial and convex extension of their
parts and according to the relation between these two forms of
extension. For example, convex spaces may become as long as
axial spaces if the system is very regular; or, as in G, many axial
lines may pass through a series of convex spaces.

Since this space structure (which can be looked at axially,
convexly, and in terms of the relation between axial and convex
extension), is the result of the arrangement of buildings, and
possibly other bounded areas such as gardens, parks, and the like,
it can also be described in terms of how the houses, shops, public
buildings, and the like, are adjacent to and directly or indirectly
permeable to it. When buildings are directly accessible to an axial
or convex space, we say that the space is constituted by the
buildings, but if the space is adjacent to buildings to which it is
not directly permeable, we say it is unconstituted. Thus the
systems of axial and convex space can be discussed in terms of
their internal configurations, in relation to each other, in relation
to the buildings which define the system, and in relation to the
world outside that system.

Two crucial concepts can now be introduced. The *description*
of a space will be the set of syntactic relations, both of buildings
and other spaces, that defines a particular space, while the
synchrony of a space will be the quantity of space invested in
those relations. The use of the term synchrony to describe space
may be seem initially curious, but it is used because it corresponds to a fundamental fact of experience, seen against the
background of the syntactic generation of settlement structures.
The term structure is normally a synchronous notion: it describes

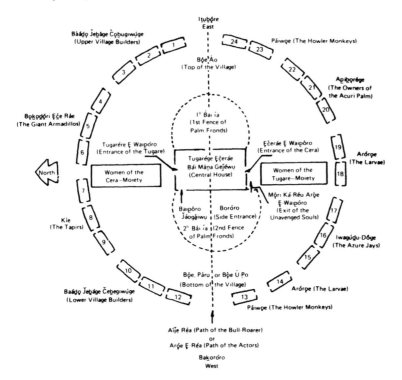

Fig. 30 Diagram of a Bororo village, after Lévi-Strauss.

a set of relations that hold at a particular point in time. The generative syntax model introduced a 'diachronic' notion of structure in which structure grew by a stage-by-stage process.

The point about investing space in particular sets of relations is that this will synchronise those relations. It will cause them to be experienced as a structure of simultaneous relations. The more space is invested in these relations, the more this synchronicity will be emphasised. Thus we can increase *convex synchrony* by increasing the quantity of two-dimensional space invested in a particular description, and *axial synchrony* by increasing the quantity of one-dimensional space invested in a description. Thus the Bororo village described by Lévi-Strauss (Fig. 30) is both strongly synchronised, in that a large amount of – convex – space is invested in its central space, and also highly descriptive, in that a large number of objects – in this case houses – are related to that space.[5]

Once the space system is represented it can be analysed as a system of syntactic relations. This means analysing the relations in terms of the basic properties of symmetry–asymmetry and distributedness–nondistributedness. To show how this is done we must first transcribe the system of axial or convex spaces as a graph; that is, as a representation in which small circles represent the spaces, and lines joining them represent their relations. For example, the axial map

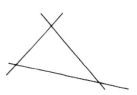

Fig. 31

Fig. 32

can be represented

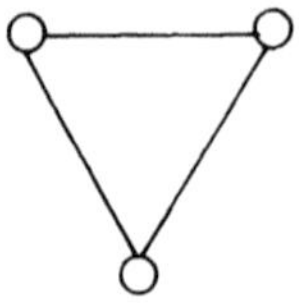

Fig. 33

or the axial map

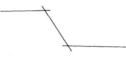

Fig. 34   by

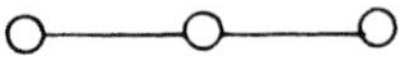

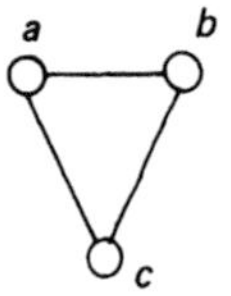

Fig. 35

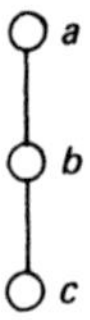

Fig. 36

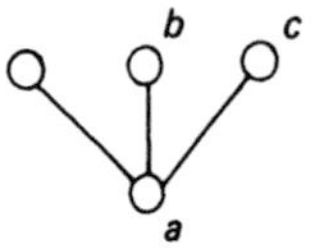

Fig. 37

Following the customary abstract mathematical use of the word, the relation of two spaces *a* and *b* will be said to be symmetric if the relation of *a* to *b* is the same as the relation of *b* to *a*. For example, in Fig. 35 the relation of *a* and *b* is symmetrical – as are the relations of both with *c*. In contrast, in Fig. 36 the relation of *a* to *b* with respect to *c* is not the same as the relation of *b* to *a*, since from *a* one must pass through *b* to reach *c*, but not vice versa. This type of relation will be said to be asymmetric, and we may note that it always involves some notion of *depth*, since we must pass through some third space to go from one space to another.

A relation between two spaces *a* and *b* will be said to be *distributed* if there is more than one non-interesecting route from *a* to *b*, and *nondistributed* if there is only one. Note that this property is quite independent from that of symmetry–asymmetry. For example, Fig. 37 combines nondistributedness with symmetry from the point of view of *a*; while Fig. 38 combines distributedness with asymmetry. In effect, in a nondistributed system there will never be more than one route from point to any other, whereas in a distributed system routes will always form rings.

These basic representational and relational concepts are enough to permit the quantitative analysis of different spatial patterns. We can, in effect, measure the degree to which any configuration of urban space is, convexly or axially, distributed, nondistributed, symmetric or asymmetric in its whole and in its parts. While alpha-analysis is aimed at providing rigorous and 'objective' descriptions that permit the comparison of urban forms with one another, the object of analysis is not merely to offer another description, but to show how it can be that these differences are generated by, and embody in their very form and structure, different social purposes. It seems that these basic concepts are enough to allow us to build a general interpretative framework for urban space structures. This framework is best presented as a series of postulates as to the basic principles of urban space and its elementary 'social logic'.

The postulates are as follows:

(a) every settlement, or part of a settlement, that we might
    select for study is made up of at least:
    a grouping of primary cells or buildings (houses, shops,
    and other such repeated elements), which we will call X;
    a surrounding space which is outside and not part of the
    settlement, whether this is unbuilt countryside or simp-
    ly the surrounding parts of a town or city. Whatever this
    is, it will be treated as a single entity, the carrier of the
    system of interest, and referred to as Y;
    possibly some secondary boundaries (gardens, estate
    boundaries, courtyard boundaries, and so on) superim-
    posed on some or all of the buildings, and intervening
    between those buildings and the unbounded space of the
    settlement. These secondary boundaries will be known
    collectively as x;
    a continuous system of open space defined by X or x,
    whose form and structure results only from the arrange-
    ment of those X or x. This open space structure will be
    known as y. Any configuration of, say streets and
    squares, would therefore be known simply as y;
    every settlement constructs an interface between the
    closed and open parts of the system; whether this is an
    X–y interface or an x–y interface (an X–Y interface being
    a fully dispersed set of buildings, and an x–Y interface, a
    fully dispersed set of secondary boundaries);
(b) every settlement can therefore be seen as a sequence
    with all, or most of X–x–y–Y. This sequence can be seen
    as a 'bi-polar' system, with one pole (the most local)
    represented by X, and the other (the most global) by Y.
    The X-pole consists of many entities, all the buildings of
    the settlement, whereas the Y-pole can be treated for our
    purposes as a single undifferentiated entity, insofar as it
    represents the world outside the system of interest that
    contains or carries the system. The interface therefore
    comprises all the structure interposed between X and Y;
(c) the two poles of the system correspond to a fundamental
    sociological distinction between the two types of person
    who may use the system: X is the domain of the
    inhabitants of the settlement, whereas Y is the domain of
    strangers (those who may appear in the system from
    outside). The interface is therefore an interface for two
    types of relation: relations among the inhabitants of the
    system and relations between inhabitants and strangers.
    Every settlement form is influenced by both types of
    relation; and every kind of syntactic analysis can, and
    needs to be, made from both points of view. It would not

be an exaggeration to say that the syntactic theory of
spatial analysis depends on comparing these two points
of view;

(d) the y-space of the settlement, the structure of public
open space, needs to be considered not only from these
two points of view, but also in the two ways mentioned
earlier; that is, in terms of its *axiality* and its *convexity*,
considered both separately and in relation to each other.
Insofar as axiality refers to the maximum global extension of the system of spaces unified linearly, whereas
convexity refers to the maximum local extension of the
system of spaces unified two-dimensionally, the sociological referents of axiality and convexity follow naturally.
Axiality refers to the global organisation of the system
and therefore its organisation with respect to Y, or in
other words to movement into and through the system;
whereas convexity refers more to the local organisation
of the system, and therefore to its organisation with
respect to X or, to put it another way, to its organisation
from the point of view of those who are already statically
present in the system;

(e) every convex or axial space in the system will have a
certain description; that is, a certain set of syntactic
relations to X, x, y and Y, which may be described and
quantified in terms of its degree of symmetry–asymmetry, and distributedness–nondistributedness. These
values indicate the degree of *unitary* or *diffused control*
of that space; that is, the extent to which it participates in
a system of ringy routes, and the degree of *integration* or
segregation of that space with respect to the whole
system, i.e. the extent to which a space renders the rest
of the settlement shallow and immediately accessible;

(f) each convex or axial space will have a certain
synchrony; that is, the investment of a certain quantity
of axial or convex space in that description. An increase
in the quantity of space, making an axial line more
extended linearly or a convex space significantly fatter,
will always increase the emphasis given to that description. On the other hand, a large quantity of space
invested in a market-place with one kind of description
will not be the same as a similar quantity of space
invested in a parade ground, since the latter will have a
different form of syntactic description. In general, a
small quantity of space will be sufficient to constitute a
description, whereas a larger quantity of space will
increasingly represent that description; that is, it will
lend it symbolic emphasis;

(g) the more descriptions are symmetric (always with respect to *X* and *Y*) then the more there will be a tendency to the *integration of social categories* (such as the categories of inhabitant and stranger), while conversely the more they are asymmetric then the more there will be a tendency to the *segregation of social categories*; while the more descriptions are distributed (again with respect to *X* and *Y*), then the more there will be a tendency towards the *diffusion of spatial control*, while nondistributedness will indicate a tendency towards a *unitary, superordinate control*;

(h) finally, these descriptions of space can be related both to the everyday buildings that make up the system and to the various kinds of public building that may be located within the urban fabric. For example, the global organisation of the system may be constituted throughout by the everyday buildings, with public buildings either hidden from the main axial system or related in the same way as the everyday buildings; or, at the other extreme, the everyday buildings may be removed from the global axial system, leaving it constituted only by the main public buildings.

A procedure for analysis

Within this framework, the analytic procedure can be set out by working through an example.[6] In order to begin alpha-analysis accurate maps are required – the best are about the scale 1:1250, although the procedure has worked successfully on maps up to the scale 1:10,000 – preferably with all entrances to buildings marked. Without precise knowledge of the location of entrances, some but not all of the key syntactic properties can be analysed. The example we will be working through is the small town of G, reproduced in Fig. 25. The support of a photographic record is also helpful, but none of the following analytic procedures depend on such a record. All can be carried out on the basis of the map alone.

Maps with some numbers

The convex map
   1.01 Make a convex map of the settlement (see Fig. 29), that is, a map of the *y*-space broken up into the fattest possible convex spaces, so that all the *y*-space is incorporated into the fattest convex space into which it could be incorporated. The formal mathematical definition of convexity is that no tangent drawn on the perimeter passes through the space at any point. It might be easier to think of convexity as existing when straight lines can be drawn from any point in the space to any other point in the space

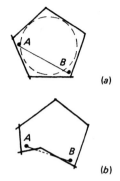

Fig. 39 (a) Convex space: no line drawn between any two points in the space goes outside the space. (b) Concave space: a line drawn from *A* to *B* goes outside the space.

without going outside the boundary of the space itself. Fig. 39 shows an example of a convex space together with a space with concavity introduced. In fact it is quite easy to make a convex map. Simply find the largest convex space and draw it in, then the next largest, and so on until all the space is accounted for. If visual distinctions are difficult, then the convex spaces may be defined in two stages; first, by using a circle template to find where the largest circles can be drawn in the *y*-space, and second, by expanding each circle to be as large a space as possible without breaking the convexity rule and without reducing the fatness of any other space. Whichever way it is done, there is one issue which must be settled in advance: one must decide what level of articulation of the *X* or *x* will be ignored. One must, in effect, decide when changes in the shape of buildings or boundaries are allowed to make a difference to the convex spaces. In practice this is not as difficult or indeterminate as it sounds and, provided the decision is applied consistently across the sample of settlements, it need not be a problem. A further problem can be raised by landscaping. Landscaping means the creation of distinctions in the *y*-space over and above those resulting from *X* or *x*: it 'fine-tunes' the environment. Since fine-tuning is itself a matter of spatial interest, the best way to handle it is to make two convex maps: a minimal map, which takes into account only *X* and *x*; and a maximal or fine-tuned map which takes account of all the further distinctions in *y*. Small articulations in *X* and *x* can also be handled in this way.

The measures of convexity

1.02 Once the convex map is complete, the degree to which the *y* is broken up into convex spaces can be measured. Normally the most convenient and informative way of doing this is to divide the number of buildings into the number of convex spaces. This will tell us how much 'convex articulation' there is for that number of buildings:

$$\text{convex articulation} = \frac{\text{number of convex spaces}}{\text{number of buildings}} \quad (1)$$

which for G will be 114/125, or 0.912. Obviously lower values will indicate less breakup and therefore more synchrony, and vice versa. If, however, we were interested in the degree of convex deformation of the grid then this can be measured by comparing the number of convex spaces we have with the minimum that could exist for a regular grid with the same number of 'islands' – defining an island as a block of continuously connected buildings completely surrounded by *y*-space. If I is the number of such islands and C is the number of convex spaces, then the 'grid convexity' of the system can be calculated by:

$$\text{grid convexity} = \frac{(\sqrt{I}+1)^2}{C} \qquad (2)$$

This formula compares the convex map to an orthogonal grid in which convex spaces extend across the system in one direction, while in the other direction, the convex spaces fit ladder-fashion into the interstices. The formula will give a value between 0 and 1, with high values indicating little deformation of the grid and low values indicating much deformation of the grid. The value for G is $(\sqrt{24}+1)^2/114 = 0.305$.

The axial map and measures of axiality

1.03 Next make an axial map of the settlement by first finding the longest straight line that can be drawn in the y and drawing it on an overlaid tracing paper, then the second longest, and so on until all convex spaces are crossed and all axial lines that can be linked to other axial lines without repetition are so linked (see Fig. 28). The degree of 'axial articulation' can then be measured. The most obvious way to do this is to compare the number of axial lines with the number of buildings:

$$\text{axial articulation} = \frac{\text{number of axial lines}}{\text{number of buildings}} \qquad (3)$$

with low values indicating a higher degree of 'axiality' and high values a greater break-up. The figure for G is 41/125, or 0.328. It is also informative in some cases to compare the number of axial lines to convex spaces in the same way, in which case low values will indicate a higher degree of axial integration of convex spaces and vice versa:

$$\text{axial integration of convex spaces} = \frac{\text{number of axial lines}}{\text{number of convex spaces}} \qquad (4)$$

The value for G is 41/114, or 0.360. The comparison to an orthogonal grid with the same number of islands can also be measured by:

$$\text{grid axiality} = \frac{(\sqrt{I} \times 2)+2}{L} \qquad (5)$$

where I is the number of islands and L the number of axial lines. Once again, the result is a number between 0 and 1, but this time higher values indicate a stronger approximation to a grid and low values a greater degree of axial deformation. In this case, of course, the equation is different since axial lines are allowed to interpenetrate, whereas convex spaces do not. The value for G is $(24 \times 2) + 2/41 = 0.288$. In general values of 0.25 and above indicate a 'griddy' system, while values of 0.15 and below denote a more axially deformed system. If there are any one-connected spaces in the system, then grid axiality should be calculated twice: once to include the one-connected spaces and once to exclude them. By definition one-connected spaces do not affect the number of islands.

The y-map

1.04 Starting from the convex and axial maps, some further useful representations of syntactic properties can be made. The first, the y-map involves the transformation of the convex map into a graph, that is, into a diagram in which spaces are represented by points (in fact we represent convex spaces by small circles) and relations between them (for example the relation of contiguity) by lines joining points – see Fig. 40(a). To make the

Fig. 40(a) The y-map of G. Each convex space is a circle, each permeable adjacency a line.

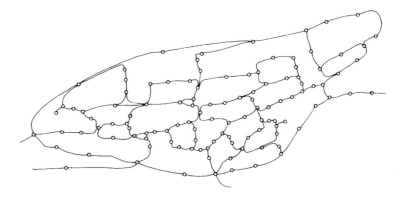

y-map, simply place a circle inside each convex space – using tracing paper of course – then join these circles by lines whenever the convex spaces share a face or part of a face (but not when they only share a vertex). A similar map can of course be made of the axial system, but in general the structure of the graph will be too complex to yield much syntactic information visually.

Numerical properties of the y-map

1.05 Even at this stage, however, it is useful to represent certain numerical properties visually, using copies of the y-map as the base and simply writing in certain values on the appropriate points and lines, so that their distribution is clear. In the following, therefore, it is probably easier to use a fresh copy of the y-map each time:

(a) *axial link indexes*: every line on the y-map represents a relation between two convex spaces. There is therefore a link that can be drawn from one space to another. In all likelihood, this link can be axially extended to other spaces. The number of convex spaces that the extended axial line can reach is the axial link index of that link on the y-map, and can therefore be written in above each link. This value will of course be 0 if the link joining the two spaces is not extendible to any further spaces. These values will indicate the degree to which one is aware, when present in one space, of other distinct spaces. In G these values are relatively high, since there are both many convex spaces and strong axial connections between them (Fig. 40(b)).

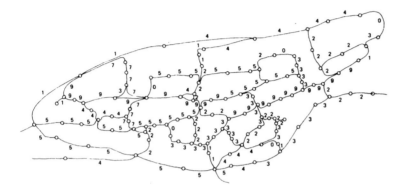

Fig. 40(b) The y-map of G showing axial link indexes. The figure above each link between circles represents the number of additional convex spaces that are traversed by the longest axial line that passes through that link on the convex map.

(b) *axial space indexes*: this time we consider the convex spaces from an axial point of view. Each space in the system will be axially linked to a certain number of other convex spaces, perhaps in several different directions. The total number of these spaces is the axial space index of a space and can therefore be written on the map adjacent to the space (Fig. 40(c)).

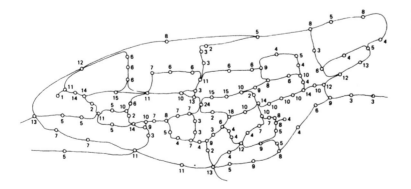

Fig. 40(c) The y-map of G showing axial space indexes. The figure above each circle represents the total number of convex spaces that are axially linked to that space in all directions.

(c) *building-space indexes*: this time we simply record on each convex space the number of buildings that are both adjacent and directly permeable to that space, i.e. the 'constitutedness' of that space. In G it should be noted how few convex spaces have a zero value (Fig. 40(d)).

Fig. 40(d) The *y*-map of G showing building-space indexes. The figure above each circle represents the number of buildings which constitute that space.

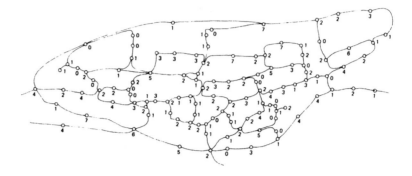

(d) *depth from building entrances*: this time record on each space the number of steps it is away from the nearest building entrance. In some cases, such as G, these values will, of course, be 1 (Fig. 40(e)'. In others, however, an interesting distribution may

Fig. 40(e) The *y*-map of G showing depth from building entrances. The figure above each circle represents the number of steps which that space is from the nearest building entrance.

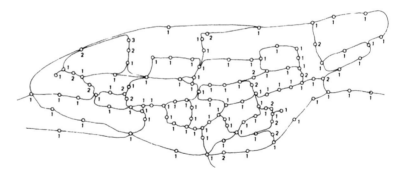

appear. For example, in many recent housing developments there is a tendency to have spaces distant from building entrances near the entrances to the system.

(e) *the ringiness of the convex system*: this is the number of rings in the system as a proportion of the maximum possible planar rings for that number of spaces. This can be calculated by:

$$\text{convex ringiness} = \frac{I}{2C - 5} \tag{6}$$

where I is the number of islands (obviously the number of islands and the number of rings is the same) and C the number of convex spaces in the system. The value for G is $24/2 \times 114 - 5 = 0.108$, which is a high value for a convex map. In effect, ringiness measures the distributedness of the *y* system with respect to itself (as opposed to X or Y).

Numerical properties of the axial map

1.06 Certain useful numbers may also be written on the axial map – though this time using copies of the map itself, rather than a graph transformation of it:

(a) *axial line index*: write on each axial line the number of convex spaces it traverses (Fig. 40(f)).

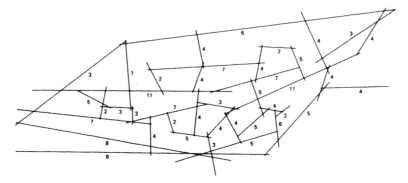

Fig. 40(f) Axial map of G showing axial line indexes. The figure above each line represents the number of convex spaces which that line traverses.

(b) *axial connectivity*: write on the line the number of other lines it interesects. (Fig. 40(g)).

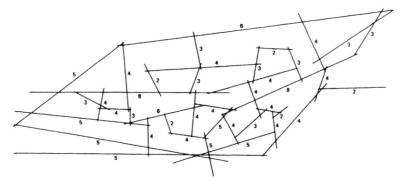

Fig. 40(g) Axial map of G showing axial connectivity. The figure above each line represents the number of axial lines that intersect that line.

(c) *ring connectivity*: write on the line the number of rings in the axial system it forms a part of, but only count as rings the axial lines round a single island i.e. rings that can be drawn around more than one island are to be ignored (Fig. 40(h)).

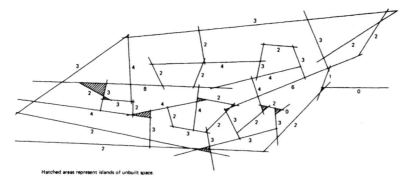

Fig. 40(h) Axial map of G showing ring connectivity. The figure above each line represents the number of islands which share a face (but not a vertex) with that line.

Hatched areas represent islands of unbuilt space.

Figure 40(i) Axial map of G
showing depth values from
Y. The figure above each
line represents the number
of steps it is from the edge
of the settlement.

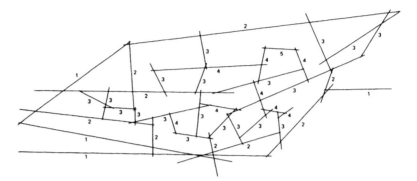

Figure 40(i) Axial map of G showing depth values from Y. The figure above each line represents the number of steps it is from the edge of the settlement.

(d) *depth from Y values:* write on each line the number of steps it is from Y in the axial map, (Fig. 40(i)). The simplest way to do this is to write in first all the lines 1-deep, then all those 2-deep and so on. The carrier, Y, is given the value 0, and so must first be identified. In the case of G, or indeed any finite settlement, simply use the roads leading to the settlement as the carrier. In an estate use the surrounding street system.

(e) *the ringiness of the axial map:* this can be calculated by:

$$\text{axial ringiness} = \frac{2L-5}{I} \tag{7}$$

where L is the number of axial lines. This value will be higher than that for the convex map, and may exceed 1, since the axial map is non-planar, though in practice values greater than 1 are unusual. The value for G is $24/2 \times 41 - 5 = 0.312$.

The interface map

1.07 A further key map is the convex interface map – Fig. 41. To make this map, take the y-map and add to it a dot for each building or bounded space in the system; then draw a line linking dots to circles wherever there is a relation of both adjacency and direct permeability from the building or boundary to the convex space. In the case of G the interface map will be, more or less, the

Fig. 41 Interface map of G. The dots are houses, the circles convex spaces, and the lines relations of direct permeability.

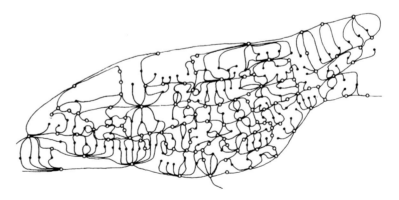

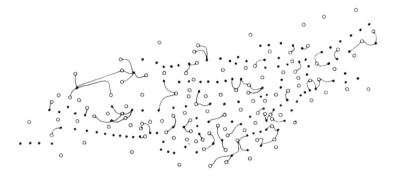

Fig. 42 Converse interface map, where lines show only relations of direct adjacency combined with impermeability.

permeability map of the settlement. But if there are a good many buildings and boundaries relatively remote from *y* then it is useful to make also a complete permeability map by proceeding from the interface map but adding relations of adjacency and direct permeability from buildings to secondary boundaries, and from secondary boundaries to each other.

The converse interface map

1.08 The converse of the interface map may then be drawn (Fig. 42) by starting from the *y*-map, drawing dots for all buildings and boundaries, but then drawing a line from each building or boundary to the convex spaces only where there is a relation of adjacency and *impermeability*. In this case, therefore, the lines linking buildings and boundaries to convex spaces will represent blank walls, whereas in the previous case they represented walls with entrances in them. The relation between the interface map and its converse will immediately show how constituted (i.e. directly adjacent and permeable) the convex spaces are with respect to buildings.

The decomposition map and its converse

1.09 This property may be explored more visually by making a decomposition map. This is drawn by starting with only the circles of the *y*-map (i.e. omitting the lines to begin with) and drawing lines linking one circle to another only when *both* are directly adjacent and permeable to at least one building entrance (Fig. 43(a)). In the case of G, this leaves the bulk of the *y*-map intact, including most of its rings. In other cases, however, the structure of *y*-space will 'decompose' into separate fragments. Cases where the *y*-map stays more or less intact will be called contnuously constituted since everywhere the convex spaces will be directly adjacent to at least one door. In other cases, hoowever what is continuous is the system of *unconstituted* space; that is, space that is remote from building entrances. This may be shown graphically by starting again with the *y*-map and then drawing lines from one circle to another only when both spaces are not

Fig. 43(a) Decomposition map of G, showing lines linking convex spaces only when both are directly adjacent and permeable to at least one house. This shows the extent to which the convex spaces are continuously constituted by front doors. In G, most of the structure of the system survives this decomposition – as will most vernacular settlement forms.

Fig. 43(b) Converse decomposition map of G. Lines are drawn between circles only when both spaces are unconstituted by building entrances.

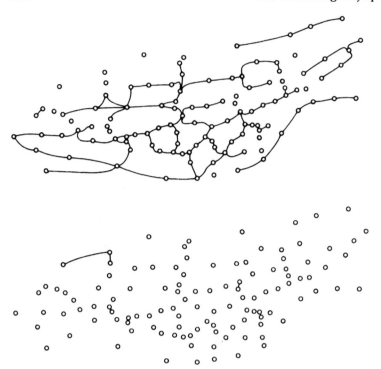

adjacent and permeable to some building. The converse map for G is shown in Fig. 43(b).

Justified maps

1.10 Other maps of properties that could be visually repre-sented at this stage might include a justified interface map or justified permeability map. A justified map is one in which some point, usually the carrier, is put at the base, and then all points of depth 1 from that point are aligned horizontally immediately above it, all points at depth 2 from that point above those at depth 1, and so on until all levels of depth from that point are accounted for. All lines between points are of course retained as in the unjustified map, although this may entail stretching the lines considerably in order to make the link in the justified map. Fig. 44((a)–(b)) is a justified axial map of G from spaces 7 and 37 drawn by computer. Justified maps are worth making when there seems to be some special depth distribution, for example of the build-ings. In many recent estates it will be found that often buildings are clustered relatively deep from *Y*, and often deep with respect to each other, perhaps in nondistributed rather than in distributed parts of the map. Such properties may hold for either axial or convex maps, and either can be justified if required. It may also at this stage be worth drawing and justifying two maps which separate out the distributed and nondistributed elements of the interface or permeability maps. The best strategy will depend on

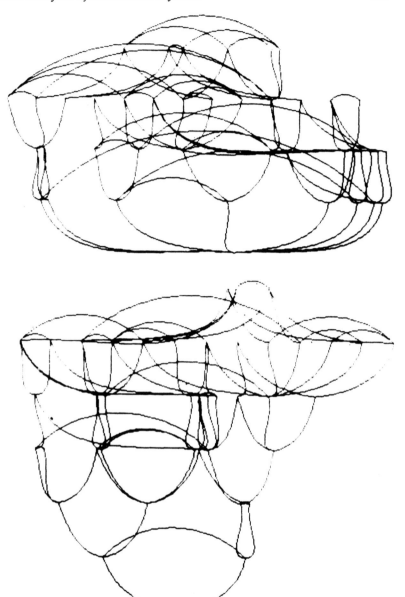

Fig. 44(a) Justified axial
map of G seen from space 7
in the numbered axial map
shown in Fig. 45. Note both
the overall 'shallowness' of
the graph and the clustering
of spaces at depths 2 and 3
from the 'root', as compared
to Fig. 44(b).
(b) Map of G seen from
space 37, which is both
'deeper' overall and has
most spaces at depths 4 and
5 from the 'root'.

what one thinks there is to be shown. Of course, all kinds of
justified maps can also be made from any point in the system. For
example, one may wish to compare what the system looks like
from an internal point and the carrier, or from two different
internal points. This can sometimes be revealing, but it will be
laborious if carried too far and if attempted without the aid of a
computer. In the numerical section that follows, the idea of looking at the system from all points in it is simplified by using com-
puter-based numerical analysis rather than visual representation.

However, it will turn out that numerical analysis will make all kinds of visual representations possible that were not possible before. On the whole these will have to do with global properties of the system that are not at all discernible with the 'naked eye'.

Numbers with some maps

Syntactic descriptions of spaces

2.01 On the basis of visual representations it is possible to see that each space, whether axial or convex (or even a building or boundary) has certain syntactic properties: it will either be distributed with respect to other spaces (have more than one way to it) or nondistributed (only one way), and it will be either symmetric with respect to other spaces (having the same relation to them as they do to it) or asymmetric (not having the same relation, in the sense of one controlling the way to another with respect to a third). The syntactic properties of a space we have called its description. The aim of the numerical side of syntactic analysis is to deepen descriptions by expressing in a concise way very complex relational properties of spaces and of the system as a whole. In particular, it is about considering individual spaces in terms of the whole system.

The measure of integration

2.02 The notion of depth has already been introduced, in the sense that axial or convex segments were either many steps – that is, deep – from buildings or from the carrier, or a few steps that is, shallow – from the carrier or the buildings. Relations of depth necessarily involve the notion of asymmetry, since spaces can only be deep from other spaces if it is necessary to pass through intervening spaces to arrive at them. The measure of *relative asymmetry* generalises this by comparing how deep the system is from a particular point with how deep or shallow it theoretically could be – the least depth existing when all spaces are directly connected to the original space, and the most when all spaces are arranged in a unilinear sequence away from the original space, i.e. every additional space in the system adds one more level of depth. To calculate relative asymmetry from any point, work out the *mean depth* of the system from the space by assigning a depth value to each space according to how many spaces it is away from the original space, summing these values and dividing by the number of spaces in the system less one (the original space). Then calculate relative asymmetry as follows:

$$\text{relative asymmetry} = \frac{2(\text{MD}-1)}{k-2} \tag{8}$$

where MD is the mean depth and k the number of spaces in the system. This will give a value between 0 and 1, with low values

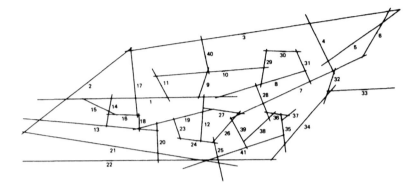

Fig. 45 Numbered axial map of G with Tables of 'integration' and 'control' values for each line. Note that low 'relative asymmetry' means *high* integration and vice versa; whereas high control values mean exactly that – high control.

indicating a space from which the system is shallow, that is a space which tends to integrate the system, and high values a space which tends to be segregated from the system. Relative asymmetry (or relative depth) can therefore be thought of more simply as the *measure of integration*. Of course, for all but the smallest systems these calculations should be done by computer. A table of 'integration' values for G is shown in the key to spaces, Fig. 45 and Table 1. Note that a *low* value means a space with a *high* degree of integration. A key figure is the mean RA from all points in the system. This is the general measure of integration for the system as a whole.

The measure of control (E)

2.03 The measure of control is calculated by a simpler, but perhaps more laborious procedure. Each space has a certain number n of immediate neighbours. Each space therefore gives to each of its immediate neighbours $1/n$, and these are then summed for each receiving space to give the *control value* of that space. In effect, each space is partitioning one unit of value among its neighbours and getting back a certain amount from its neighbours. Spaces which have a control value greater than 1 will be *strong* control, those below 1 will be *weak* control spaces. Note that control is a local measure, since it only takes into account relations between a space and its immediate neighbours, whereas integration is a global measure since it takes into account the relations of a space to every other space in the system. A table of control values for G is given in Table 2.

Converting values for different sized systems

2.04 Some words of warning about RA values. For any given system the list of RA values for spaces will give a true account of the distribution of integration. The same will hold true when we compare across systems approximately equal in syntactic size, i.e. number of spaces. But if we wish to make comparisons across systems which differ significantly in size, we must make one more transformation to eliminate the considerable effect that size can

Table 1.

Point number	Relative asymmetry	Real RA
37	0.15000000	0.99580078
30	0.13589744	0.90217849
33	0.13333333	0.88515625
10	0.13076923	0.86813401
23	0.12692308	0.84260066
29	0.12564103	0.83408954
18	0.12435897	0.82557843
16	0.12179487	0.80855619
35	0.12051282	0.80004507
11	0.11923077	0.79153395
38	0.11666667	0.77451172
36	0.11666667	0.77451172
40	0.11666667	0.77451172
15	0.11666667	0.77451172
5	0.11538462	0.76600060
9	0.11025641	0.73195613
34	0.10897436	0.72344501
14	0.10769231	0.71493389
20	0.10384615	0.68940054
39	0.10000000	0.66386719
22	0.09871795	0.65535607
32	0.09743590	0.64684495
13	0.09743590	0.64684495
41	0.09615385	0.63833383
25	0.09615385	0.63833383
31	0.09615385	0.63833383
6	0.09487179	0.62988272
24	0.09487179	0.62982272
19	0.08974359	0.59577825
17	0.08974359	0.59577825
26	0.08846154	0.58726713
4	0.08846154	0.58726713
28	0.08846154	0.58726713
8	0.08846154	0.58726713
3	0.08717949	0.57875601
12	0.08589744	0.57024489
21	0.08461538	0.56173377
27	0.08205128	0.54471154
1	0.07564103	0.50215595
2	0.07435897	0.49364483
7	0.07307692	0.48513371

Mean	0.1041	0.6913
Standard deviation	0.0185	0.1231
Coefficient of skewness	0.3599	0.3599
Coefficient of kurtosis	−0.6776	−0.6776
Minimum	0.0731	0.4851
Maximum	0.1500	0.9958
No. of non-zero elements	41	41

Table 2. *List of points with control values (E)*

Element number	Control value
1	2.3667
7	2.1167
19	1.7833
3	1.7000
10	1.5000
36	1.3333
35	1.2000
34	1.2000
13	1.2000
16	1.1667
24	1.1500
32	1.1250
41	1.1000
22	1.1000
26	1.0750
25	1.0500
21	1.0500
8	1.0417
29	1.0000
28	0.9583
2	0.9417
14	0.9083
31	0.8750
4	0.8750
39	0.8583
12	0.7917
20	0.7667
38	0.7500
40	0.7500
5	0.7500
27	0.7417
17	0.7417
9	0.7083
30	0.6667
15	0.6250
6	0.6250
18	0.6167
37	0.5000
33	0.5000
23	0.4167
11	0.3750

have on the level – though not the distribution – of RA values in real systems. In effect, what we do is compare the RA value we have with the RA value for the 'root' (the space at the bottom of a justified map) of a 'diamond-shaped' pattern. This has nothing to do with geometric shape. It simply means a justified map in which there are k spaces at mean depth level, $k/2$ at one level above and below, $k/4$ at two levels above and below, and so on until there is

Table 3. *Table of D-values for k spaces, i.e. RA values for diamond-shaped complexes (see text) of k cells.*

k	D	k	D	k	D	k	D	k	D	k	D
1		51	0.132	101	0.084	151	0.063	201	0.051	251	0.044
2		52	0.130	102	0.083	152	0.063	202	0.051	252	0.043
3		53	0.12	103	0.083	153	0.063	203	0.051	253	0.043
4		54	0.127	104	0.082	154	0.062	204	0.051	254	0.043
5	0.352	55	0.126	105	0.082	155	0.062	205	0.051	255	0.043
6	0.349	56	0.124	106	0.081	156	0.062	206	0.050	256	0.043
7	0.34	57	0.123	107	0.081	157	0.061	207	0.050	257	0.043
8	0.328	58	0.121	108	0.080	158	0.061	208	0.050	258	0.043
9	0.317	59	0.120	109	0.080	159	0.061	209	0.050	259	0.043
10	0.306	60	0.119	110	0.079	160	0.061	210	0.050	260	0.042
11	0.295	61	0.117	111	0.079	161	0.060	211	0.050	261	0.042
12	0.285	62	0.116	112	0.078	162	0.060	212	0.049	262	0.042
13	0.276	63	0.115	113	0.078	163	0.060	213	0.049	263	0.042
14	0.267	64	0.114	114	0.077	164	0.060	214	0.049	264	0.042
15	0.259	65	0.113	115	0.077	165	0.059	215	0.049	265	0.042
16	0.251	66	0.112	116	0.076	166	0.059	216	0.049	266	0.048
17	0.244	67	0.111	117	0.076	167	0.259	217	0.049	267	0.042
18	0.237	68	0.109	118	0.075	168	0.059	218	0.048	268	0.041
19	0.231	69	0.108	119	0.075	169	0.058	219	0.048	269	0.041
20	0.225	70	0.107	120	0.074	170	0.058	220	0.048	270	0.041
21	0.22	71	0.106	121	0.074	171	0.058	221	0.048	271	0.041
22	0.214	72	0.105	122	0.074	172	0.058	222	0.048	272	0.041
23	0.209	73	0.104	123	0.073	173	0.057	223	0.048	273	0.041
24	0.205	74	0.104	124	0.073	174	0.057	224	0.047	274	0.041
25	0.200	75	0.103	125	0.072	175	0.057	225	0.047	275	0.041
26	0.196	76	0.102	126	0.072	176	0.057	226	0.047	276	0.041
27	0.192	77	0.101	127	0.072	177	0.056	227	0.047	277	0.040
28	0.188	78	0.100	128	0.071	178	0.056	228	0.047	278	0.040
29	0.184	79	0.099	129	0.071	179	0.056	229	0.047	279	0.040
30	0.181	80	0.098	130	0.070	180	0.056	230	0.046	280	0.040
31	0.178	81	0.097	131	0.070	181	0.055	231	0.046	281	0.040
32	0.174	82	0.097	132	0.070	182	0.055	232	0.046	282	0.040
33	0.171	83	0.096	133	0.069	183	0.055	233	0.046	283	0.040
34	0.168	84	0.095	134	0.069	184	0.055	234	0.046	284	0.040
35	0.166	85	0.094	135	0.068	185	0.055	235	0.046	285	0.040
36	0.163	86	0.094	136	0.068	186	0.054	236	0.046	286	0.039
37	0.160	87	0.093	137	0.068	187	0.054	237	0.045	287	0.039
38	0.158	88	0.092	138	0.067	188	0.054	238	0.045	288	0.039
39	0.155	89	0.091	139	0.067	189	0.054	239	0.045	289	0.039
40	0.153	90	0.091	140	0.067	190	0.054	240	0.045	290	0.039
41	0.151	91	0.09	141	0.066	191	0.053	241	0.045	291	0.039
42	0.148	92	0.089	142	0.066	192	0.053	242	0.045	292	0.039
43	0.146	93	0.089	143	0.066	193	0.053	243	0.045	293	0.039
44	0.144	94	0.088	144	0.065	194	0.053	244	0.044	294	0.039
45	0.142	95	0.087	145	0.065	195	0.053	245	0.044	295	0.039
46	0.140	96	0.087	146	0.065	196	0.052	246	0.044	296	0.038
47	0.139	97	0.086	147	0.064	197	0.052	247	0.044	297	0.038
48	0.137	98	0.086	148	0.064	198	0.052	248	0.044	298	0.038
49	0.135	99	0.085	149	0.064	199	0.052	249	0.044	299	0.038
50	0.133	100	0.084	150	0.064	200	0.052	250	0.044	300	0.038

one space at the shallowest (the root) and deepest points. A table of D-values, i.e. RA values for the diamond-shaped pattern, for systems of different sizes is given in Table 3. All one has to do is find the D-value for the system with the same number of spaces as in the real example, then divide that value into the value obtained for each of the spaces. This will give the 'real relative asymmetry' or RRA of the space:

$$RRA = \frac{RA}{D_k} \tag{9}$$

or system:

$$\overline{RRA} = \frac{\overline{RA}}{D_k} \tag{10}$$

which for G is $0.1041/0.151 = 0.689$. The D-value is the means to arrive at RRA in all cases except when calculating RRA from X in a settlement. In this case, because we are calculating the depth from a large number of roots (all the buildings in the system), instead of comparing to a diamond we compare to a 'pyramid-shaped' pattern, or half a diamond. The table of P-values is given in Table 4. Otherwise, everything is as before. To repeat, RRA values will only be needed when comparing across systems of different sizes. For looking at any particular case the ordinary values printed by the computer will be all that is needed. When they are used, however, whether D- or P-based, RRA values will not be simply between 0 and 1, but above and below 1. Values well below 1 (of the order of 0.4 to 0.6 will be strongly integrated, while values tending to 1 and above will be more segregating.

Integration from X for the convex spaces

2.05 In general, numerical analysis will be based on the axial map. Before proceeding to this, it is worth establishing one or two numerical properties of the convex map: RRA from X of the convex spaces; and E-values for the convex spaces. RRA from X can be calculated on the basis of the depth values already assigned to the convex spaces: those adjacent and permeable to some buildings being given the value of 1, those two steps away the value of 2, and so on. Simply add these, divide by the total number of convex spaces, which gives the mean depth; then calculate RA as per the equation and divide by the P-value for that number of spaces. The value for G is 0.168, which is extremely low. Much higher values will be found in recent housing layouts, which characteristically distance convex space from the building entrances.

Control values for convex spaces

2.06 The E-values are best calculated and recorded on the convex map itself, rather than on the y-map. The interest here will lie in the relation between the convex size of spaces, their distance from the nearest building entrances and their E-value. In G, for example, there is very little depth from buildings in the convex system, and the larger convex spaces are distinguished by having higher E-values than their neighbours. They do not, on the other hand, have any special degree of connectivity to the buildings. Convex size is therefore associated with increasing connectivity to segments of space, rather than increasing

Table 4. *Table of P-values for k spaces, i.e. RA values for pyramid-shaped complexes (see text) of k cells. Use only to calculate the real relative asymmetry (see text) from X.*

k	P	k	P	k	P	k	P	k	P	k	P
1		51	0.036	101	0.0188	151	0.0128	201	0.0097	501	0.0039
2											
3	0.410										
4	0.331										
5	0.278	55	0.034	105	0.0182	155	0.0125	225	0.0087	550	0.0036
6	0.241										
7	0.212										
8	0.190										
9	0.172										
10	0.157	60	0.031	110	0.0174	160	0.0121	250	0.0078	600	0.0033
11	0.145										
12	0.135										
13	0.126										
14	0.118										
15	0.111	65	0.029	115	0.0167	165	0.0117	275	0.0071	650	0.0030
16	0.105										
17	0.099										
18	0.094										
19	0.090										
20	0.086	70	0.027	120	0.0160	170	0.0114	300	0.0065	700	0.0028
21	0.082										
22	0.079										
23	0.076										
24	0.073										
25	0.070	75	0.025	125	0.0153	175	0.0111	325	0.0060	750	0.0026
26	0.068										
27	0.065										
28	0.063										
29	0.061										
30	0.059	80	0.024	130	0.0148	180	0.0108	350	0.0056	800	0.0025
31	0.058										
32	0.056										
33	0.054										
34	0.053										
35	0.051	85	0.022	135	0.0142	185	0.0105	375	0.0052	850	0.0023
36	0.050										
37	0.049										
38	0.048										
39	0.047										
40	0.045	90	0.021	140	0.0137	190	0.0102	400	0.0049	900	0.0022
41	0.044										
42	0.043										
43	0.042										
44	0.042										
45	0.041	95	0.020	145	0.0133	195	0.0100	450	0.0044	950	0.0021
46	0.040										
47	0.039										
48	0.038										
49	0.038										
50	0.037	100	0.019	150	0.0129	200	0.0097	500	0.0039	1000	0.0020

permeability to buildings – although this is always maintained through the continuous constitution principle.

The system seen from X

2.07 In general RRA from X of the convex spaces and the E-values of the convex spaces will index key aspects of how the

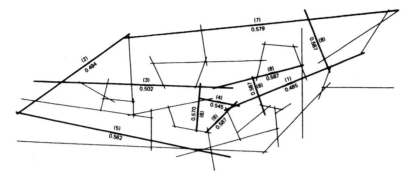

Fig. 46 Integration core of G, i.e. in this case the 25% most integrating spaces, with RA values numbered in order of the degree of integration. Where spaces have the same RA value they have been included in the core, making the core larger rather than smaller than 25% of axial lines.

system looks from the buildings which make up the settlement – that is, from the point of view of the inhabitants. A high RRA from X – and certainly a value over 1 – will index the degree to which buildings are to be found in groups segregated from each other, although it says nothing about the size of those groups. The distribution of E-values for convex spaces in relation to building entrances will then indicate the degree to which the convex system is controlled from the buildings. These may constitute all or most of the convex spaces (as at G) or concentrate on the strong or the weak E-value spaces. In a prison, for example, the strong control convex spaces are never constituted by the cells – for obvious reasons.

The axial integration 'core'

2.08 Let us assume that we have integration and control values for all the spaces in the axial system. What we are interested in is the distribution of these values. A good way to begin is by re-drawing the axial map starting with the lowest RA line – i.e. the most integrating – and working from low to high. It will always be interesting to see where the most integrating lines are and what they relate to in the system; but more important is what type of pattern the strong integrating spaces make. A useful device is to make a map of the 10%, 25% or 50% most integrating spaces, or of a given number of spaces if the system is large and complex. Fig. 46 shows that at G these make a system strongly biased towards one end of the town in the direction of the nearest large neighbouring town, and towards much of the periphery, but strong integrating lines also pass through the centre and make two rings, one close to the centre of G, and the other linking the centre to the periphery. This map might be thought of as the *core* of the settlement. We may then take the other extreme and map the 25% least integrating spaces, i.e. those with the highest RA values. Fig. 47 shows their distribution at G, showing that they tend to cluster in the quieter zones of the settlement.

High and low integration maps

2.09 We may extend this and map all the axial spaces below mean RA on one map, and all those above on another. Fig. 48(a) shows that at G the low RA system makes a kind of circle with a Y-shape inside it, while the high RA system fills in the three interstices formed by the Y and the outer circle (Fig. 48(b)). How many spaces there are in each map is itself of interest, since fewer will imply more integrative or segregative spaces. Fig. 49 shows Figs. 48(a) and (b) combined.

The control core

2.10 With E or control values we may proceed slightly differently. Instead of taking the 'best 25%' of lines, we may take instead the least set of lines that accounts for 25% of the control in the system. All we need to do is to draw an axial map starting from the highest E-value line, and work down until we have accounted

Fig. 47 25% most segregating spaces in G.

Fig. 48(a) Spaces above mean integration at G. (b) Spaces below mean integration at G.

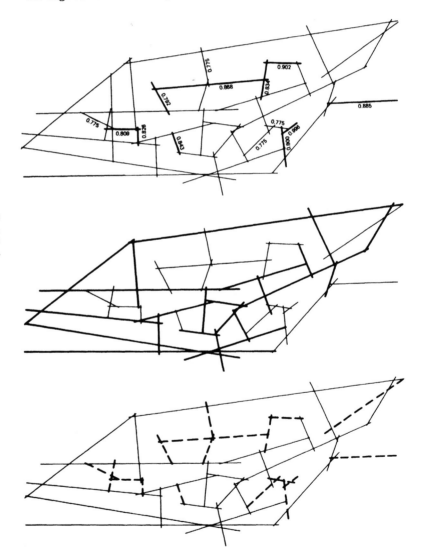

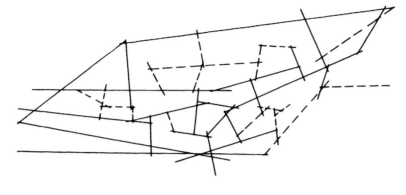

Fig. 49 Integration–segregation map of G. Integrating spaces are represented by solid lines and segregating spaces by dotted lines.

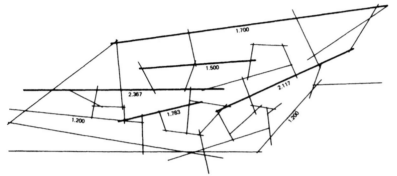

Fig. 50 Axial spaces at G which account for the top 25% of the total control value – in effect, the 'strong control' map. Space 37 has been eliminated to give a figure for the distributed system only.

for 25% of the E-value in the system. Fig. 50 shows how few lines this implies at G (excluding the effect of the nondistributed space (37 in Fig. 45)).

Combined maps

2.11 We may then make a whole series of maps by permutating these properties, i.e. a map of spaces with both high integration (low RA) and high control (high E), with low integration and high control, with high integration and low control, and with low integration and low control. These may be made both at the 25% level $(++/--)$ and at the 50% $(+/-)$ level as in Table 5, taking percentages of the numbers of spaces in the case of RA, and total value for E – again excluding the effect of nondistributed space 37 from high control maps.

Table 5. *Key to Figs. 51–58(a).*

Integration RA		Control E-value		Integration RA		Control E-value	
		Strong E++	Weak E−−			Strong E+	Weak E−
	Strong RA−−	Fig. 51	Fig. 52		Strong RA−	Fig. 55	Fig. 56
	Weak RA++	Fig. 53	Fig. 54		Weak RA+	Fig. 57	Fig. 58(a)

Some main dimensions of the settlement

2.12 On the basis of these maps a series of points can be made which reveal something of the local and global structure of the settlement:

(a) only three lines are in both the integration++ (RA− −) and control++ (E++) maps. One of these lies on the edge of the settlement, (Fig. 51), while the other two are the lines that link the centre to the two ends, one in the direction of another main neighbour. Both of these lines go to but not through the centre. Since association with high integration must make high control high global control (integration being the global measure), it is clear

Fig. 51 Spaces at G with both strong integration and strong control (RA− −E++).

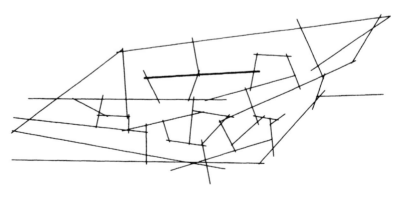

Fig. 52 Spaces at G with strong integration and weak control (RA− −E++).

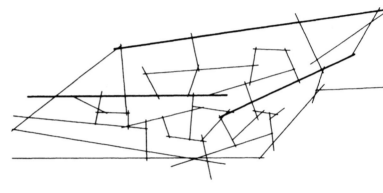

Fig. 53 Space at G with weak integration and strong control (RA++E++): the 'balcony access' space in G.

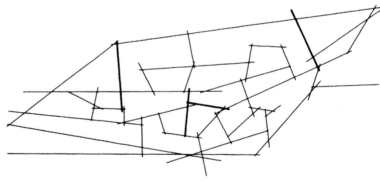

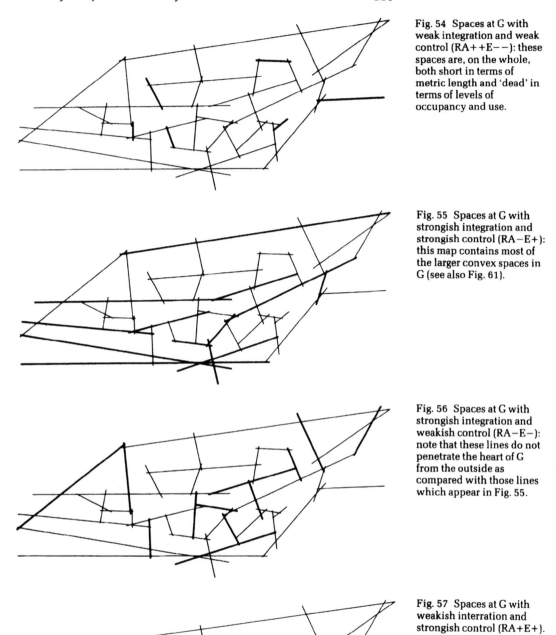

Fig. 54 Spaces at G with weak integration and weak control (RA++E−−): these spaces are, on the whole, both short in terms of metric length and 'dead' in terms of levels of occupancy and use.

Fig. 55 Spaces at G with strongish integration and strongish control (RA−E+): this map contains most of the larger convex spaces in G (see also Fig. 61).

Fig. 56 Spaces at G with strongish integration and weakish control (RA−E−): note that these lines do not penetrate the heart of G from the outside as compared with those lines which appear in Fig. 55.

Fig. 57 Spaces at G with weakish interration and strongish control (RA+E+).

Fig. 58(a) Spaces at G with
weakish integration and
weakish control (RA+E−).

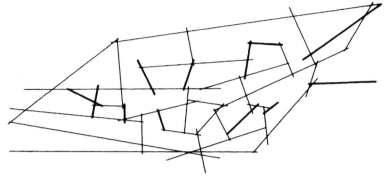

Fig. 58(b) Spaces at G with
weakish integration and
either weakish or strongish
control (Figs. 57 and 58(a)
combined).

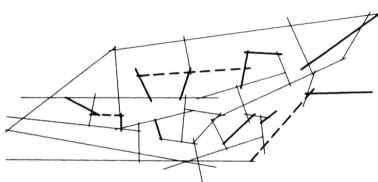

that the strongest global control structure of the settlement must
be given by these three lines;

(b) the strongest difference between the high integration and
high control maps lies in the number of vertical lines that have
high integration (RA−−) but low control (E−−). A careful
inspection of the maps (Fig. 52) will show that each of the four
best such lines intersects one of the three strongest high integration–high control lines (Fig. 51). These lines therefore integrate
the system across its global control lines, and in doing so, bring
each of the three low integration zones within a short section of
global control space of each other.

(c) in the high control map there are exactly three free-standing
spaces (see Fig. 59). Two of these spaces are also found in the low
integration (RA+)–high control (E+) map (Fig. 57). If all three
spaces in Fig. 57 are added to the low integration (RA+)–low
control (E−) map (Fig. 58(a)), itself very fragmented, then they
have the effect of forming the three clusters of the low integration
zones (Fig. 58(b)).

Linking axiality to convexity

2.13 Finally, if we extract from the convex map all the
interior spaces with marked convex extension (Fig. 60) and

experimentally overlay these on the various maps, we find that by
far the best fit is with the high integration (RA−)–high control
(E+) map (Fig. 61). This axial map links together nearly all the
major convex spaces, with the exception of the one adjacent to the
church. On all other maps the distribution of strong spaces
appears more random.

Interpretation

The global orientation of the system

3.01 These points by no means exhaust the possibilities of
visual and numerical analysis, but they do permit us to sketch an
interpretation of G using the postulates set out earlier in this
Chapter (pp. 95–7). The last point made was perhaps the most
fundamental: in G, convex space is invested in the strong global

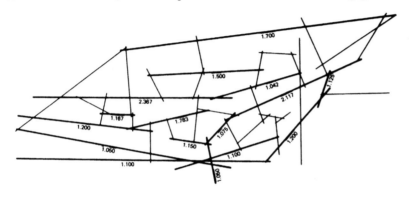

Fig. 59 Spaces at G with
50% of the top control
value, i.e. the strong control
map.

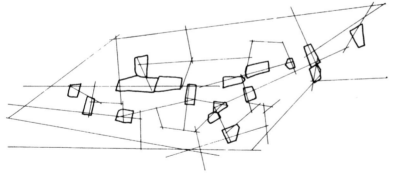

Fig. 60 Largest convex
spaces in the interior of G.

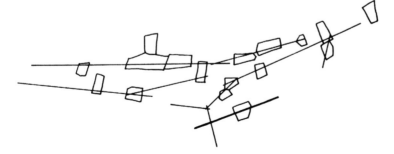

Fig. 61 Map showing the
interior lines of the high
integration, high control
axial map superimposed on
the largest convex spaces.
This shows that more space
is invested in global rather
than local relations in the
system.

system, that is, in the set of spaces that have both high integration and high control. Space is not invested in local relations, as would be required if the settlement were to be given a territorial interpretation. This is confirmed by the lack of any special investment of buildings in convex expansion. It is also confirmed by the fact that the global internal structure of the settlement forms the Y-within-the-circle shape, the points of which are the three main routes into the system from the outside. The conclusion is unavoidable that G is globally structured to make the inhabitant–stranger interface rather than the inhabitant–inhabitant interface.

The local control of the system

3.02 This is only a part of the story. There is also the division of the settlement into the core – the Y-in-a-circle – and the three low integration zones. These zones are where strangers are less likely to penetrate. They are also among the zones where the buildings are densely congregated. These 'quiet' areas are achieved without cutting them off from the main structure of the settlement. This has the effect that, although the system as a whole is geared to the accessing and control of strangers, there is also an inhabitant-orientated global structure which is made up of these quieter areas plus their strong transverse connectivity with each other, and with the main stranger interface, through the strong vertical lines. The inhabitant can thus see a very different settlement to the one the stranger sees. The high permeability of the low integration areas seems geared to allowing the inhabitant out more than letting the stranger in. The advantage to the stranger on the control dimension is counterbalanced by the advantage to the inhabitant on the integration dimension. The system as a whole is geared to the accessing, but at the same time to the control of strangers.

Systematic interpretation

3.03 Interpretation is, of course, more of an art than a procedure and it is never possible to establish in advance which spatial dimensions are likely to be the most relevant. It does, however, help to work systematically, insofar as this is possible. Working systematically means essentially three things at this stage:

(a) working from a summary of the main spatial features of the system as shown by the visual and numerical analysis – plus any other features which one feels are present but which have not yet been expressed through representations or numbers;

(b) using the set of postulates as a general interpretative framework – always remembering that this aspect of space syntax is only a theory and may well not be adequate to explain one's material in a way that is satisfactory;

(c) finally, and most simply, trying to see the settlement as an interface between the two kinds of social relations: those among inhabitants and those between inhabitants and strangers. Try to build a general picture of how the structure of the interface generates and controls these relations. When attempting to do this, however, never forget that the internal structure of the dwelling may be important to a full understanding of the system.

Some differences

These global and local properties of G will turn out to be genotypical for a substantial class of settlements. Equally, other classes will vary and even invert these properties. There is no scope in this primarily theoretical exposition for an exhaustive examination of such cross-cultural variations. This will be the theme of a subsequent volume. For our present argument it will be more important to show that the analytic technique can pin-point and elucidate certain key aspects of different settlement forms crucial to the social theory of space, which it is the aim of this book to develop.

We may begin with an example close to home: the piecemeal development in the nineteenth century of the area of Inner London now known as Barnsbury, bounded on the west by the Caledonian Road, on the east by the Liverpool Road, on the north by Offord Road and on the south by Copenhagen Street (Fig. 62).[8]

The convex map of the area is not given, but it has an RRA from X of 0.105 (i.e nearly all the convex spaces are constituted) and a grid convexity of 0.372; both figures are close to those of G, but an improvement in the direction of better constitutedness and a more convexly synchronised form.

The axial map is shown in Fig. 63. This map has a grid axiality of 0.232, slightly less than G (the non-axial organisation of the squares is responsible) and an axial ringiness of 0.316, slightly more than G. Its mean integration from all lines is 0.704, slightly less integrated than G. The axial map becomes especially interesting when we plot its integration core and its most segregated lines.

Figure 64 shows the eleven most integrating lines (chosen to be the same number as in G) numbered in order of integration. The most integrating line of all is – gratifyingly, but far from obviously – the 'village-line', that is, the relatively short line where the grid deforms, and where the main shop, pub and garage are located. The second connects the village-line to the west carrier, the third is on the east carrier itself, the fourth connects the village-line to the north carrier, and so on. In other words, the integrating lines quickly construct a pattern very similar to G: long axial lines in from the carrier, with shorter lines at the centre, and with some parts of the carrier included as well. The remainder of the integrating map then amplifies this into a partial grid.

Fig. 62 Ordnance Survey
map of Barnsbury area,
North London.

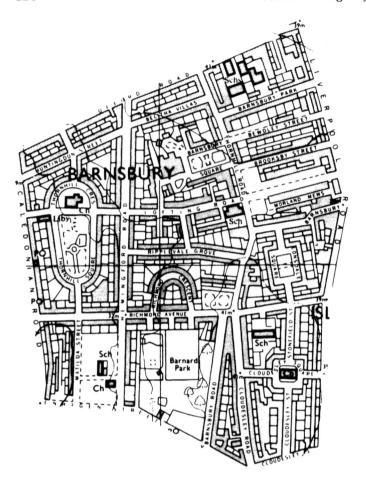

Topologically, therefore, both G and Barnsbury are, axially speaking, incomplete wheels, with a hub at the syntactic centre and spokes connecting the centre to a partially realised rim. As with G, the high segregation (though still for the most part highly connected) axial lines (Fig. 65) are then to be found forming zones in the interstices of the wheel; and in this case it turns out that these lines circumscribe more or less, all the main squares. This is a reversal compared to G, where the larger convex spaces were located on the integrating structure. Here the larger spaces – albeit with boundaries around them – are conspicuously located in the relatively segregated areas, although these areas remain very shallow to the integrating structure.

This is one of the ways in which the relation between axiality and convexity creates the characteristic pattern of Barnsbury. But there is also another, concerning not the most segregated structure but the main integrating lines. It concerns how the village is defined. Axially the village is conspicuous not only by being the most integrating line in the system, but also by being a sudden,

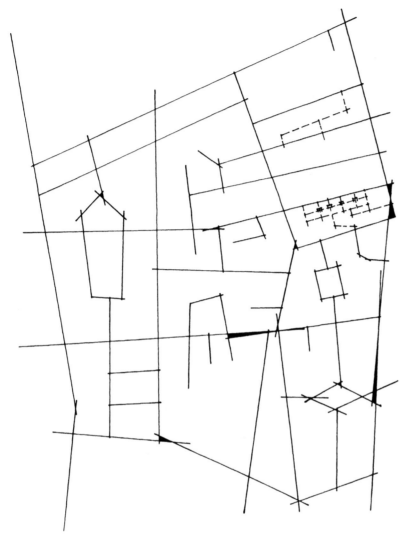

Fig. 63 Axial map of
Barnsbury.

fairly marked, *local deformation* of the grid; not only this, but in
each direction a long axial line links the village-line direct to the
carrier. Axially, therefore, the village is recognisable both in terms
of a local deformation and in terms of its global connectivity. The
village deformation is only one step from the carrier and therefore
visible globally; whilst its local identity as a space is created by
the deformation. These properties will turn out to hold for a large
class of urban areas in London, and constitute one of its most
characteristic morphological effects.

The village is also convexly recognisable in that it is the only
series of relatively small convex spaces in the system covered by a
single axial line. This is a common way in which local areas are
defined spatially in London. A sudden sharp increase in the

Fig. 64 Integration core of
Barnsbury, numbered in
order of integration values.

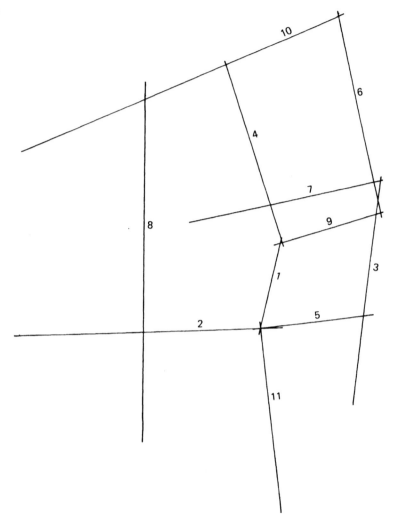

frequency of convex spaces, coupled to their strong axial linking, shows again that at the local level also the spatial definition of the 'village' in Barnsbury has convex correlates. This permutation of our major spatial variables will again turn out to provide a characteristic means of local definition of areas in London.

Now let us turn to a very different kind of system: a purpose-built modern estate (in fact about half of it) in which a conscious and careful attempt has been made (in reaction against the high-rise era) to reproduce many of the generic properties of traditional European settlements. The task for syntax is to try to show whether these properties have been genuinely reproduced and, if not, to detect the differences.

A glance at the ground plan will show immediately why the estate appears to be a true copy (Fig. 66). The layout clearly has a locally beady ring form. Equally clearly it also attempts to

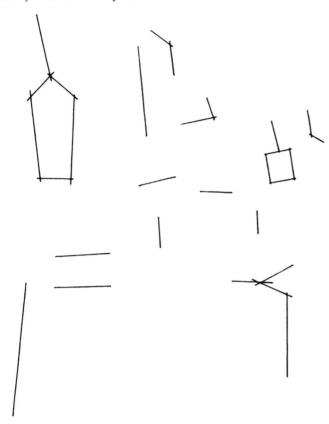

Fig. 65 Segregation map of Barnsbury.

constitute the open space structure by opening the dwellings – admittedly by way of high-walled front gardens – directly on to it. The question therefore becomes: how far does it reproduce the global spatial properties of traditional settlements?

We may begin by looking at the most global level, the level at which the estate is embedded in the surrounding area. Fig. 67 is an axial map of the area prior to the building of the estate. Fig. 68 is the same map after the building of the estate. Even a cursory inspection of the new map reveals some rather startling properties. Of course the axial map immediately shows a dramatic change in the scale of the new estate compared to the surrounding area, in that in general axial lines are much shorter. But more important is the way in which the shorter lines are related both to each other, and to the outside, to create both a high degree of axial discontinuity from the surrounding area – there are no axial lines that go from the surrounding area into the interior of the scheme – coupled with a great deal of depth once the estate is entered. This property on its own ought to be enough to virtually eliminate the passage of strangers through the scheme, ensuring that most of the spaces will be deserted for much of the time.

But it is not only with respect to the outside that the estate uses

Fig. 66 Part of Marquess
Road estate in Islington.

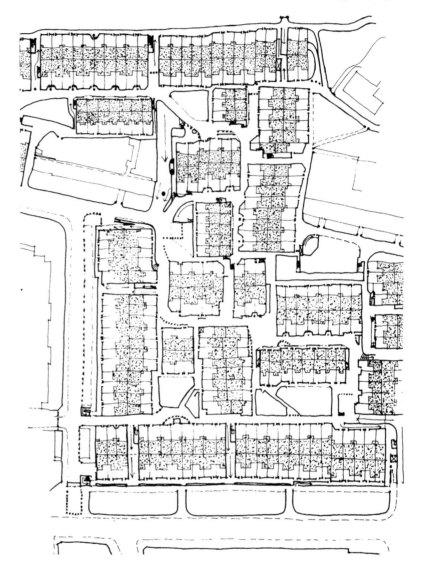

depth in a most untraditional way. Internally the axial map is far
more segregated than G, its mean RRA being 0.9, as opposed to G's
0.664, which is a very substantial increase for a system of that
size. The reason is fairly obvious. A substantial proportion of lines
add depth by going from only one line to another. Rings do not
therefore on their own produce integration. The axial ringiness of
the system is in any case not what it appears to be at first. The
axial ringiness is 0.160 compared to G's 0.277. On grid axiality too
a substantial reduction is shown by the value of 0.121, compared
to G's 0.263.

Looked at from the point of view of X, also, the estate bears little
resemblance to a traditional settlement. Convex RRA from X is

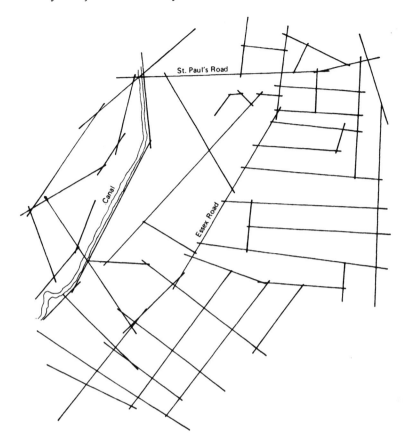

Fig. 67 Marquess Road area
in 1897 – axial map.

0.91 compared to G's 0.203. To amplify this, if we mark depth
values from the building entrances on the convex spaces, we find
high values crowded round the entrances to the estate – one of the
more subtle, probably unconscious, ways in which modern
estates are cut off from the outside world. Internally too the
convex system is broken up. The decomposition map in Figure 69
shows how the clusters of constituted spaces tend to form islands
separated from others by unconstituted spaces.

Finally if we take the best eleven spaces (the same number as
we used for G to describe the integrating core), then we see that
they form a structure that hugs the edges of the estate, and
completely fails to penetrate the deeper parts of the scheme (Fig.
70).

The 25% control map is also revealing. It shows a strong control
system which is fragmentary, and dispersed through the estate.
We must conclude, all in all, that the estate is a spatial pattern
without an effective global structure.

In spite of its strong, genotypical differences in comparison to
traditional settlement forms, the estate is still a distributed
system. The properties we have found in it, however, are found to

Fig. 68 The Marquess
Road area after the building
of the Marquess estate —
axial map.

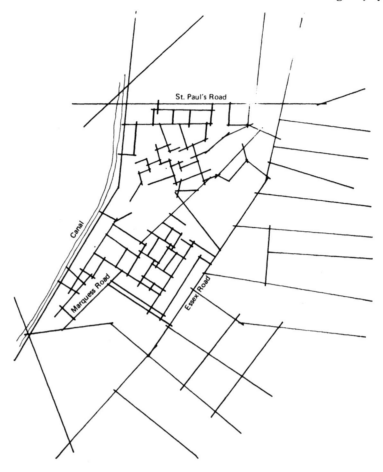

a much greater degree in the – far more prevalent – modern layout
forms which superimpose hierarchies of boundaries on the primary cells – bounded estates internally composed of bounded
blocks, for example. These are strongly nondistributed systems.
Such systems are of great interest – as is their social logic –
because in many ways they have properties which are syntactically the direct inverse of traditional forms. Since the contemporary
'pathology' of space is largely concerned with such systems, it is
worth trying to uncover some typical properties.

   We may begin with the pathology of a concept. Modern theories
of space in almost all cases stress three related principles: that
space should be hierarchically arranged through a well-marked
series of zones from 'public to private';[9] that the object of spatial
organisation must be to encourage specific groups of people to
identify with particular spaces by excluding others from access;[10]
and that those spaces identified with particular groups should be
segregated from each other.[11] These ideas are pervasively present
when space is discussed, often appearing to act as a taken-for-

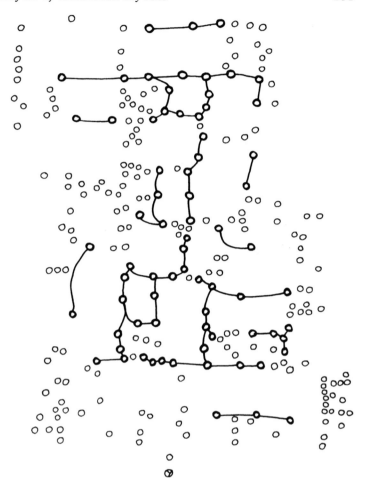

Fig. 69 'Decomposition' map of part of Marquess estate, showing how convex spaces adjacent to doors form islands segregated from other islands by 'unconstituted' spaces, i.e. spaces faced with blank walls. Note that this is the most generous interpretation possible. If all the articulation of the convex spaces is taken into account, then the 'decomposition' effect is much stronger.

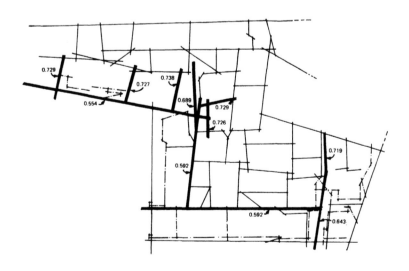

Fig. 70 Integration core of part of Marquess estate.

granted model of 'good' spatial order rather than as an explicitly stated theory. Curiously, they are often assumed (and sometimes even stated) to be the guiding principles of traditional settlements, although our examination of G would suggest almost the opposite.[12]

However, these principles are realised today in whole families of different-seeming forms, and the abstract spatial model that they imply can be succinctly stated. It is that of an asymmetric, nondistributed structure, or more simply a 'tree', everywhere branching and becoming deeper, with the primary cells at the deepest points of the tree (Fig. 71).

If instead of looking at this model from the point of view of Y, the carrier, we look at it from the point of view of a single building or primary cell, and to clarify this we set it out as a left–right progression from this building to Y, then it can immediately be seen to have one consistent property when viewed from the building: as one moves away from the building entrance, at every step one is as many steps away from the nearest other entrance as from the original. For this reason we may call it the 'no neighbours' model – although it might be better to talk about the 'no neighbours' principle since the model itself is rarely likely to be realised in its pure form (Fig. 72).

However, as a guiding principle, we may see how – with some licence – it underlies the compound form of the unfortunate Ik (Fig. 73), which can be represented from one of its constituent buildings as in Fig. 74, with a new convention adopted for the nondistributed elaboration of the system: each time a higher order boundary is superimposed on a building or group of buildings it is also represented by a dot, with a loop joining the dot to itself, showing the scope of the boundary.[13]

In spite of its density and contiguity, the syntax of boundaries,

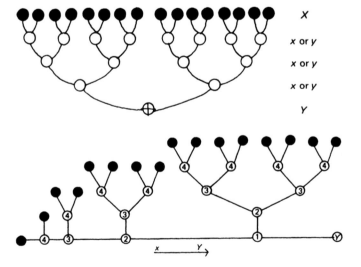

Fig. 71 An 'everywhere branching' tree.

Fig. 72 An 'everywhere branching' tree seen, left–right, from one of its endpoints.

Fig. 73 Ik compound.

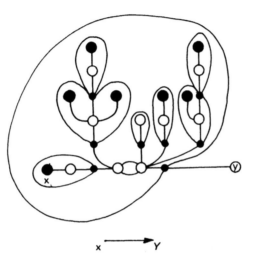

Fig. 74 Ik compound, seen left–right from one of its primary cells.

x ———▶ Y

spaces, and permeabilities guarantees that the conduct of every-day life will exclude accidental contact with neighbours *as neighbours* – that is, in the vicinity of their own dwellings. Whatever contacts may occur accidentally – and the axial breakup of the space guarantees that these will be as little as possible in any case, as contact is obviously minimised if lines are short – they are as it were projected away from the dwelling itself. This is exactly the opposite of G, of course, where accidental contacts will inevitably occur in the vicinity of dwellings, and where any sight lines minimise the reductive effect of local breakup of space on numbers of such contacts.

Let us now look at a very ordinary area of London – part of Somerstown, just north of the Euston Road – in the two phases of its growth. Fig. 75 is the area as it originally grew in the nineteenth century and Fig. 76 is the interface map of its closed

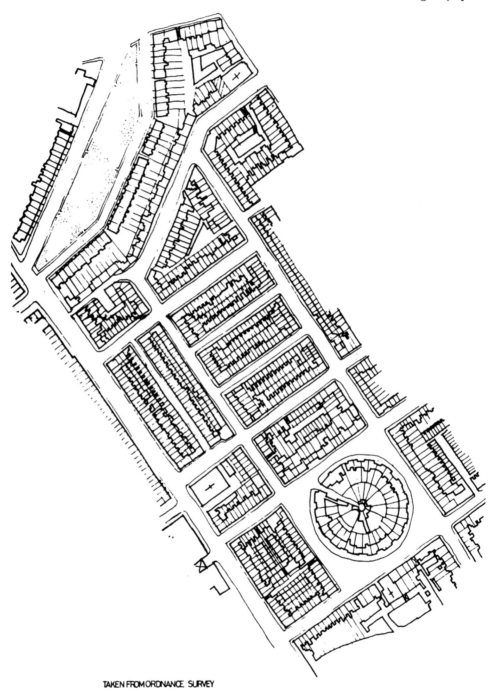

TAKEN FROM ORDNANCE SURVEY

Fig. 75 Somerstown,
London, in the nineteenth
century.

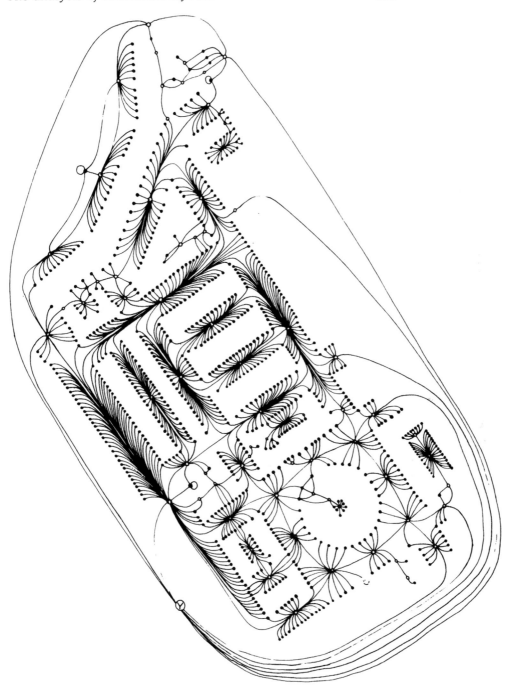

Fig. 76 Interface map of
nineteenth-century
Somertown.

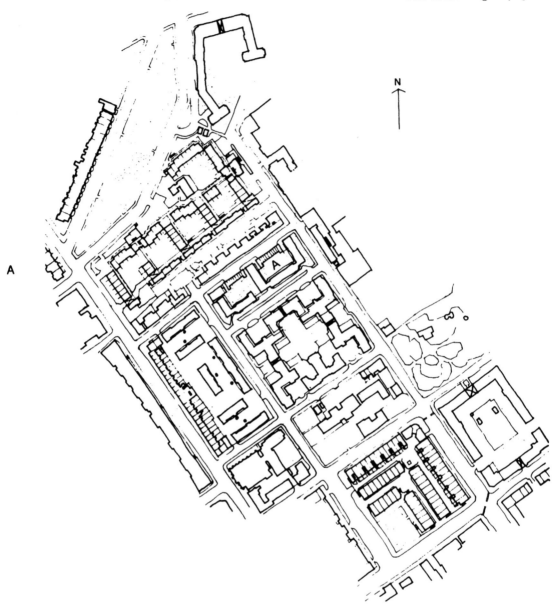

A

Fig. 77 Somerstown as it
has been gradually
redeveloped in the
twentieth century.

and open parts. Fig. 77 is the same area as it has been gradually
redeveloped over the past half-century or so, and Fig. 78 is its new
interface map, with the same convention as that used for Ik (Fig.
74), of a dot with a loop joining the dot to itself, used here to
represent the boundary of each estate. Fig. 78, since it shows only
the interface, exhibits only these superordinate boundaries
together with their loops, since this is what will be experienced by
an observer moving in the open parts of the system.

We then take the block marked A, and first magnify it (Fig. 79)

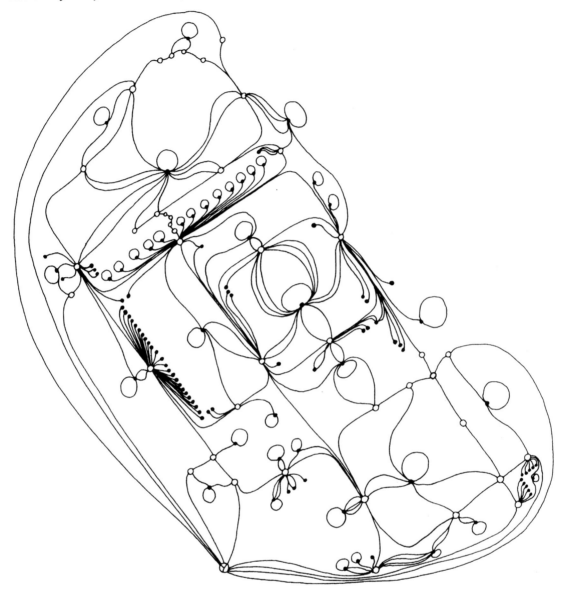

Fig. 78 The interface map
of Somerstown now.

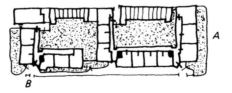

Fig. 79 The block marked
A in Somerstown (Fig. 77).

Fig. 80 Permeability map
of block marked A in Fig.
77.

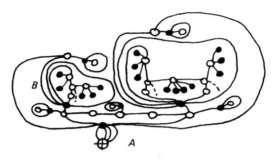

Fig. 80 Permeability map
of block marked A in Fig.
77.

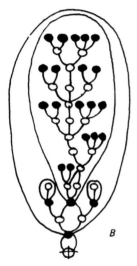

Fig. 81 Justified
permeability map of sub-
block B in Fig. 80.

then draw an unjustified permeability map of the whole estate
(Fig. 80), and justify the block marked B (Fig. 81).

The larger interface map and the justified map of the block
together give a graphic representation of how the syntax of this
system will be experienced. It is not a pure 'no neighbours' model
but it is not an exaggeration to say that its logic pervades the
whole arrangement. The structure of open space everywhere
intervenes, as it were, between the small isolated groups of
dwellings, whereas previously the spaces constituted by the –
much larger – groups of dwellings were continuous. Note that in
Fig. 80 only the ground level of the scheme has been represented.
The syntactic effects discerned become even more pronounced
when the – in this case few – higher storeys are included, as in Fig.
81.

Thus the ground level logic of the earlier street scheme is
inverted in ways that will be sustained as buildings become
higher. There is nothing syntactically new about high-rise housing
forms: syntactically their generic logic is established in the typical
low-rise public housing schemes that preceded them. For this
reason if no other we can begin to discern that perhaps high-rise is
not in itself the problem, and low-rise is not itself the answer.

The problem of the modern urban surface lies, we would
suggest, in its complete reversal of virtually every aspect of the
spatial logic of urban forms as they evolved. A careful syntactic
examination of the new type of surface will show how numerous
and, in some instances, how subtle these reversals are. They can
most succinctly be explained in terms of the X-x-y-Y model with
which we began alpha-analysis, coupled to the main syntactic
relations and the ideas of size (synchrony) and numbers of
relations (description).

It is clear that the system that was shallow from Y (the outside)
has become remarkably deep, (or asymmetric): also the system
that was distributed, or ringy, has become more and more tree-
like, or nondistributed, as movement occurs from Y to X. What
was a direct, single interface has become a complex, multilayered
interface with various levels of x intervening between X and y. As
a result, the closer convex spaces are to Y (i.e. in the surviving
street system, which by our definition of Chapter 2 is no longer a

street system), the less likely it is to be constituted by building entrances – that is, to have relations of direct adjacency and permeability. On the contrary, the street is dominated by relations of adjacency and impermeability from buildings to convex spaces. Blank walls face the stranger wherever he moves.

Another way of formulating this is to say that, seen from the point of view of X, the system of y-space has become like a pyramid, with more and more space projected away from X, just as it has already been seen to be away from Y. This is important, since it means that the system of space is deep from X (the dwellings) as well as deep from Y (the outside). This two-way introduction of indirect, or asymmetric relations is one of the key reasons for the curiously fragmentary and disembodied character that much modern space possesses. These properties can, of course, be expressed numerically: in Fig. 82 the RRA from Y (treating the street system as carrier) is $RRA_d = 2.262$, while the RRA from X is $RRA_p = 1.285$. This 'two-way depth' property can be seen even more strikingly when we consider where the larger spaces are. In most cases it will be found that the larger (fatter) the space, the more likely it is to be deep from building entrances and deep from Y. In other words, symbolic emphasis is given to spaces that exactly express this principle of the spatial segregation, both from the primary cells and from the outside. This property will usually hold regardless of the geometric location of the larger spaces. For example, in the block immediately below the one we have illustrated in Somerstown, the vast central convex space is several convex steps from both dwellings and the outside in spite of its geometric position. Such spaces are, of course, amongst the least used of spaces in the new urban surface, as would be inferred from their syntactic description.

A further genotypical relation between size and syntax is related to the above. In general, the closer the movement towards the entrances to buildings the smaller the convex spaces are likely to be. But there is also a relation between the description of spaces (i.e. the number of relations) and depth, in that the most relations to spaces (those with the primary cells) occur in these convexly small, deep spaces.

But in spite of the relation between description and depth, the

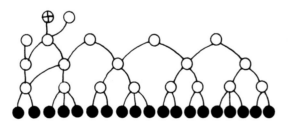

Fig. 82 Pyramid map of how the space structure of sub-block *B* in Fig. 80 looks from the point of view of the dwellings.

effect of the arrangement of y-space is to make the groups of dwellings deep from each other. They become locally concentrated, but globally segregated from each other. Seen in terms of the formal model, these X, the dwellings, are segregated within themselves from y-space (increasingly as convex spaces become larger), and from Y, the outside world. In other words, the double interface – between inhabitants and inhabitants, and between inhabitants and strangers – has been prised apart in terms of *both* its constituent relations. Inhabitants no longer relate to each other as neighbours, other than in the smallest groups, as a result of the increased internal segregation of X; while inhabitants never interface with strangers in their role as inhabitants, because of the depth of y from X; and strangers never penetrate to X, because of the depth from Y.

In spite of its superficial appearance of greater order then, the modern surface is characterised above all by a loss of the global structure that was so pronounced a property both of an organic town and an area of piecemeal redevelopment in nineteenth-century London. It is extraordinary that unplanned growth should produce a better global order than planned redevelopment, but it seems undeniable. The inference seems unavoidable that traditional systems work because they produce a global order that responds to the requirements of the dual (inhabitants and strangers) interface, while modern systems do not work because they fail to produce it. The principle of urban safety and liveliness is a product of the way both sets of relations are constructed by space. Strangers are not excluded but are controlled. As Jane Jacobs noted many years ago, it is the controlled throughput of strangers and the direct interface with inhabitants that creates urban safety.[14] We would state this even more definitely: it is the controlled presence of passing strangers that polices space; while the directly interfacing inhabitants police the strangers. For this reason, 'defensible space', based on exclusion of strangers and only on surveillance of spaces by inhabitants can never work.

An excursion into social interpretation: two social paradigms of space?

Thus we see in the old and new urban surface two completely different paradigms of spatial organisation, in many senses the inverse of each other. But where in society can we find the origins of such differences? And how can it be explained that under some circumstances society seems to generate one type of spatial order, and under others a quite different one?

The answer to this question is the subject of the rest of the book. But even at this stage, and using only those concepts so far introduced, it is possible to sketch some broad theoretical ideas about why this bifurcation of spatial forms should be found. In the brief analysis of societies seen in terms of their spatial and transpatial properties sketched in Chapter 1 (pp. 41–2), it was suggested that every society has spatial groups of people, who live and move in greater proximity to each other than to others, and transpatial groups based on the assignation of different labels to different groups of individuals. A label grouping was called transpatial because the grouping in no way depends on spatial proximity, although it could coincide with a spatial grouping. Two different pathways of development of such a system were noted: cases where spaces and labels corresponded to each other, that is, all the members of the spatial group shared the same label; and cases where spaces and labels were in a noncorrespondence relation, that is, the label groups were distributed among the various spatial groups.

Now if they are to reproduce themselves as systems, these two types of system will have quite different internal logics. In a correspondence system, encounters resulting from physical proximity, through membership of the same spatial group, and encounters resulting from label sharing, through membership of the same transpatial group, will reinforce each other, and will do so at the expense of relations with members of other spatial – and by definition transpatial – groups. Of its own logic, therefore, the system will tend to become locally very strong, and will require not only restrictions on encounters, but also strongly defined spatial boundaries. The strength of the system will be a function of its ability to maintain correspondence, and this must inevitably lead in the direction of exclusivity, strong rules, strong boundaries, and an internally hierarchical organisation. This is the natural logic of the correspondence principle (which is another name for the territorial principle). It does not mean that all systems with correspondence at any level will behave in this way. It does mean however, that to the extent the system depends on correspondence at more than the primary cell level in order to reproduce itself as a system, the more it will tend to follow its internal logic.

A noncorrespondence system in contrast will only succeed in reproducing itself if it works on the contrary principles. In such a system the two types of grouping are split; the spatial grouping works locally, as it must, but the transpatial grouping works across space, relating individuals in different spatial groups to each other, and causing them to encounter each other. The labelling will only remain powerful in the system as it reproduces itself to the extent that the label group is realised in terms of encounters between members of different spatial groups. The system must therefore aim to maximise encounters across space if it is to reproduce itself. However, since the local encounter system does not depend on labels to reinforce it, then locally also the system must tend to maximise encounters, and this means maximising encounters between members of different transpatial groups. Transpatial labels must in effect be disregarded locally if the system is to work. A noncorrespondence system therefore tends, insofar as it succeeds in reproducing itself, to be globally rather than locally strong. Both within the spatial group and between spatial groups it must seek to maximise its encounter rate, and the function of the transpatial grouping will be to promote these encounters across space. Of its own logic, therefore, the system must depend on non-exclusivity, weaker rules, weak boundaries and lack of hierarchy. It must seek to maximise local encounters regardless of labels, and global encounters regardless of spatial group. It is, for example, an important generative principle for urban systems that key facilities – those that generate most movement in the system – are located to organise their potential in the global encounter system rather than purely the local. Of their very nature, therefore, probabilisatically used facilities will tend to generate a noncorrespondence system rather than a correspondence system.

It follows naturally that a noncorrespondence system will depend spatially on exactly the kind of openness in both inhabitants' and inhabitants–strangers' relations that we find in systems like G, coupled to the relatively weak and diffused local organisation that orientates the system towards the global level; and, of course, a correspondence system will need by some means or other to construct a system with the properties associated with closedness, coupled to a strong and bounded local organisation. In both cases there will be an intimate link between the principles of spatial organisation and how the society works. This leads us to define a principal axiom for the whole syntax theory of space: *spatial organisation is a function of the form of social solidarity*; and different forms of social solidarity are themselves built on the foundations of a society as both a spatial and a transpatial system. This will be our guiding principle from now on. But before proceeding to a more extensive examination of the social determinants of space, we must first expand our syntactic arguments in the direction of the social by looking at the internal structure of buildings. Buildings are distinguishable from settlements by their tendency to embody a much higher degree of social information in their spatial form. Their analysis will require an expansion of the theoretical arguments in such a way as to show that many more dimensions of social meaning can be assimilated to the syntax model by a simple extension of its principles. In this way we can approach the relation of society to space with a unified model.

4

••

Buildings and their genotypes

SUMMARY

This chapter adapts the analytic method to building interiors, arguing that these are different in kind to settlement structure, and not simply the same type of structure at a smaller scale. The method shows how buildings can be analysed and compared in terms of how categories are arranged and related to each other, and also how a building works to interface the relation between the occupants and those who enter as visitors. Small and large examples of domestic space are examined to show in principle that spatial organisation is a function of the form of social solidarity – or the organising principles of social reproduction – in that society.

Insides and outsides: the reversal effect

A settlement, as we have seen, is at least an assemblage of primary cells, such that the exterior relations of those cells, by virtue of their spatial arrangement, generate and modulate a system of encounters. But this only accounts for a proportion of the total spatial order in the system, namely the proportion that lies between the boundary of the primary cell and the global structure of the settlement. No reference has yet been made to the *internal* structure of the primary cells, nor to how such structures would relate to the rest of the system. This section concerns the internal structures of cells: it introduces a method of syntactic analysis of interior structures, which we will call gamma-analysis; it develops a number of hypotheses about the relation between the principal syntactic parameters and social variables; and it offers a theory of the relations between the internal and external relations of the cell as part of a general theory of the social logic of space. Since the shape of the general theory is not at all obvious from what has gone before, some theoretical problems must be explored before questions of analysis and quantification can be opened.

One of the most common assumptions about space, sometimes explicit, more often implicit, is that human spatial organisation is the working out of common behavioural principles through a hierarchy of different levels. Thus from the domestic interior, or even from the individual space, through to the city or region, it is assumed that similar social or psychological forces shape space, differing only in involving larger numbers of people and larger physical aggregates.[1] The assumption is so common that it deserves a name: we might call it the 'continuum' assumption. If the continuum assumption were true, the analysis of interiors would simply be a matter of taking the principles and techniques for the analysis of aggregates and applying them on smaller scale. Unfortunately, this would lead us to overlook a very fundamental fact, one which when taken account of adds a whole new dimension to the system. We might call it the fact of the boundary.

A settlement presents itself to our experience as a continuous object by virtue of the spatial relations connecting the outsides of boundaries. By moving about the settlement we build up knowledge of these exterior relations until we have a picture of some kind of the settlement structure. The spaces inside the boundaries have a quite contrary property: they are a series of – potentially at least – separate events, not a continuous system. The same drawing of boundaries that constructs a settlement as a continuous spatial aggregate with respect to the outsides of cells creates a set of discontinuous spaces on the insides of those cells, which do not normally present themselves to experience as a continuous spatial system with a global form, but as a series of discrete events, expressly and explicitly disconnected from the global system. They are experienced one by one as individuals, not as a single entity sustained by physical connections. This property lies in the very nature of a boundary, which is to create a disconnection between an interior space and the global system around, of which it would otherwise be a part.

By virtue of this fact of disconnection, the set of spaces interior to boundaries creates a different kind of system, one whose basic properties have already been discussed at some length: a transpatial system. A transpatial system, we may remember, is a class of spatially independent but comparable entities which have global affiliations, not by virtue of continuity and proximity but by virtue of *analogy* and *difference*. In such a system the nature of our spatial experience is different from our experience of a spatially continuous system. We enter a domain which is related to others not by virtue of spatial continuity, but of *structural comparability* to others of its type. We experience it as a member of a class of such interiors, and we comment on it accordingly. The relations between interiors are experienced as conceptual rather than as spatial entities, and the mode of organising global experience out of local observations is transpatial rather than spatial.

This is the fundamental fact of the boundary. There is no homogeneous continuum of spatial principles from the very large to the very small. In the transition from large to small there is a fundamental discontinuity where the system in effect reverses its mode of articulation of global experience out of local events. In moving from outside to inside, we move from the arena of encounter probabilities to a domain of social knowledge, in the sense that what is realised in every interior is already a certain mode of organising experience, and a certain way of representing in space the idiosyncrasies of a cultural identity.

Even the continuous scale of spatial organisation is shown to be illusory by the reversal effect of the boundary. Behind the boundary, the reference points of space do not become correspondingly smaller. On the contrary they expand through their primarily transpatial reference. As a consequence of the nature of the boundary, the most localised scale of spatial organisation tends to become the most global in its reference. The boundary refers to the principles of a culture.

The duality of inside and outside adds a new dimension to the relation between *social solidarity* and space. A solidarity will be transpatial to the extent that it develops a stronger and more homogeneous interior structuring of space and, in parallel, emphasises the discreteness of the interior by strong control of the boundary. The emphasis in such a case will be on the internal reproduction of a relatively elaborate model. Words like ritualised and conformist might well be applied to such types of organisation. The essence of a transpatial solidarity lies in the local reproduction of a structure recognisably identical to that of other members of the group. The stronger and more complex the structure, therefore, and the more exactly it is adhered to, the stronger will be the solidarity. Such a solidarity requires the segregating effect of the boundary to preserve the interior structure from uncontrolled incursion. Solidarity means in this case the reproduction of an identical pattern by individuals who remain spatially separated from each other, as well as from the surrounding world. A transpatial solidarity is a solidarity of *analogy* and *isolation*: that is of analogous structures realised in controlled isolation by discrete individuals.

In contrast, a *spatial solidarity* works on the contrary principle. It builds links with other members of the group not by analogy and isolation, but by *contiguity* and *encounter*. To realise this it must stress not the separateness of the interior but the continuity of interior and exterior. Movement across the boundary, which would undermine a transpatial solidarity, is the fundamental condition of existence for a spatial solidarity. In such circumstances an elaborate and controlled interior cannot be sustained, but nor is it necessary. Encounters are to be generated, not limited, and this implies the weakening of restrictions at and within the boundary. A spatial solidarity will be undermined, not strengthened, by isolation. In a spatial solidarity, therefore, the weakening of the boundary is associated with a weaker structuring of the interior. Informality rather than ritual must prevail if the principles of the system are to be sustained.

Thus the reversal of space that occurs naturally at the boundary of the primary cell generates a dualism in the principles of solidarity that can relate society to space. An analysis of spatial patterns internal to the cell, and those relating the interior to the exterior, must therefore aim to capture the spatial correlates of these bifurcating principles. This will be possible because the dualism reflects only the dual nature of the boundary, which at one and the same time creates a category of space – the interior – and a form of control – the boundary itself. This dualism is invariably present in spatial patterns within buildings. The method of analysis to be outlined in this section on gamma-analysis will centre on these two dimensions and their inter-relations. It will turn out that category and control are closely related to the basic parameters of alpha-analysis. Relative asymmetry in gamma-analysis will articulate the relations of the space, that is, of the category embodied by the space; and ringiness – i.e. distributedness – in gamma will articulate the relations of the boundary, that is the relations of control on the category.

A building is therefore at least a domain of knowledge, in the sense that it is a certain spatial ordering of categories, and a domain of control, in the sense that it is a certain ordering of boundaries. Sociologically speaking, a building relates this dualism to the universe of inhabitants and strangers by reversing the spatial and transpatial relations that were identified in alpha. Every building, even a single cell, identifies at least one 'inhabitant', in the sense of a person with special access to and control of the category of space created by the boundary. An inhabitant is, if not a permanent occupant of the cell, at least an individual whose social existence is mapped into the category of space within that cell: more an inhabitant of the social knowledge defined by the cell than of the cell itself. Inhabitant is thus a categoric concept, and therefore a transpatial entity, and in that sense the inhabitant is part of a global categoric reality as a result of being mapped into the local bounded space of the cell, as well as being a member of a local spatial reality.

With strangers the effect is the opposite. Every building selects from the set of possible strangers a subset of 'visitors' who are persons who may enter the building temporarily, but may not control it. Pupils in a school, patients in a hospital, guests in a house, and prisoners in a prison all fall within this category of being more than strangers, in that they have a legitimate reason to cross the boundary of a building, but less than inhabitants, in that they have no control over that building and their social individuality is not mapped into the structure of space within that building. In this sense a building also localises the global world of strangers, by the same means as it globalises the local world of inhabitants. It realises a categoric order locally, then uses the boundary to interface this categoric order with the rest of the social world.

A building may therefore be defined abstractly as a certain ordering of categories, to which is added a certain system of controls, the two conjointly constructing an interface between the inhabitants of the social knowledge embedded in the categories and the visitors whose relations with them are controlled by the building. All buildings, of whatever kind, have this abstract structure in common; and each characteristic pattern that we would call a building type typically takes these fundamental relations and, by varying the syntactic parameters and the interface between them, bends the fundamental model in one direction or another, depending on the nature of the categories and relations to be constructed by the ordering of space.

In the sense that it is some ordering of space, then, a building is at least some domain of unitary control, that 'unitariness' being expressed through two properties: a continuous outer boundary, such that all parts of the external world are subject to some form of control; and continuous internal permeability, such that every part of the building is accessible to every other part without going outside the boundary. To express this set of relations, and to avoid confusion with definitions of a building that depend on it being, for example, under a single roof, the term 'premises' will in future be used instead of 'building'. Premises are a domain of unitary control with the boundary and permeability properties given above, whose internal relations are developed by syntactic means into a certain kind of interface between inhabitant and visitors. Gamma-analysis is therefore the analysis of these spatial relations and controls realised though the permeability pattons of the subdivided cell.

The analysis of the subdivided cell

Formally speaking, gamma-analysis is alpha-analysis interpreted for permeability. The relation of contiguity in alpha becomes the relation of direct permeability in gamma; and the relation of containment in alpha becomes the relation of controlling permeability in gamma. The elementary objects in gamma are cells with certain permeability properties. The gamma equivalent of the alpha closed cell is the cell with only one access from the carrier (Fig. 83); while the equivalent of the alpha open cell is the cell with more than one access from the carrier (Fig. 84).

The translation into graphs, or *gamma maps*, is more straightforward than with alpha, since every interior of a cell or subdivision of a cell can be conceptualised as a point and represented as a circle, with its relations of permeability represented by lines linking it to others. Thus the cell with one entrance can be conceptualised as a unipermeable *point* and represented as in Fig. 85, while the cell with more than one entrance can be conceptualised as a *bipermeable point* and represented as in Fig. 86. The

Fig. 83

Fig. 84

Fig. 85

Fig. 86

carrier for any gamma structure is the space outside the cell considered as a point, and represented as a circle with a cross. When the carrier is added, the two structures in Figs. 85 and 86 will become those in Figs. 87(a) and (b).

From these inital elements, the same configurational generators as in alpha may be used to construct patterns with the properties of symmetry, asymmetry, distributedness and nondistributedness. In gamma two spaces a and b will be: symmetric if a is to b as b is to a with respect to c, meaning that neither a nor b control permeability to each other; asymmetric if a is not to b as b is to a, in the sense that one controls permeability to the other from some third space c; distributed if there is more than one independent route from a to b including one passing through a third space c (i.e. if a space has more than one locus of control with respect to another); and nondistributed if there is some space c, through which any route from a to b must pass. Thus, Fig. 88 shows a and b in a symmetric and distributed relationship with respect to c; while Fig. 89 shows a and b in a symmetric and nondistributed relation with respect to c. Fig. 90 shows a and b in a nondistributed and asymmetric relationship with respect to c. Fig. 91

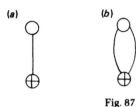

Fig. 87

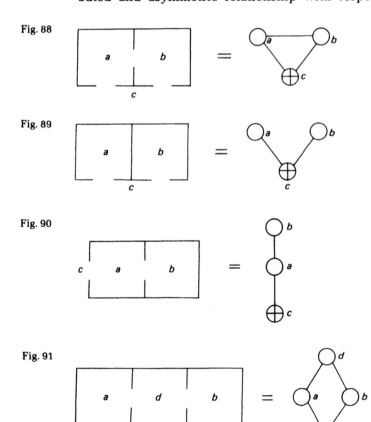

Fig. 88

Fig. 89

Fig. 90

Fig. 91

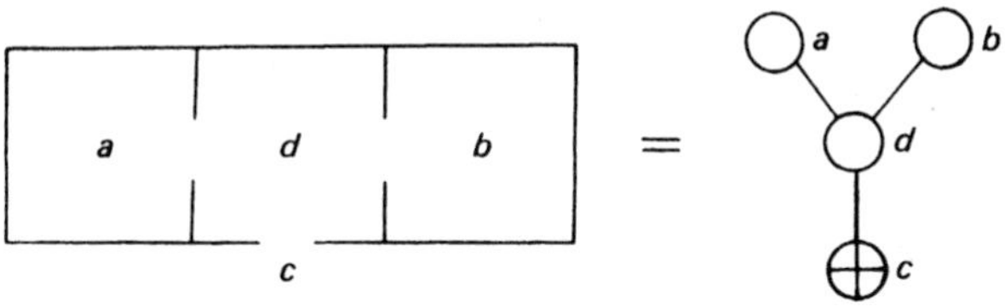

Fig. 92

shows a slightly more complicated case, where a and b are symmetric to each other with respect to c, but d is an asymmetric relation to both with respect to c. This example therefore illustrates a relation that is both asymmetric and distributed. Fig. 92 inverts this and places d in a nondistributed and asymmetric relation to a and b, which still remain symmetric to each other with respect to d (or to c).

We can now use the basic dimensions of the model to set up a technique for the representation and analysis of permeability structures considered as gamma maps. The first stage is a representational device (already introduced in alpha), which we call a *justified gamma map*, and which is constructed in the following way. Every space in the premises can be assigned a depth value according to the minimum number of steps that must be taken to arrive in that space starting from the carrier, a step being defined as a movement from one space to another. A justified gamma map is a graph in which spaces are represented as before by circles and permeabilities by lines, and all spaces of the same depth value are lined up horizontally above the carrier, with the lines representing direct permeabilities between spaces drawn in, however long they have to be to make the necessary connections. The procedure is rather like dissection: the premises are 'sliced' down the middle and 'pinned out' so that their internal structure is visible. The justified gamma map has the great advantage that it renders the basic syntactic properties of symmetry and asymmetry, distributedness and nondistributedness very obvious – far more obvious than in an ordinary layout diagram. Because justified gamma maps are also graphs, they also permit easy measurement of these syntactic properties. Thus justified gamma maps are intended to allow a form of analysis that combines the visual decipherment of pattern with procedures for quantification.

Take, for example, the four simple structures in Fig. 93, whose justified gamma maps are set out in Fig. 94. Certain global syntactic properties of the structures are immediately visible as a result of this representation. For example, it is clear that b and c are distributed forms, whereas a and d are nondistributed. While cutting across this, b and d are relatively deep, or asymmetric, compared to a and c which are comparatively shallow, or symmetric. In short, the four structures can easily be seen to be permutations on the two underlying dimensions of the syntax model.

Fig. 93 Four theoretical
buildings with identical
geometrics and adjacency
graphs.

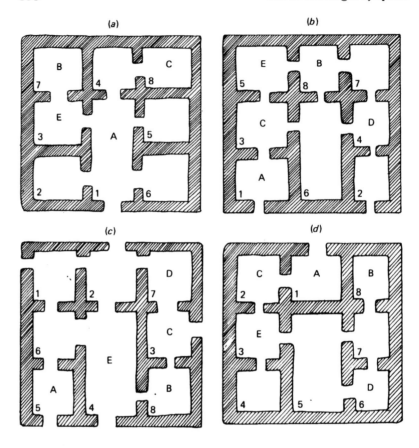

This simple procedure shows that, from a syntactic point of view, the four premises are very different from each other. There appears to be no syntactic genotype when considered from the point of view of the spatial pattern, in spite of the fact that in terms of either geometry or their adjacency graphs all four are identical.

If we consider the labels, and more precisely the relation of the various labels to the spatial configuration, certain regularities can be found. For example, space *A* is always as shallow as any other in the complex, while *B* is always as deep as any other. *D* is always on a ring, and where there is no ring, as in case (a), there is no space *D*. Space *E* is always on a shortest path from *A* to *B*. And finally, in contrast to all of these, the position of *C* is randomised. Since it is the only one that is so, then this in itself might be considered significant. In other words, in terms of the relations between syntactic positions in the complex and the labels common to all the complexes there are certain genotypical trends. These are not strong, of course, but they illustrate the basic strategies of gamma analysis. First, we consider the spatial pattern alone and look for invariants and common syntactic themes.

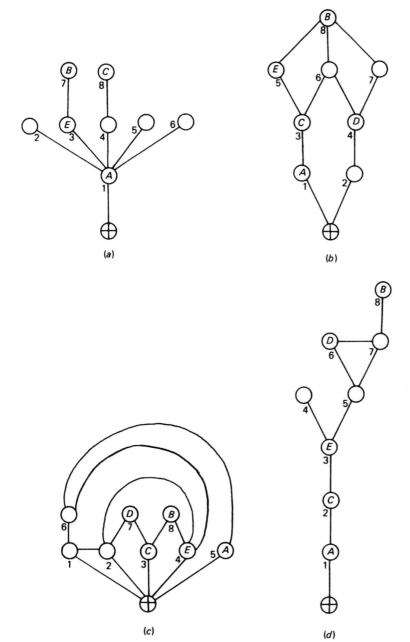

Fig. 94 Justified permeability maps for Fig. 93.

(a)

(b)

(c)

(d)

Second, we consider the relations of labels to syntax. Obviously there will be cases where both syntactic and label genotypes exist for a sample of premises, but the examples show that, formally at least, the two can exist independently.

Both the analysis of spatial patterns alone and the analysis of labels can be made much more precise by adapting and developing

		Depth	RA	RR of	RR from			Depth	RA	RR of	RR from
	⊕	0	0.321				⊕	0	0.392	0.125	0.099
	1	1	0.071				1	1	0.357	0.125	0.116
	2	2	0.321				2	1	0.357	0.125	0.116
	3	2	0.250				3	2	0.250	0.250	0.173
1	4	2	0.250			2	4	2	0.250	0.250	0.173
	5	2	0.321				5	3	0.392	0.125	0.139
	6	2	0.321				6	3	0.214	0.375	0.231
	7	3	0.500				7	3	0.392	0.125	0.139
	8	3	0.500				8	4	0.321	0.250	0.173
	Mean	2.125	0.317				Mean	2.375	0.365	0.194	0.151
		Depth	RA	RR of	RR from			Depth	RA	RR of	RR from
	⊕	0	0.107	0.500	0.347		⊕	0	0.786	0.025	0.015
	1	1	0.214	0.250	0.277		1	1	0.536	0.031	0.019
	2	1	0.111	0.500	0.347		2	2	0.357	0.042	0.026
	3	1	0.214	0.375	0.308		3	3	0.250	0.063	0.038
3	4	1	0.143	0.500	0.347	4	4	4	0.500	0.043	0.026
	5	1	0.286	0.125	0.213		5	4	0.286	0.125	0.078
	6	2	0.250	0.250	0.198		6	5	0.464	0.125	0.078
	7	2	0.285	0.250	0.231		7	5	0.429	0.125	0.078
	8	2	0.285	0.280	0.347		8	6	0.571	0.063	0.038
	Mean	1.375	0.202	0.306	0.291		Mean	3.750	0.464	0.071	0.044

Fig. 95 Values for all points in the four complexes of Fig. 93.

some of the syntactic measures outlined in the earlier discussion of settlement analysis. For example, the relative asymmetry (RA) of a complex (see pp. 108–9) from any point can then be calculated simply by taking the point as the carrier of the system and calculating from that point as though it were the carrier. Variation in this will indicate the degree to which a particular space or label is integrated into or segregated from the spatial pattern of the complex as a whole. The values for the four complexes of Fig. 93(a)–(d) are given in Fig. 95.

The variation in RA for different points in a complex can often be very striking. Take for example the highly ringy complex given in Fig. 96(a) and (b). From the carrier the RA is 0.43, which is nearly half that possible for that number of spaces. Taking point 4 as the carrier, and redrawing the justified gamma map from that point (Fig. 96(b)) the RA changes completely, giving a value of only 0.095, less than a tenth of that possible. No less striking is the difference in RA from the primary cells and from the carrier in the 'no neighbours' model, discussed on p. 132 and illustrated in Fig. 72. Taking the example in Fig. 97(a) and 97(b), show first the justified gamma map from the carrier, with the primary cells in the deepest spaces, and in this the RA of the carrier is 0.219. From any deepest point, that is from any primary cell in the 'no neighbours' model, the RA is 0.472. The 'no neighbours' model is

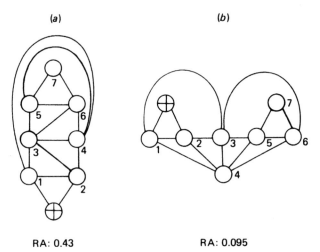

(a)   (b)

RA: 0.43   RA: 0.095

Fig. 96 The same complex justified from two different points.

in fact a form that maximises the differences in relative asymmetry between the carrier and the deepest points, and since the deepest points always number one more than the rest of the points in the system, then the 'no neighbours' model is, formally as well as intuitively, a powerful way of achieving the greatest segregation of the greatest numbers. The social politics of space in effect takes advantage quite systematically of this elementary mathematical fact.

If relative asymmetry in its various forms captures the symmetry–asymmetry dimension of the syntax model in numerical form, then parallel measures of *relative ringiness* capture the distributed–nondistributed dimension, perhaps more than the control values used in alpha-analysis. (However, recent research in building interiors at UCL has increasingly used control values, rather than ringiness values for individual spaces.) Here we may begin with a very simple fact, one that has already been discussed (p. 94). Since the least number of lines to connect a system of k points is $k-1$, and since $k-1$ points can only give the form of a

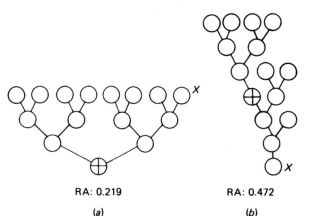

RA: 0.219   RA: 0.472

(a)   (b)

Fig. 97 The 'no neighbours' model (see Figs. 71 and 72) seen from its carrier and an endpoint.

ringless tree (whether the tree is bushy or linear – symmetric or asymmetric – is immaterial), then any increase in the number of lines will result in rings forming in the complex.

Since distributedness can be defined in gamma as a relation with more than one locus of control, then increasing the ringiness of the system will increase the distributedness both of the complex as a whole and of those points within it affected by the rings. The relative ringiness of the complex will be (as with alpha) the number of distinct rings over the maximum possible planar rings for that number of points: $2p - 5$ where p is the number of points in the complex. The relative ringiness of a *point* (RR of) in the complex will be the number of independent rings that pass through that point over the maximum that can pass through it, which will be $p - 1$ for p points since any further lines from any particular point will only repeat a link that has already been made. The relative ringiness from a point (RR from) can then take into account not only the number of rings in the complex, but also the distance from the point to all other rings in the complex, by multiplying the relative ringiness of the complex as a whole by 1 over the mean distance that the point is from each of these rings (adding 1 to exclude zeros). This measure can then be applied not only to the points that lie on rings, but also to those that do not: that is, it can be applied also to points in the nondistributed parts of a complex. Ringiness measures for the structures given in Figs. 93 and 94 are also given in Fig. 95.

The essential proposition of gamma-analysis is that buildings transmit social information through their interior structures both through general variations in the basic syntactic parameters, and also – perhaps primarily – through the variations in the syntactic parameters which appear when the complex is looked at from the points of view of its various constituent spaces. We may define a space syntactically in terms of how the complex is seen syntactically from that space. The richness in this differentiation is the means by which interior structures carry more social information than exterior relations. An alpha or settlement system is characterised by the general syntactic homogeneity of the bulk of its primary cells, a gamma or interior system by the absence of such homogeneity. For this reason labels are more significant in gamma. If a genotype in alpha can be defined in terms of parametrised syntactic generators governing encounter probabilities, a genotype in gamma can be defined in terms of associations between labels of spaces and differentiations in how those spaces relate to the complex as a whole, in terms of the syntactic dimensions. As in alpha, genotypes will be the result of relations of inhabitants with inhabitants and inhabitants with visitors, but the more controlled interfaces of gamma will articulate differences and similarities in forms of social solidarity with greater precision and greater differentiation than in alpha. In the sense that all buildings, of whatever kind, map relations between the inhabitants and between inhabitants and visitors, through some parametrisation of the syntactic dimensions of symmetry–asymmetry and distributedness–nondistributedness, then all buildings share the same abstract genotype. As the forms of solidarity to be mapped into the buildings change, and as the relations between inhabitants and visitors change accordingly, consequent changes in the syntactic dimensions will construct a building of a certain type, and with a certain individuality.

Some examples of domestic space

The need for this rather complicated model of what a building is can be shown by considering what might be expected to be an elementary case: the organisation of domestic space in an ordinary household. Fig. 98(a) is the plan of a fairly standard English cottage built in the latter part of the nineteenth century, together with its justified gamma map, (adding a convention by which each transitional space – halls, lobbys, etc. – is represented by a solid dot rather than a circle), and RA measures from the three main downstairs spaces, and from the carrier. Fig. 98(b) is the same for a conversion of the house for middle-class occupants in the 1960s. Taking the original house first, a number of familiar themes in traditional English domestic space organisation can be seen to have both a syntactic and numerical form. First, the principal spaces on the ground floor – the parlour, which is the best and least used room, the kitchen and the living room – all have markedly different RA values. The space with the highest value is the parlour, the second the kitchen and the lowest the living room, indicating that the parlour is relatively speaking the most segregated from the rest of the complex (in spite of being next to the front door and at the front of the house), and the living room the most integrated.

This family of spaces, the order of RA values, and the spatial relations those values imply, constitute an immensely powerful genotypical theme in English domestic space organisation and reappear under an enormous number of geometric and syntactic transformations as can be seen in Fig. 99, where these relations are invariant in all cases. For immediate purposes, it can immediately be seen that the order of RA values survives in the radically transformed house in Fig. 98b. The values are in all instances lower, but the order remains the same: the 'best' room is the highest, the kitchen second and the principal living area lowest, in spite of the complete alteration of the permeability relations holding among these spaces.

The maintenance of the order of RA values for the principal downstairs spaces is not the only significant RA figure in the transformation from old to new. In general, the RA values in the

Fig. 98 A typical English
cottage as built in the
nineteenth century (Fig.
98(a)) and as recently
converted (Fig. 98(b)).

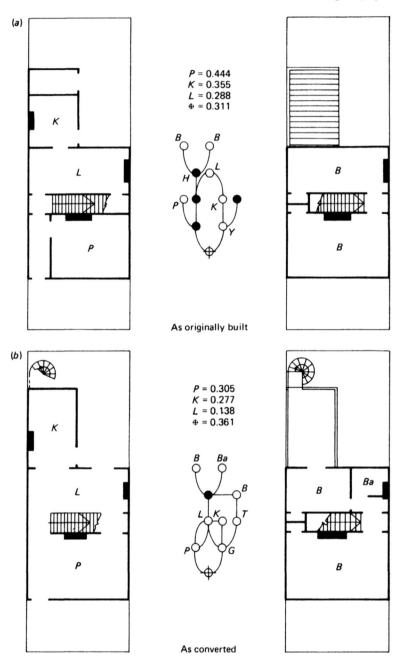

$P = 0.444$
$K = 0.355$
$L = 0.288$
$\oplus = 0.311$

As originally built

$P = 0.305$
$K = 0.277$
$L = 0.138$
$\oplus = 0.361$

As converted

transformed house are substantially lower in the traditional
house, but there is one value which *increases* from old to new,
and that is the carrier. Not only is there an increase in absolute
terms, but compared to other RA values in old and new, the
carrier moves from lowest equivalent in the old to highest
equivalent in the new. The change is therefore much more marked

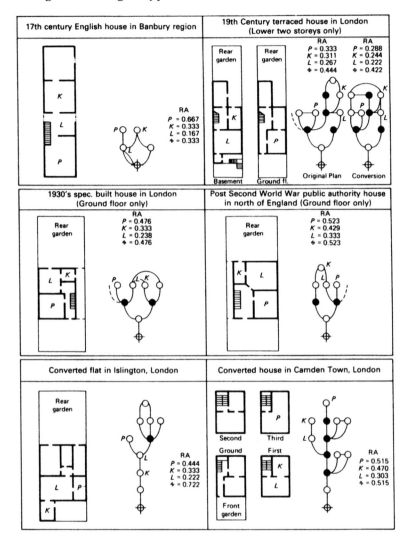

Fig. 99 Six English houses of different periods and sectors of the market, with different building forms, but all preserving the order of integration values for the main use spaces of P (best room), K (kitchen) and L (main living space).

then might at first appear, when all the spatial relations of the two complexes are taken into account. Slightly surprisingly, perhaps, the interior of the house is more segregated from its exterior in the transformed version. The garden, on the other hand, goes the other way: the new house is much more integrated with its garden than the old. Only the bedrooms – again in spite of a major change on the ringiness dimension for one of them – retain their RA values more or less comparably to other spaces in the changes from old to new. Finally, in both cases the lavatory, in one case situated in the yard and in the other in the bathroom, has highest, or highest equivalent RA of all.

On the ringiness dimension the transformations from old to new are no less striking. Overall, the mean relative ringiness of spaces in the new is two-and-a-half times that of the old. But this increase in quantity is not the only point of interest. The *form* of ringiness is if anything more significant. In the old house there is only one ring, and that is not internal to the house but passes through the carrier. The 'living room' or everyday space, is at the deepest point of this ring with respect to the carrier. The ring that the everyday space lies on is therefore only a ring with respect to the relation between the interior and exterior. Moreover, since the everyday space is at the deepest point on this ring with respect to the carrier, it can be seen as the most important space in mediating the relationship of the domestic interior to the outside world. In the transformed house, all the new rings that are added are interior rings. The everyday space, marked L, is now the hub of a set of internal rings and one carrier ring. The everyday control due to this space passes, as it were, from the interior–exterior relation to a much stronger interior emphasis. This shift will be confirmed by observation of everday use. In the new house, the difference between front and back door ceases to be a fact of cultural and practical importance in spatialising different kinds of relationships. In all likelihood the back door ceases to be functional, and all access is controlled through the front door. At the same time, the front door will be more strongly controlled, again reflecting the shift in the controlling ring space inside from an interior–exterior orientation to a purely interior one.

To account for the social significance of these spatial changes, we must refer back to the abstract model of a building as some parametrisation of syntactic variables to articulate relations among inhabitants, and between inhabitants and visitors, in terms of – possibly different – forms of social solidarity. In the case of the household, the relations of inhabitants are, of course, simply the basic family relationships between men and women and parents and children, and visitors are simply those who, either as friends or relations or in some more formal capacity, might have reason to cross the threshold. It ought to be possible to move from a superficial description of how these relations are mapped into the spatial structure of the household to a theoretical description by transcribing these relations into the abstract structure of the model of a building.

An initial point immediately suggests itself. It has often been observed that a standard feature of English domestic space in the recent past, at least for certain sections of the population, has been a space with a rather puzzling combination of properties: the front parlour.[2,3] The space is the best room in the house in the sense that it contains the best furniture and effects; on the other hand, it is used only rarely, perhaps on Sundays, perhaps only on formal and ceremonial occasions. Moreover, although the space contains the best that the household has to offer, and is also at the front of the house, it is invariably concealed from the outside by curtains, lace and otherwise, and ornaments that prevent the passer by from

seeing in. Syntactically, it can also be that this space has pronounced features distinguishing it from the ground-floor spaces: it
has the highest relative asymmetry; and it is the only major space
on the ground floor that is not on a ring – that is, it is a
nondistributed space. Both these properties can immediately be
referred to the concept of a transpatial solidarity, that is, a form of
solidarity realised through the control of categories in isolation,
rather than the interpenetration of categories by spatial contiguity
and random movement. The front parlour is, quite simply, a
transpatial space. As such, it must be insulated from its immediate surroundings and from everyday transactions. Its function is to
articulate relations across greater distances, both spatial and social,
and to achieve this it must be unlinked as far as possible from the
surrounding spatial system. The syntactic values of the space
express this requirement.

In complete contrast to the front parlour, the living room, the
theatre of everyday life and interaction, has the contrary syntactic
properties: it is on a ring, and it has the lowest relative asymmetry
of any ground-floor space – that is, it is the most integrated with
the rest of the household. It is also the most powerful space in that
it occupies the central position on the ring when seen from the
carrier. Syntactically, it is a kind of centre to the household. Most
routes from one space to another in the system as a whole,
including the carrier, will pass through the living room. Its
theoretical nature is as simple and as basic as that of the parlour: it
is the key locus of *spatial* solidarity, as opposed to transpatial
solidarity. It is the space to which all members of the household
have equal access and in which they have equal rights. But it is
also a space in which local interaction dependent on spatial
proximity – relations with neighbours and locally based kin –
normally takes place. In its more developed forms some neighbours will even have rights of access to this space.

The third major ground-floor space, the kitchen, has a combination of the properties of the other two. It has a higher relative
asymmetry, but it is also on a ring. The explanation of both is
simple and inter-related. The high relative asymmetry of the
kitchen articulates a categoric segregation, that between men and
women; while the fact that the kitchen is interposed between the
carrier and the *locus* of spatial solidarity articulates the substantially greater dependence of that spatial solidarity on relations
among women. Thus the relations of this space articulate in a very
strong way the domination of everyday transactions in the household by women. The household is a 'sociogram' not of a family but
of something much more: of a social system.

Finally, the spatial organisation of the upper floor is much
simpler: bedrooms are simply separate spaces off a common hall.
This nondistributed form has in fact one important property: it
maximises the relative asymmetry of all the spaces (except the

hall) with respect to each other, and thus achieves the maximum segregation effect with the fewest number of spaces. This maximum segregation principle is, of course, an articulation of the most fundamental social rule of all: the incest taboo. For sleeping purposes, members of the same household must be as strongly segregated from each other as possible.

How then is the transformation to be accounted for? That is, how can it be theoretically described in terms of shifts in the abstract model? One important aspect of the old genotype that survives, of course, is the order of relative asymmetry values for the major spaces on the ground floor. The best space still has the highest asymmetry, the most used space the lowest, and the kitchen lies in between. However, these categories of use are much weaker than they were. Everyday life spills into the best space, and ceremonial visitors equally use the everyday space. It is this weakening of categoric distinctions that is reflected in the considerable overall reduction of relative asymmetry values for these spaces. The merging of use and the reduction of the degree of segregation are parallel phenomena. The one is the means by which the other is defined. The reduction of relative asymmetry values reflects a general law that associates strong categoric spaces with high relative asymmetry, a law that depends on the simple proposition that the maintenance of a strong category depends on a spatial event: the relative segregation of that category from the less controlled encounters of everyday life.

But there is one ground-floor space that actually increases its relative asymmetry in the transformed house, and that is the carrier. The segregative focus is, as it were, shifted from the interior spaces to the relations between interior and exterior, that is, to the boundary itself. Again this spatial change is associated with a behavioural one. In the old house, the front door might often be left open for a while, even for quite prolonged periods, and free interaction could be expected to take place in the vicinity of the door. In the transformed house this is much less likely. In general the door, with its quasi-traditional furniture carefully burnished, will be firmly shut and hardly ever left casually ajar. Yet, in apparent contradiction, the front window, previous carefully curtained at all times, offers no impediment to the passing observer. On the contrary, the interior of the dwelling is boldly manifested to the outside world, especially after dark, so that a street of such transformed houses appears to the casual passer-by almost as a carefully contrived exhibition of interiors.

The reason for this radical change, and for its apparent contradiction, is of course that a change in the solidarity principles has taken place, with a reshuffling of what is meant by an inhabitant and a visitor. The underlying organising principle of the traditional interior was that of a spatial solidarity which, under controlled conditions, penetrated the boundary and related the interior of the house to its exterior relations. The transpatial space was the obverse side of this principle: it was necessary to deal with relations that were too problematical to be easily accommodated in everday living patterns, especially relations involving ceremonial transitions or class relations. In the transformed house the principles are reversed. The fundamental organising principle is that of a transpatial solidarity. The inhabitants do not relate to their proximate neighbours in a spatial, relatively informal way. Their social networks are much more selective, built up at a distance, and require the much stronger control of the boundary to eliminate the contingent and the spatial. If the traditional interior therefore articulated two kinds of solidarity, the spatial and transpatial – and this was what led to the strong differentiation of space in terms of relative asymmetry – the transformed interior articulates only one form: the transpatial form. The spatial relations to the proximate external area have been eliminated from the internal ones by the newly strong boundary. And just as the spatiality of the traditional model on the internal–external dimension was counterbalanced by the strongly asymmetric and controlled transpatial space, so the interior–exterior transpatiality of the transformed model is counterbalanced by the ringy and less asymetric relations of the new domestic interior. It is that the passing observer sees: an inaccessible spatiality, manifested to the world as a symbol and yet absolutely unlinked to those who merely pass by in spatial proximity. It is *because* interior–exterior relations are so despatialised that the interior can be manifested. The inhabitant has nothing to do with those who only in a relation of spatial proximity to him. It is in this disjunction of the spatial and transpatial that these apparently contradictory principles of behaviour have their origin.

The essentially transpatial nature of the transformed system thus finds its expression at the boundary, rather than in the interior relations. These can be far freer because there is only one form of solidarity to articulate: the solidarity of a transpatial class realised spatially. The interior space develops as a system orientated towards syntax rather than semantics: that is, the emphasis is on building complex patterns of relations between spaces that in themselves represent only weak categories of use. The associated behavioural code emphasises exactly this more developed connectivity. Visitors, usually dinner guests, are moved from one space to another during the course of their entertainment, and often as a result experience much of the interior as a series of connected spaces. In contrast, in the old code visitors of whatever kind were strongly confined to a particular part of the interior. The difference between the two interiors (though not the whole code) reflects with some precision what Bernstein has characterised as the difference between a personal and a positional system.[4] A positional system deals with the control of categories, that is, of people considered as categories; a personal system considers them as persons. In the language of the present model, positions are transpatial, while persons are spatial. The increase in the ringiness of the interior, which increases the potential controlling influences which spaces can have on each other, and some more than others, articulates precisely this change to a system based on persons as spatial entities: the syntactic transformation literally expands the scope of persons to act and control the system at the expense of the relative protection afforded by categories and their more controlled, rather than controlling, spaces.

In contrast to both of these cases, the classic suburban domestic space organisation takes features of both and assembles them in the image of yet another form of social solidarity. In the suburban house, the segregation of interior and exterior is even stronger, usually mediated by a front garden which, like the traditional parlour, is carefully maintained but never used by people; and behind this protective belt the space organisation is even more uniformly categoric and controlled than in the traditional model. The downstairs interior approximates a simple tree form, governed by a hall. The tree form maximises the asymmetry and the control of the principal spaces, while the space that segregates and controls them, the hall, is yet another instance of a ritualised, unused space. The non-use of the least asymmetric and most controlling space by persons perfectly illustrates the non-personal, but highly positional nature of the suburban system. The orientation of the domestic space and its life towards a ritualisation of everyday existence finds its perfect spatial expression in these subtly different spatial relations.

By contrasting all three types of domestic space in terms of their solidarity principles, a deeper analysis of their social nature is possible. All are in effect the spatial forms of a class society, where each form of domestic space organisation has to deal both with relations within and between classes. The front parlour itself is characteristic of 'respectable' working-class life, that is, of those who invest in the control and articulation of relations across the class divide within their own homes. The transpatial space is at root a means of dealing with relations across classes, while maintaining the principles of a spatial solidarity that are characteristic of working-class living patterns more or less everywhere. The suburban interior is the domestic space of the upwardly mobile aspirer, who invests both living space and everyday life in crossing the class divide. It is a spatial order dedicated to the promotion of one form of solidarity at the expense of another – hence its maximal orientation towards both control and strong categories. The transformed urban interior is the spatial organisation of an achiever, one who has crossed the class divide and who uses space to express his membership of, not aspirations towards

an ascendent class in our society: the class of those people who
earn their living by the transformation – as opposed to the mere
reproduction – of symbols, such as writers, designers, and
academics.

All three reflect the fundamental proposition that spatial order
is a function of social solidarity. All three also reflect a certain
underlying lawfulness in the ways in which differential solidarities turn themselves into spatial forms and rules: that categoric
differences within classes (including differential solidarities) are
realised through variations in relative asymmetry; while relations
across classes are realised in variation in relative ringiness, that is,
in the form of control. The space of the new middle-class
domestic interior is ringy and relatively low on asymmetry
because it is the space of a single class, protected by a highly
selective boundary, and of a single solidarity, that is, of common
patterns of solidarity among men, women and children.

Two large complexes from the ethnographic record

Thus the sociological character of variations in domestic space
organisation in different sub-cultures of English society can be
given a precise structural and numerical form through the agency
of the abstract model of a building – but only because the
examples are small scale and a good deal of data on the use of
space is easily available. The larger buildings become, and the
more removed from intuitive experience, the more hazardous
becomes the use of the abstract model to try to construct a
sociological picture of a particular type of building. Fortunately,
gamma-analysis provides us also with a means of slowing down
the argument and exploring the syntactic organisation of a more
complex building through a stage by stage procedure, which, at its
best, will reveal a series of clues leading at least to informed
conjectures as to the sociology of their spatial structure.

Take, for example, 'premises' (if that is the right term) like the
'Kuanyama' kraal of the Ambo tribe drawn by Walton, after Loeb,
in his study *African Village* (Fig. 100),[5] whose justified gamma
map (treating each segment of the rather extraordinary 'passages'
as a dot, following the domestic space convention, and allowing
no segment of space to be larger than its axiality, following the
alpha convention) is as in Fig. 101.

The visual transformation from the plan to the gamma map
immediately makes two points obvious. First, the deepest space
from the carrier – a nondistributed space – is that of the head man
of the kraal; second, the deepest distributed space is the meeting
place. In other words, from the point of view of the world outside
the deepest space is that of the chief inhabitant, while the principal space on the deepest ring is that of the principal inhabitant–
visitor interface. Reversing the system and looking at the complex

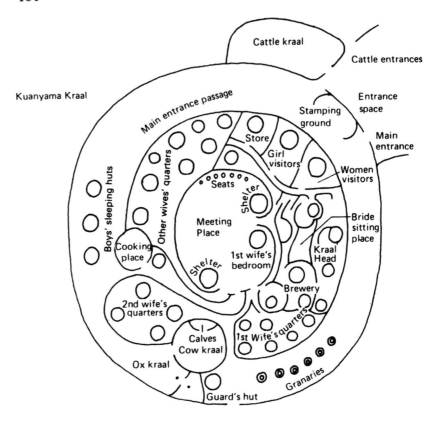

Fig. 100 'Chiefly' kraal of the Ambo people, after Walton.

from the point of view of these two spaces, similar properties hold: the kraal head's space has the highest relative asymmetry of any space in the complex (0.262) by a substantial margin; while the meeting place has the lowest, (0.093) again by a substantial margin, the former being nearly three times the latter. In other words, looking at the relations of inhabitants to each other, similar properties hold: the kraal head's space is the most segregated; while the meeting place is the most integrated.

The principal internal relations mapped into the structure are the most basic: those between the sexes, and those between age groups. In all these relations both the depth measures (i.e. relative asymmetry from the carrier) of the spaces and their relative asymmetries are informative. For example, all the wives' quarters (with the exception of the first wife's bedroom, which is located in the meeting place) have relative asymmetry well above the average for the complex, though well below that of the sub-complex belonging to the head man. At the same time the boys' quarters not only have a lower asymmetry, but they are also located in a shallower position in the complex than either the wives or the headman. There is also a difference on the ringy dimension, in that the space governing the boy's hut is on a shallow ring, whereas the spaces governing the women's huts are

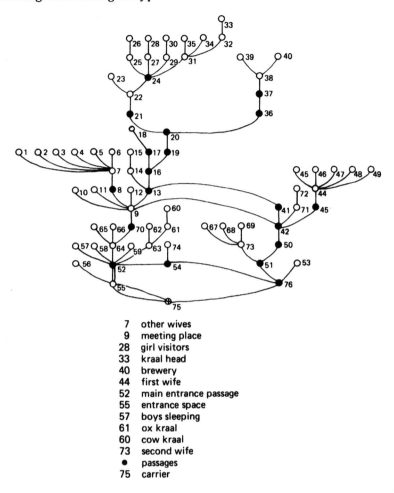

Fig. 101 Justified permeability map of Fig. 100.

7	other wives
9	meeting place
28	girl visitors
33	kraal head
40	brewery
44	first wife
52	main entrance passage
55	entrance space
57	boys sleeping
61	ox kraal
60	cow kraal
73	second wife
●	passages
75	carrier

in all cases themselves nondistributed. The headman himself has two principal spaces: his own quarters and the meeting place. The former is the least ringy space in the complex, the latter the most, being the only space that lies on two rings.

An abstract statement of these relations can perhaps clarify their underlying genotype. Since in general relative asymmetry is associated with strong categories – that is, with the transpatial – and ringiness with control – that is, with the spatial – then it can easily be seen that, insofar as he occupies a positional label (headman of kraal), the headman has the highest relative asymmetry realised in the most controlled space; on the other hand, insofar as he interfaces spatially with others through the meeting place, he has the lowest relative asymmetry realised through the highest ringiness, that is, the highest control. This is the situation when considering the meeting place from an internal point of view. If we look at it from the carrier, that is from the point of view of visitors, then the meeting place is still deeper in the building than any other distributed space. From the point of view of the visitors, therefore, the meeting place has a high relative asymmetry. We can therefore associate the meeting place itself with a strong categoric ordering of the relations between inhabitants and visitors – and this, of course, finds its expression through the location of the sacred fire in this space. Thus the spatial relations of the meeting place combine a high asymmetric, or meaning value on the inhabitant–visitor dimension, with a high spatial control value on the inhabitant–inhabitant dimension, that is, in the relation between the headman and the other categories of people in the complex. The close association of the wives' complexes, in a nondistributed relation, with the ringy complex on which the meeting place is the dominant space, articulates this control. All routes from wives' spaces pass through this ringy complex at a point close to the dominant space.

The relation between those parts of a building that lie on the ring system that includes the carrier, and those that are removed

Fig. 102 Fig. 100 divided into its distributed ('ringy' – Fig. 102(a)) and nondistributed (tree-like – Fig. 102(b)) sub-systems.

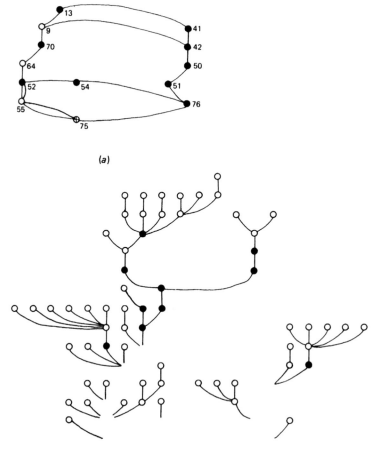

(a)

(b)

from it, is one of the keys to a sociological account of spatial organisation in buildings generally. In most, but by no means all cases, as we shall see, the distributed system is the set of spaces through which the visitor, subject to more or less control, may pass; while the nondistributed system, (that is, the set of trees connected to each other only through the distributed system) is the domain of the inhabitants, with stronger sanctions against penetration by the visitor. Fig. 102(a)–(b) divides the Ambo kraal into its distributed and nondistributed sub-systems. As with the introduction of the gamma map itself, this transforation has the immediate advantage of visually clarifying several of the spatial relations that have been described and expressed numerically, in the sense that the meeting place is at the apex of the distributed system, the kraal head at the apex of the deepest nondistributed complex, and the relation between them is that of the former governed by the latter from the point of view of the carrier.

The structure is made very much clearer if we contrast the Ambo kraal with another 'chiefly' building from Africa: one of the 'palaces' of the Ashanti chiefs, as illustrated and described by Rattray.[6] Fig. 103 shows the layout given in Rattray, while Fig. 104 shows the full justified gamma map, and Fig. 105 and 106 the division into distributed and nondistributed systems. Visually, the difference is immediately obvious. While both buildings have a similar number of spaces, the Ambo kraal has a far more elaborate nondistributed structure than the Ashanti palace, and a far simpler distributed structure. More precisely, the Ambo kraal has more asymmetry in its nondistributed structure, while the Ashanti palace has more ringiness in its distributed structure. Counterbalancing this, the Ambo kraal has more asymmetry in its distributed structure and the Ashanti palace more symmetry in its nondistributed structure. Overall, the Ambo kraal is two-and-a-half times as asymmetric as the Ashanti palace, while the Ashanti palace is three times as ringy as the Ambo kraal.

In terms of individual spaces and their use labels, the comparison is no less striking. The Ashanti palace, for example, has no single deepest (nondistributed) space, although the place where the chief sleeps, space 33, is one of the spaces at the deepest level, and the only one that is a single space governed by a courtyard. Taking the complex as a whole, therefore, depth from the carrier does not distinguish any space or set of spaces very strongly, in complete contrast to the Ambo kraal. In terms of the distributed spaces, the contrast is more intriguing. In the Ambo kraal, the principal space for interfacing inhabitants and visitors was the deepest distributed space, whereas in the Ashanti palace it is at the shallowest level (space 2). However, in spite of the difference in depth from the carrier, in both buildings the main interface space has the property of having the lowest relative asymmetry of any space in the building – 0.041 in the Ashanti case, 0.093 in the

Fig. 103 Ashanti 'palace', after Rattray.

Plan of an Omanhene's 'Palace'

2 Where the chief presides over important cases and holds big receptions.

7 court of restricted access in which internal disputes are heard.

13 court known as the approach to the big mausoleum.

19 court of the mausoleum.

27 court in which lesser ordinary cases are heard.

32 an open space where small boys attending the chief's wives play.

34 where any subject or stranger may come for hospitality at the chief's expense.

36 the big sleeping place–the chief sleeps in a room off.

40 the yard behind the sleeping quarters.

47 the yard leading to the lavatory in which rations are issued and sheep slaughtered.

51 court in which the chief and his elders discuss in private.

58 'street' of the women.

Ambo case. If we then contrast the location of the most sacred object – the sacred fire in the case of the Ambo, the 'blackened stools' in the mausoleum in the case of the Ashanti – in the Ambo case it is found in the meeting place, that is in the deepest distributed space with the lowest relative asymmetry, whereas in the Ashanti case it is to be found in a nondistributed sub-complex, in a space with the highest relative asymmetry in the complex – space 22 (RA = 0.99).

The spatial relations between men and women are even more radically different. In the Ashanti case, not only are women located in the shallowest spaces in the complex, but also their 'street' (as Rattray calls the elongated courtyard complex occupied by the women) has the highest ringiness value of any space in the building, some of it stemming from the high degree of connectivity to the carrier, but due also to the connections to what would

otherwise be relatively deep and segregated spaces dominated by
the chief. The spatial shallowness of women goes beyond that of
their living quarters. The room of the 'ghost wives' is the only
nondistributed cell directly permeable to the carrier. It is therefore
the shallowest nondistributed space – in spite of which it also has
a high relative asymmetry, meaning that it is strongly segregated
from the remainder of the complex.

Rather more obviously, the buildings can be contrasted in terms
of the nature of the spaces, as well as in terms of their relations.
For example, in the Ambo kraal, most of the spaces in the

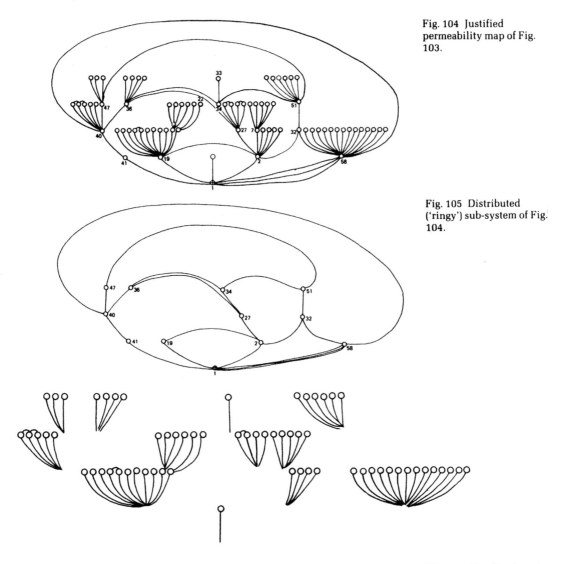

Fig. 104 Justified
permeability map of Fig.
103.

Fig. 105 Distributed
('ringy') sub-system of Fig.
104.

Fig. 106 Nondistributed
(tree-like) sub-system of
Fig. 104.

distributed system are called passages: that is, they have the lowest convex synchrony (i.e. are narrowest). In the Ashanti palace, the opposite is the case. The distributed spaces are for the most part those with most convex synchrony (i.e. the fattest). In other words, space is invested in the distributed system, not in the nondistributed system, as is the case with the Ambo kraal. There are also differences between spaces in the distributed system in the Ashanti case. For example, the lowest convex synchrony space – that of the women's street – is also the largest in terms of area, and has the highest description, in the sense of relations synchronised by the space – in this case the individual dwellings of the women. In contrast, the space with most convex synchrony is space 32, which is only described as a place for boys to play in. However, this space alone among the distributed courtyards has no primary cells constituting it. The high synchrony therefore synchronises no important local descriptions. As soon as the synchronisation of local descriptions is taken into account, the highest synchrony is found, as with the Ambo case, in the principal interface space, the entrance court, or space 2. In both cases, therefore, in spite of their different locations, space is invested where most emphasis on manifest symbolic meaning is required.

In order to interpret the Ashanti palace in terms of the abstract model of a building – that is, in terms of relations of differential solidarity among inhabitants and between inhabitants and visitors, we must take account of one further important fact about the buildings: that two of the entrances (those marked 63 and 64 by Rattray) are described as 'private ways'. This means at least that these routes are open to inhabitants and not to visitors, and possibly also they are open to some inhabitants but not to others. Rattray is unfortunately not explicit on this latter point. But even with what we do know, we can redraw the gamma map of the building with and without these private ways. Since the effect of these is on the distributed courtyards, we will also eliminate all primary cells from the map. This will have the effect of clarifying the relations of spaces in the distributed system, which have so far been somewhat obscured by the numerical and visual effects of the presence of so many primary cells. Fig. 107(a) shows the justified gamma map of the distributed courtyards without the secret ways, Fig. 107(b) shows it with them. The principal measures are tabulated below, with RA values translated to 'real RA' values to allow for size differences. The most obvious change that results from the addition of the private ways is that the relative asymmetry of the complex from the carrier reduces to about half. This means, simply enough, that the building has a higher relative asymmetry from the point of view of visitors than it does from the point of view of inhabitants. This is graphically shown by the continuous increase in the number of spaces at each

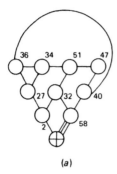

(a)

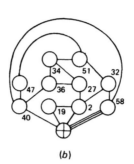

(b)

Fig. 107 Justified permeability maps of the courtyard structure of Fig. 103 without (107(a)) and with (107(b)) the 'private ways'. 107(c) shows changes in syntactic values resulting from the transformation.

(c)

Changes in syntactic values resulting from the transformation of RA values to 'real RA' values.

	RA	RRA	RR	RA	RRA	RR
⊕	0.305	1.003	0.251	0.178	0.605	0.340
2	0.222	0.729	0.251	0.155	0.529	0.318
58	0.222	0.729	0.297	0.200	0.680	0.318
19				0.266	0.907	0.251
40	0.194	0.638	0.251	0.133	0.453	0.298
21	0.222	0.727	0.218	0.200	0.680	0.265
32	0.194	0.638	0.272	0.178	0.605	0.298
51	0.194	0.638	0.251	0.200	0.680	0.251
36	0.222	0.729	0.218	0.200	0.680	0.251
47	0.277	0.911	0.204	0.244	0.831	0.227
34	0.222	0.727	0.204	0.222	0.756	0.227

level of depth in the complex, ending with no less than four spaces – nearly half of those available – at the deepest level. Of these four spaces, one (space 47) has a markedly higher relative asymmetry with respect to the rest of the complex – that is, on the inhabitant–inhabitant dimension – than the others: this is the space in which sheep are slaughtered and which leads to the lavatory. This seems to indicate that on internal relations asymmetry is invested in the space housing the most earthy and bodily of functions.

When the private ways are added, however, a number of interesting effects appear. First, the space with the highest relative asymmetry in the distributed system is now the most sacred space: namely the courtyard containing the mausoleum with the blackened stools, that is, the ancentral, most transpatial objects. Second, from the point of view of the carrier, two spaces have now become joint deepest spaces, both spaces with conspicuous functions in terms of the general model. Space 34 is the place where the chief must entertain any subject or stranger, implying that the space is concerned with the realisation of relations across space rather than with local relations. Space 51 is the space where the chief and his elders confer in private: that is, it is the space in which is realised locally the most political function, meaning by 'political' that it is concerned more with open ended negotiations than with the closed and predetermined ritual. Third, these last named spaces, 34 and 51, are the only ones that actually increase their relative asymmetry when the private ways are added, even if only by a relatively small margin in both cases. Finally, space 40 becomes the space with the lowest real relative asymmetry of all. This seems odd at first, since the space is the only one that appears to have no particular function, being only the yard behind the sleeping quarters. However, examination of some of the rooms adjoining the courtyard suggests an answer. Space 40 turns out to be the place where the chief goes when he wants to be alone. In other words, in his private capacity, as opposed to his public function, the chief goes to occupy the most strategic space in the building.

How can this rather strange collage of facts be assembled into a coherent picture? The best approach is through a proper comparison between the distributed system of the Ashanti palace and that of the Ambo kraal, and then between their nondistributed systems. It has already been noted that the Ambo kraal has more mean relative asymmetry than the Ashanti palace. Calculated by the 'real' formula, it can be seen to have twice as much: an average of 1.237 as opposed to 0.673. But in spite of this, the Ashanti palace has much more *differentiation* of distributed spaces in terms of their real relative asymmetry values. It has a relatively larger range and a good spread through the range: whereas the Ambo kraal has a smaller range with no less than seven spaces sharing the same value and the remainder being more or less three pairs of duplicates. As far as the nondistributed system is concerned, the figures are the other way round. The RA values for the nondistributed sub-complexes are far less differentiated in the Ashani palace than in the Ambo kraal. There are two spaces with a very high real relative asymmetry value in terms of their sub-complex: the two deepest spaces in the mausoleum, which have a real value of just over 2 – a very high value for the system, indicating a very strong category. But for the most part, nondistributed spaces are only one deep from the distributed system. Moreover, most of the nondistributed spaces have low synchrony compared to the distributed spaces, just as with the Ambo the distributed spaces, with one strong exception – the meeting place – have low synchrony in comparison with the nondistributed spaces. All these facts seem to point the same way: the Ashanti palace invests spatial structuring in the distributed system, that is, in the relations between inhabitants and visitors, while the Ambo kraal invests spatial structure in the relations among inhabitants.

Investigation of the use labels of the distributed spaces in the Ashanti palace confirms this orientation. Space 2 is the space where major cases are heard; space 27 has lesser cases; space 34 is where the chief entertains strangers; space 51 is where the chief and his elders (from other parts of the settlement) meet and discuss; space 19 is the setting for major religious functions. Even the distributed spaces that do not have a conspicuous inhabitant–visitor function suggest this relation in a more informal way. The women's court, space 58 for example, with its three direct ways to the carrier, space 32 where the sons of visitors play, and the court where the chief eats alone, space 40, with its private way direct to the outside all seem, in one way or another, to emphasise the relation with the outside world rather than the internal structure of the complex. Only the places for sleeping and bodily functions, spaces 36 and 47, seem to be exceptions to this general rule.

In the Ambo kraal, the inhabitant–visitor relation seems collapsed into one space in the distributed system, the meeting place, and apart from that, into the most asymmetric complex of the nondistributed system – the spaces for women and girl visitors are to be found deep in the kraal head's sub-complex. One more generalisation is thus possible. Because nondistributed complexes form a discrete system, it can be said that in the Ashanti palace the inhabitant–visitor relations are both complex and form a continuous system while in the Ambo kraal, the spaces forming the relation are a discontinuous system. In the Ashanti case, therefore, the inhabitant–visitor relation is in the spatial dimension, while the Ambo kraal it is primarily in the transpatial dimension.

Another component of the underlying genotypes of the buildings is brought to light by a more careful examination of the relative ringiness of points in the distributed courtyards. In the private ways version of the Ashanti distributed sub-complexes, the highest internal ringiness values belong to space 2, the principal interface space between the chief and outsiders, and space 58, the women's street. But without the private ways, the highest value belongs to space 58 alone. The private ways therefore balance relations between the sexes on the ringiness dimension. But even with the private ways added the values, although equal, are not equivalent. The ringiness of the women's street is biased strongly in the direction of the carrier, not in the direction of the building. The principle is clear. The chief male has the highest ringiness when considered from the point of view of the internal structure of the building; but the women have the highest when considered from the point of view of the relations between the inside of the buildings and the outside. The men and the women point, as it were, in different directions – the women in the direction of the outside, and therefore of spatial relations; and the men in the direction of the inside, and therefore of transpatial relations. It appears then that differential solidarities between men and women are inscribed in the ringiness structure of the building, and are not, as in the case of the Ambo kraal, differences on the same dimension, implying inequality, but differences based on strength in different dimensions, implying some kind of counterbalancing and relative equality.

This point is accentuated if we consider the effect of removing the women's space from the distributed complex of the Ashanti palace with and without the private ways. If the private ways are available, then removal of the women's space makes little difference to the structure of the gamma map, and no space changes its depth. But if the women's space is removed from the gamma map with the private ways, the effect is dramatic, and the gamma map takes on the form shown in Fig. 108: of which the real relative asymmetry from the carrier is no less than 1.582. The introduction of the private ways therefore has two effects on the spatial structure of the complex, one on the inhabitant–inhabitant dimension, the other on the inhabitant–visitor dimension. On the former, it restores some closer balance between male and female on the ringiness dimension, and on the latter, it restores differentials between inhabitants and visitor on the asymmetry dimension.

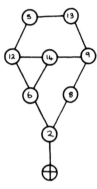

Fig. 108 Distributed sub-system of Fig. 104 without women's complex and without 'private ways'.

If we now return to the most basic proposition of all, that of associating the interior of a boundary with a transpatial solidarity and the relation of inside and outside with a spatial solidarity, and link this to the proposition that the distributed structure of a building normally articulates inhabitant–visitor relations while the nondistributed structure maps inhabitant–inhabitant relations, then the contrasting genotypes of the Ashanti palace and the Ambo kraal can be drawn at the most fundamental level. The Ambo kraal, with its investment of boundaries rather than space in its distributed system, its limitation of the distributed system to little more than a single dominant asymmetric ring, its deepening of a single interface space, and its investment of space in the nondistributed asymmetric components of the deeper reaches of the building, is very clearly a system orientated towards the interior of the boundary, and thus towards of solidarity that does not depend on external spatial connectivity, but on internal conceptual strength and structure. It is therefore a system which in general selects the pathway towards transpatial solidarity and the elimination of immediate spatial relations. The Ashanti system works on the contrary principle. The investment of space in the elaborate distributed system, and the lack of investment in the nondistributed system, the complex ringiness of the distributed system and the complex relations between inside and outside, all indicate a system selecting the pathway towards spatial solidarity. Much of the elaborate ceremonial of the palace is aimed at this direct spatial interface, and much of the relationship between chief and people articulated through the spatial structure of the building requires this interface – judgements, enthronements, and so on. In both cases, there are, of course, the opposite tendencies also. The orientation towards one form of solidarity or the other is not uniform. Each uses the other in effect to articulate internal relations among inhabitants. Thus the Ashanti palace invests more transpatial structure in males and more spatial structure in females, but taken as a whole the building has far less asymmetry and far less nondistributedness that the Ambo kraal, which in its turn invests more symmetry in females than in males, but nevertheless remains a system predominantly orientated to the value of asymmetry.

The correlates of this genotypical divergence in social structure and overall settlement morphology are not hard to find. The Ashanti live in relative dense, semi-urbanised settlements, and have traditionally a social structure in which both residence and descent pass through the female rather than the male line. Often this entails husbands and wives not cohabiting, but remaining within the household of their matrilineal group, with husbands visiting wives and wives sending food across to husbands. This type of social arrangement clearly requires a locally dense settlement form, and also generates an orientation to the exterior relation of the boundary as much as to the interior relations. The use of the space outside and between houses for everyday activities is indeed a common feature of Ashanti village life. The notion of a system orientated towards a spatial solidarity has roots in these social morphological trends. The Ambo, by contrast, are a society in which residence passes through the male line: women move away from their maternal family on marriage and are expected to have unequivocal loyalty to the household dominated by their husbands. From the settlement point of view, the Ambo live in relatively dispersed conditions – conditions that facilitate the maintenance of a system orientated towards the control of society through the boundary rather than through interior–exterior relations. The power of these principles of social solidarity to imprint themselves on the spatial structure of the society is shown with great emphasis by the way in which generic traditional social relations still pervade these two elaborate buildings of the embryonic 'state'.

5

••

The elementary building and its transformations

SUMMARY

This chapter tries to outline a general theory of buildings in terms of their spatial form by considering the elementary building and its social relations, and examining cases as they evolve away from this basic form into different types of complexity. It is argued that 'type of interface' is a missing conceptual component of the analysis of buildings into types. The chapter ends by discussing certain kinds of contemporary complex buildings within this framework, and argues that buildings play a fundamental role in organising certain kinds of social relations.

Elementary buildings

There is no scope in this book for an extensive review of building types and their evolution. However, it is relevant at this stage to try to erect on the basis of the definitions and procedures used so far, a more general theory of spatial structure in buildings, illustrating certain very fundamental types of structure and ending with a review of the principal themes in spatial organisation in contemporary buildings.

Any general theory must start from fundamentals, and in order to sketch a general theory of spatial structure in buildings we must return to the most elementary concept of a building. The elementary cell was, the reader will recall, a closed cell with a permeability defining a contiguous open cell (Fig. 109). This structure is also the *elementary building*, seen from the point of view of the abstract model. The open segment of space is the distributed component and the closed cell is the nondistributed component. The closed cell is the domain of the inhabitant alone, while the open cell is the locus of the inhabitant–visitor interface. This elementary building is not confined to the distant past and primitive societies. Instances can still be found today. For example, the traditional shop, which during the day lays out its goods in the space in front of the closed cell and at the same time makes the interior of the closed cell as continuous as possible with the outside space, is exploiting the basic potential of this structure. At night, all the goods are put inside the closed cell and the

Fig. 109 The elementary building.

permeability is sealed. The whole structure as it were becomes the closed cell alone. During the day the opposite occurs. The disposition of goods in the open cell and the opening of the closed cell implies that as far as possible the whole structure becomes the open cell alone. The elementary structure appears not because of an inherited tradition, but because of structural necessity: a shop has a very definite spatial model. It must maximise the probability of random visitors at its interface and minimise the controls over them as far as is consistent with the control of the removal of its goods. The structural isomorphism of the shop with, for example, certain simple house types in various societies, is a result not of cultural diffusion of an artefact, but of the internal structural necessities of an abstract model realising itself in physical form. Wherever the logic of circumstances dictates the maximising of random encounters without losing a minimal spatial control, this elementary structure will be regenerated.

The evolution of this elementary building in different directions following the internal logic of social solidarities can be briefly sketched by considering some of the buildings which, on the surface, appear to be among the simplest on earth: the tent and hut dwellings of nomads. Take, for example, a Bedouin tent as illustrated by Torvald Faegre.[1] Fig. 110 shows a basic structure to which key details must be added – all mentioned in Faegre's text but not indicated in his plan – if the genotype is to be understood.

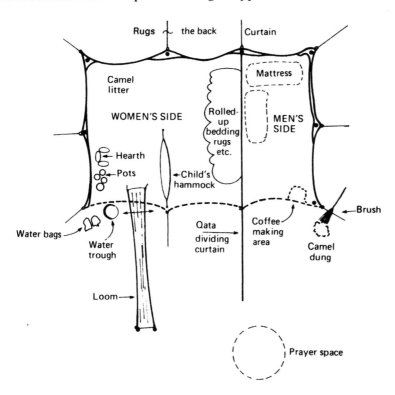

Fig. 110 Bedouin tent, after Faegre.

Fig. 111 A Tuareg tent, after
Faegre.

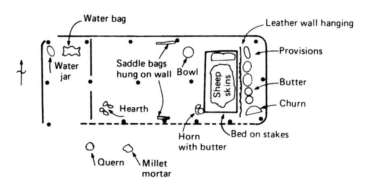

First, the host's camel saddle is set on the mattress in the deepest
part of the men's side, and the host and 'guest of honour' sit either
side and talk across it. Second, the space outside has a mark
indicating that it is a place for prayer, and this implies of course
that it is a male-dominated space. Third, although the rules for
hospitality are extremely strong – a Bedouin must give three days'
hospitality even to his enemies – there is a strong prohibition on
guests seeing into the women's side of the tent. With these extra
details the abstract model of the system is extremely clear. The
inhabitant–visitor relation is realised on the depth dimension –
that is, asymmetry from the carrier – in that the guest–host pair
occupy the deepest space; while the inhabitant–inhabitant relation – that between men and women – is realised on the relative
asymmetry dimension, first in that the boundary strongly segregates one from the other, and second in that the space with minimal relative asymmetry – the space outside – is controlled by the
men through a male orientated transpatial function – literally transpatial in that the prayer mats are turned in the direction of Mecca.
This space, being the only space on a ring – the carrier – is also the
strongest point of control in the system.

If we then compare this with a Tuareg tent (Fig. 111, again taken
from Faegre, but checked with a direct informant), once the detail
from the text is added we find a great contrast. First, the space
outside is not a transpatial space, but a space of practical
functions. As Faegre says, 'mats are often stretched well out in
front of the tent, making an enclosure courtyard that is an
extension of the space inside the tent. The hearth is set in this
space . . . just outside the tent are placed the wooden millet mortar
and the stone quern for grinding grain.'[2] The functions are, of
course, more orientated to women than to men. Second, men
receive guests outside the tent, and even outside the settlement,
where men spend much of their time. The plan already shows the
third property: that the distinction between men and women is
not made inside the tent. On the contrary 'the bed is set in the
middle of the floor . . . in small tents it takes up most of the floor
area'.[3] In other words, both in its internal organisation and in the

relation of interior to exterior the system completely lacks the strong model that existed in the Bedouin case. Women are not divided from men inside, there is equal control of the outside space, and visitors are not distinguished according to different categories of inhabitant (that is, men and women).

To say that the system lacks structure would be an error. Properly speaking, it has the minimal structure of the elementary model: the interior to exterior asymmetry dimension distinguishes only inhabitants from visitors; no internal structure distinguishes inhabitants from each other; while the ringy space, the space outside, serves to link the inhabitant and visitor in a less controlled system. The precise theoretical nature of this type of system, where the structure is less obvious and more probabalistic, is part of the subject matter of Chapter 6 (see pp. 217–22). In the meantime, it is perhaps no surprise to learn that the Tuareg have an entirely different system of social relations between men and women. Not only are they matrilocal, but women have the highest developed craft – the leather work that dominates the tents decoratively – and even, it is said, they may take initiative in sexual matters. As Faegre observes, the status of the Tuareg women is a constant source of irritation to their Arab neighbours. This liberation is amply manifested in the virtual reversal of the spatial model of the Bedouin tent.

Moving half way across the world, the Mongolian yurt is comparable to the Tuareg tent in its lack of internal subdivisions, yet comparable to the Bedouin tent in the development of its internal model (Fig. 112). Compared to the previous two, its structures appears almost paradoxical. In the interior, every

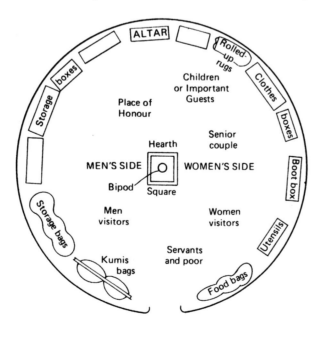

Fig. 112 A Mongolian yurt, after Faegre.

aspect of position is developed in terms of some social difference, all broadly within two dimensions: the depth or asymmetry from the carrier indicates differences in rank for both inhabitants and visitors with a new form of emphasis added in the form of an 'altar' in the deepest space; while the internal differentiation of space records every possible difference in status, whether by sex, age or degree of wealth. But all this it does without boundaries of any kind. In other words, this most extreme development of a structured interior that we have yet encountered is brought into being not by the multiplication of boundaries but by their elimination. Yet so strong is the symbolic structure of the yurt that 'through the centuries, the yurt has become a sacred universe to its inhabitants. To the Mongols the roof is the sky, the hole in the roof the Sun – the Eye of Heaven through which comes the light'.[4] The yurt, it seems, is one of those striking cases where the interior of the dwelling is seen as a microcosm of the universe.

This is a clue to its spatial nature. The structure of space inside the yurt is as much a transpatial structure, embodying relations of identity with all other yurt dwellers, as it is a spatial structure organising the daily life of its occupants. The existence of an altar in the deepest space is a direct corollary of this. Like the Bororo village (see Fig. 30) it is a structure of categories rather than a structure of control. As such, like the Bororo village, its categories and relationships must be seen to co-exist as a structure; that is, it must be synchronous. Since it has already been argued that the synchronisation of relationships into a unified system of space is a means of moving from a constitutive reality to a representative, or symbolic one, then it is clear that in saying this we are saying nothing that has not been said before, only that if finds its most powerful form in the interior of the boundary. There is therefore a deep association between the lack of internal boundaries and the existence of an altar. In fact, so far as we have been able to observe, these two phenomena are nearly always correlated: given a strong internal synchronous model there will be a sacred deepest space. Here everything is synchronised: but above all the relationships of inhabitants to each other are synchronised and made parallel to the relations between inhabitants and visitors, and both are realised in a powerful and complex model which depends on the non-existence of boundaries. The yurt is a structural interior that is maximally orientated towards the global structure of society: it builds its local relationships in the image of society as a whole.

The twin themes of the synchronised interior and the sacred deepest space provide a stepping stone to another of the fundamental building types: the shrine, or building for institutionalised religous observation. Take for example a typical Ashanti abosomfie or shrine, a building based on the same general arrangement as the dwelling, and its gamma map (Fig. 113). A deepest space is created by a series of differentiations of level, of

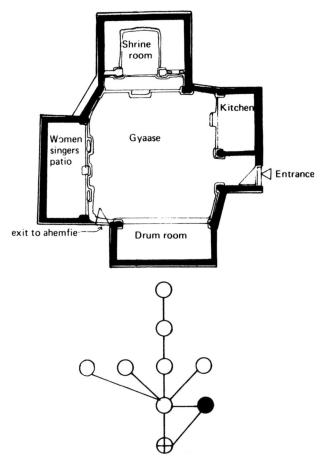

Fig. 113 An Ashanti abosomfie, or shrine, after Rutter.

which the real relative asymmetry is 2.170. The courtyard space is at once the space of visitors, and thus a bipermeable space and at the same time it synchronises all the significant spaces in the system. This deepening of a single unipermeable space – the domain controlled by the inhabitants – coupled to a bipermeable space, often of considerable size, for the visitors is, it would appear, the underlying genotype for a vast family of buildings for religious observance across many cultures and times. The English parish church (see Fig. 114) for example, has the same basic model. The pervasive tendency to axialise the relations between deepest space and visitor space is a direct by-product of the genotype: a deep space must be synchronised with a large shallow space.

Yet in spite of its frequent elaboration the genotype is a simple development of the structure of the elementary building. The closed cell is extended to a deeper, but still unipermeable sequence; the open cell is expanded to accommodate more visitors; while the axiality retains the direct relation of synchronisation. The religious building as a type in effect maximises both

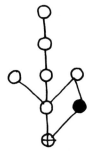

Fig. 114 An English parish church, after Bannister Fletcher.

components of the spatial–transpatial model underlying the elementary building: it maximises the spatial interface to a maximally transpatial space. It assembles the inhabitant in his closed cell and the visitors in their open cell (in the sense of being functionally bipermeable) into a direct interface, while making the inhabitant as deep as possible and the visitors as numerous and synchronised as possible.

Further light can be cast on the genotype by references to a concept due to Victor Turner: that of *communitas*. In his book *The Ritual Process* Turner proposes that there exists a state of what he calls *communitas* in which social structures are rescinded, and all participants in ritual becomes identified with each other through common status and community of belief.[5] The difference between the semi-sacred interior of the yurt and the shrine might be interpreted in relation to this. The yurt has the basic structure of a ritual space, but retains the complex set of social differentiations and statuses through its local spatial differentiations. A shrine does the opposite. It obliterates these structural differences and locates all visitors in a single, undifferentiated space, in which their relation is made only and exactly by their synchronous presence with the objects of the shrine in the deepest space. The visitor space in a shrine, both according to Turner and according to the logic of our model, is the space of *communitas*.

In terms of its abstract genotype, therefore, a shrine can be seen as certain syntactic and parametric transformation of the elementary building. Other types of building can be seen as different transformations, but as transformations nonetheless. A theatre, for example, differs from the shrine in that the principal space of the inhabitants – that is, the stage – is as shallow as possible with respect to the space of the visitors, rather than as deep as possible. Following the logic of the model, this implies an interface that is not based on a strong transpatial category, requiring a local ritual to preserve its clarity, but on a directly spatial interface, only one step removed from physical contact. In common with shrine the theatre tends to develop a 'stage door'. At first sight, this is a rather curious phenomenon, since it is the most important inhabitants who use the stage door, in spite of the fact that it is nearly always a concealed, unceremonious, even furtive entrance. The stage door is, in fact, a common feature of spatial genotypes where the inhabitant is located in a deep space, and must be seen to emerge from its depths rather than frⁿm the profane visitors' space which, to the visitors, appears to control the pathway to the deep space. The stage door is a pervasive feature because it is a means of maintaining an illusion. But it also illustrates an important principle about the spatial structure of buildings. The spatial genotype of inhabitant–inhabitant and inhabitant–visitor relations to be realised in a building may not be easily realised or easily reconciled with practical and functional requirements. A factory, for example, genotypically prefers the social segregation of workers from each other and their integration only through the productive process. However, the functioning of the productive process cannot tolerate the spatial segregation that the ideal genotype requires. Wherever this type of contradiction occurs we invariably find one of two things: either we find an inconspicuous spatial strategy developed to overcome the functional difficulty and preserve the genotype, as is the case with the stage door; or we find that rules are added to the system in order to preserve the genotype – in the case of the factory, rules forbidding or hindering movement and lateral interaction of individual workers with each other.

A building *type* may be defined in general as a characteristic genotypical transformation of the underlying abstract model of a building, realised in, and identifiable through, a certain arrangement and parametrisation of the basic syntactic dimensions. The identifying features of a type are discoverable in broad terms by simply asking which of the relations of the elementary building are amplified or restricted, and in what ways. For example, a department store is a building which, while being as large as possible, minimises the nondistributed component associated with the inhabitants and maximises the ringiness of the visitor space. The control remains with the inhabitants – the sales people – but realised as minimally as possible in order to maximise the useful route potential of the distributed system – the spaces between the counters – for the visitors.

A museum, on the other hand, is a building in which both the inhabitants and their nondistributed domains have all but disappeared, and in their place is only the knowledge they control, interfaced everywhere with the distributed system. But this distributed system is not maximally ringy. On the contrary, it tends to have few asymmetric rings rather than many symmetric rings, reflecting the high categoric investment in the displayed objects in museums compared to those in department stores. But in the museum a new phenomenon appears: uniformed agents of the inhabitants – but not the inhabitants themselves (that is, those who control the knowledge invested in the building) deploy themselves in the distributed structure, a by-product of the take-over of the entire building by a spatial system that permits and even requires the visitor to penetrate everywhere in it.

Reversed buildings and others

All the buildings touched on so far have, in spite of their great variety in form and function, one common feature: they all have the elementary relation between the inhabitant and visitor, in the sense that the inhabitant is in the deeper, often nondistributed parts of the building, and interfaces with the visitor through the

shallower, often distributed parts of the building that form its
principal circulation system. But the reader will not find it
difficult to think of instances where this elementary relation does
not hold: hospitals, for example, or asylums, certainly prisons,
and possibly schools would be very hard to see in this way,
although banks, police stations, most types of office and factory all
seem to be based on this relation. A cursory review suggests that it
is when buildings have what we might call a public institutional
character that the elementary relation does not hold: and since
buildings of this kind have evolved and diversified substantially
in the past two centuries, then it becomes a key issue to examine
these kinds of building as a species, and to try to discover why
they seem to be so characteristic of society today and less so of
societies in the past. In what follows it will be argued that there is
a very fundamental building genotype that is characterised exactly by the reversal of positions of inhabitant and visitor, in the
sense that the visitors – those who do not control the knowledge
embodied in the building and its purposes – come to occupy the
deeper primary, usually nondistributed cells; while inhabitants –
those who do control the knowledge embodied in the building
and its purposes – or their representatives come to occupy the
distributed circulation system. For convenience this species
could be called the *reversed* building – reversed in the sense that
patients and prisoners occupy the primary cells, while guards and
doctors occupy the distributed system and move freely in it. Such
buildings have a general sociological character, hence the common theme of reversal, but at the same time the species has
significantly different sub-varieties. These varieties need to be
examined in some detail before any useful conclusions can be
drawn about the sociological character of the reversed genotype.

The most general feature of all the buildings so far examined,
apart from the elementary relation of inhabitant and visitor, has
lain in the fact that the spatial structure of each building embodies
knowledge of social relations. It is through this embodied knowledge that buildings act as rule systems and function to reproduce
forms of social solidarity. Another way of expressing this would
be to say that buildings are spatially about social knowledge – that
is, taken-for-granted knowledge of rules governing the relations of
individuals and the relation of individuals to society. Social
knowledge is about the unconscious organising principles for the
description of society. Often a building is a concretisation of these
principles. In fact we might say that insofar as buildings are
elementary in their organisation of relations between inhabitants
and visitors, then they are expressions and realisations of these
organising principles in a domain that is more structured than the
world outside the boundary.

But insofar as they reverse the elementary relations of inhabitant and visitors, buildings are about the *pathology* of descrip-

tions: that is, they are about the restoration, purification and instillation of descriptions. The building exists not to create a domain where established relations are embodied and enacted, but in order to create a more highly controlled domain in which the restitution, re-creation and transmission of descriptions can take place. In an elementary building, the function of the asymmetry available in the primary cells is to control a social category by defining its permissable relations. In a reversed building, the function of the primary cell is to *eliminate* relations, relations that are presumed to be dangerous and contaminating to descriptions. The primary cell thus becomes a singularity, a point without relations, rather than a point defined by its relations. Likewise, in an elementary building, the function of the distributed system is to articulate the relations by which visitors have differential access to inhabitants, thus confirming the differences between inhabitants; in a reversed building, the distributed system is the means by which inhabitants have uniform access to and control of visitors, thus confirming their homogeneity. The essential structure of the reversed building thus predicates the elimination of social knowledge. Except for the interface between inhabitant and visitor, knowledge of social relations is suspended. We are in the domain of *reflexive* knowledge, that is, knowledge that suspends the enactment of its own principles in order to reconstitute them. In this domain, because the building is no longer ordered by the local realisation of the transpatial categories of society, the interface becomes a *spatial interface of control*. Instead of embodying a ritual, the building embodies a confrontation between the pathology of descriptions – the sick, the indigent, the disturbed and the uneducated – and those by virtue of whose special powers and knowledge descriptions can be restored.

From its inception as a building type there are two fundamental variants on the reversed building, the one concerned with the pathology of individuals, the other with the pathology of society. The spatial genotypes of the two are different but related. The first is the infirmary, in which the disturbed descriptions of individuals are to be restored by being brought into direct contact with and put under the control of those whose knowledge of the interior workings of nature can restore them to their proper state. This interface must have two properties: it must be direct, without intermediaries or intervening spatial structures; and it must be one of control. The spatial genotype for this interface is easily derived from that of the elementary building by way of the shrine building, through which it appears to have evolved historically. Take for example the infirmary of Tonnerre at about the year 1300 (Fig. 115). The main body of the building is identical to the shrine, but with certain features added. First, in the synchronised and bipermeable visitor space, subdivisions have been added without impeding the axial flow of the distributed space. Second, two new

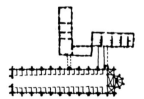

Fig. 115 The medieval infirmary of Tonnerre, after Thompson and Goldin.

sub-complexes have been added that house the new inhabitants of the system, those whose attentions can restore the patient to health. Third, these new sub-complexes control the distributed structure in that without them the structure has become unipermeable: in other words, reversing the previous situations, the building has become genotypically unipermeable for the visitors, who now occupy a set of primary cells, and bipermeable (manifestly rather than secretly) for the inhabitants. These features now construct the essential structure of the first variant of the reversed building. The distributed structure is now the domain of the inhabitants; the visitors have been rendered asynchronous with respect to each other, but synchronous in their relations to the inhabitants; and in the distributed system, as though in a street (but with roles reversed), there now exists a direct interface without intervening hierarchy between the inhabitants and visitors.

Nowhere is this genotypical structure more aptly shown than in the picture given in Thompson and Goldin's book *The Hospital*, which shows a 'nursing brother', probably St John of God, kissing the wounds of a patient.[6] The patient is sitting on a bench just outside his cubicle. In the background are other patients in their cubicles, with curtains drawn back in some cases, drawn to in others. In the distance is a doorless permeability leading into another space where other activity is seen to be going on. This is the essence of what is to become in our time the 'professional' relationship between doctor and patient in hospital. The principal inhabitants, those whose special knowledge gives them the power to cure, are brought into a direct physical relation with sufferers, but at the same time the relation between the two is unequal: insofar as this relation exists, it exists by virtue of the control of the distributed structure of the building by the inhabitants. This transformation is necessitated by the fact that for the purpose of the interface between inhabitant and visitor the higher asymmetric value of the inhabitant space no longer maps his superior status. He does, of course, have such a space: he can retreat to the sub-complexes away from the distributed system, where the traditional positional and status differences between inhabitant and visitor are still inscribed – in the Tonnerre case the spaces in the sub-complexes can easily be seen to have higher relative asymmetry than the space of the patients. But the unequal interface between the two is no longer recorded on the asymmetry or meaning dimension, but on differential relation to the ringiness, or control dimension. The need for the direct interface, however, means that the control dimension is inherently weak. It cannot be realised in a hierarchically arranged system of boundaries, since these would separate the inhabitants from the immobilised visitors. But another kind of control dimension is already present: a transpatial control dimension. The space of the interface is the space of *communitas* as witnessed in the pervasive presence of altars in such space. The homogeneity of members of *communitas* is singularly well-suited to the homogeneity of controlled visitors in the genotype. The weakness of the spatial control dimension is thus compensated by the strength of the transpatial control dimension.

The second variant of the reversed building refers to the pathology of society rather than of individuals. In this case it is the spatial control that is strong and the interface that is weak. Take for example the Narrenturm of the Allgemeines Krank-enhaus of Vienna built in 1784 (Fig. 116). The origins of the genotype of this classical structure lie not in the need to construct a direct interface between the holders of knowledge and those whose descriptions are to be restored, but in the need to restore society to health by segregating from it those elements which undermine its description. In this case, not only are the relations among the visitors rendered asynchronous by their location in primary cells, but also the relation of inhabitants to visitors is also rendered asynchronous by the addition of nondistributed and asymmetric spatial relations between them. This asynchrony of inhabitant and visitor is rendered the more obvious by the fact that it is guards, the hierarchical agents of those who control the knowledge of descriptions that are to be restored by segregation, who move in the ringy spaces adjacent to the primary cells. The building is reversed, but only in the interests of spatial control, not in the interests of constructing the restitutive interface. In effect, the building is about the pathology of social knowledge, but not about the reflexive knowledge that can restore it. All that can be achieved is the purification of the description of social knowledge in the society at large by the maximal segregation of those random elements that destabilise descriptions.

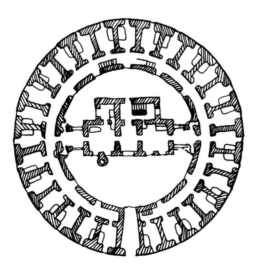

Fig. 116 The Narrenturm of the Allgemeines Krankenhaus of Vienna, 1784.

Fig. 117 Jeremy Bentham's
'Panopticon' of 1791.

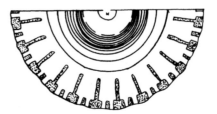

Fig. 117 Jeremy Bentham's
'Panopticon' of 1791.

The reversed building thus has a genotype with two elements: the direct interface of reflexive knowledge and the reversed non-interface of control. To the extent that knowledge is to be applied to restore descriptions the direct interface will be the dominant formative feature of the building; to the extent that society is to be cured by the elimination or control of random elements the elimination of the interface will be the dominant theme. It is now possible to give an account of the genotype of Jeremy Bentham's 'Panopticon' proposal of 1791, which is both precise and very simple (Fig. 117). The design is nothing more nor less than an attempt to have both aspects of the genotype of the reversed building at once. The building retains the strong asymmetric nondistributed structure of the control dimension, and at the same time through visual links from centre to periphery it attempts to construct a direct interface between the inhabitant possessors of knowledge and the prisoners. Moreover, the genotype was held to be constructable because reflexive knowledge at the level of society was held to exist: society could be reformed not simply by the removal of people from society but by the reconstitution of social relations through the direct interface with this reflexive knowledge, given the elimination of existing social relations by the control dimension of the building. The Panopticon is perhaps a famous building not because its influence was pervasive, but because it represented a unique synthesis of a socio-spatial genotype whose two primary dimensions had hitherto been realised only at the expense of one another.

It is perhaps the fact that the Panopticon represents such a powerful, if largely unrealisable, genotype, that has misled historians to overstate the importance of the building and to simplify accounts of its influence on subsequent trends in the architectural organisation of space. To understand the evolution of the important species of reversed building in the last two centuries it is necessary to once again separate the two dimensions of the genotype, and to look for the continuation of their conflict and mutual irreconcilability, rather than their assumed unification. This is particularly important because the conflict between the direct interface and segregative control becomes in our time the conflict between the professional and the bureaucratic models of the socio-spatial interface constructed by buildings, and as such is

a critical feature of the uneven evolution of many common types
of building today. To give even a brief account of these factors we
must first give some account of the relation between these two
spatial modes and different approaches to the application of
reflexive knowledge to the stabilisation and of descriptions in
society – that is, through what we have come to know as
bureaucratic 'intervention' and professional 'judgement'.

In society today the difference between what is legitimised as a
professional mode of operation – lawyers, doctors, architects, and
so on – and a bureaucratic mode lies in the nature of the
knowledge that underlies the activity. What we call professions
are legitimised where the application of important knowledge,
involving some elements of risk, is thought not to be reducible to
rules and procedures. There can be many reasons for this irreduci-
bility. For example, knowledge may be radically incomplete, as it
is in medicine, and require some degree of interpretation before it
can be applied to cases; or knowledge may change and develop
rapidly, following other trends and as new situations arise, as in
the case of architecture, and require constant revision to be
considered up to the mark; or it may be that too high a proportion
of the cases where the knowledge is to be applied and decisions
are to be taken raise special problems that makes them unique, as
is so often the case with the law. In practice, all three factors are
pervasive in all professions, and indeed the very existence of
profession depends to a large extent on this being the case.
Whatever the details of the particular instance, it is generally true
that professions are characterised by a high degree of *indeterminacy* in the application of knowledge to cases.[7] Decisions
cannot be taken by rote, nor by reference to a rule book that covers
all cases. Judgement and interpretation are held to be required.
The essence of the professional mode follows: responsibility for
the application of such knowledge is invested not in procedures
but in persons – persons who as individuals accept the risk
involved in decisions in particular cases, and as a collectivity take
responsibility for the body of knowledge on which these decisions
are based. In professions, therefore, persons are all-important. In
the bureaucratic mode the contrary is the case. Cases can be dealt
with bureaucratically to the extent that the knowledge on which
decisions are to based can be reduced to rules and procedures.
Once the reduction has been made then procedures not persons
are the order of the day. Persons become unimportant because a
standardised procedure can be carried out by anyone.

The two modes of applying knowledge have consequences for
the type of organisation that is appropriate to the way in which
each deals with its cases. In the professional case, because
personal judgement must be applied in each case, it is not
possible to have a series of intermediaries between those who
hold the knowledge – that is, those who have knowledge of the

principles to be applied – and those who deal with cases. The essence of a profession, seen organisationally, is that those with most knowledge of principles deal directly with cases. Professional work consists in the direct application of principles to cases. If organisations are structured so as to best control risk, then a professional organisation must be structured so as to maintain this direct interface between principles and cases as far as is feasible. In a bureaucracy, where the central discipline is procedures, not persons, the opposite is the case. If procedures are to control risk then they must both be set out and be seen to be followed. The mode is essentially hierarchical. Those at the top of the organisation concern themselves with principles – policy, as they would call it – while those at the very bottom deal with cases. Usually there will be a series of layers in which each layer inherits principles from above and transmits procedures down below. At the bottom level are those who deal with cases – that is, who pay over the social security or interview the unemployed. In bureaucracies the distance between those who deal in principles and those who deal in cases is as great as possible; and the internal logic of such an organisation must tend to make it more so, since the elimination of indeterminacy at the point of contact with cases must depend on procedures that can deal with every conceivable type of case, and this must in turn lead to an even more complex hierarchy of control. But the same organisational elaboration that in bureaucracies controls risk at the interface with the case will increase risk if applied to professional organisations. If knowledge involves a substantial component of judgement by persons with knowledge of principles, then it follows that the distance between principles and cases must be as small as possible.

The importance of this digression into the relationship between forms of knowledge and forms of organisation is that the different modes have fundamentally different consequences for space. More precisely, they have different consequences for the type of interface they construct between inhabitant and visitor, and this in turn leads to generic differences in the spatial genotypes of buildings. Under the influence of the different organisational arrangements the relationships of the elementary buildings are re-shuffled in a way no less fundamental than in the reversed building. An analysis of some of the variations can lead to two useful outcomes: first, a theory of the species of interface that underlie the much larger family of varieties of building type – the species of interface is the most fundamental spatial feature of any building, and a comparative analysis of these is therefore a necessary step to any theory of building types; and second, a theory of the relations between different species of interfacing tendencies that can occur in buildings as they become larger and more complex, and accommodate a more diverse range of – often conflicting – organisational forms.

Take for example the standard genotype for a purely bureaucratic building, that is, one which is organisationally hierarchical and which interfaces inhabitants and visitors mainly at the lowest level. The common form for such a building involves a large space for visitors, as shallow in the building as possible, and on the deep side of this space there is a series of booths or separated windows, each of which both acts as a barrier between inhabitants and visitors and provides the interface across which interaction is to take place. As in the shrine, the visitor space synchronises the visitors. But it is no longer a distributed space. There is now only one way in and out for the visitor. At the deep edge of this space the booths have a curious effect: they make the inhabitants asynchronous with respect to each other (that is, they each occupy a discrete space), and insofar as the inhabitants interface with the visitors, this asynchrony is retained for them. But for the visitors the interface is not asynchronous. All the booths are visible from the body of the visitor space. This closedness of the inhabitants' spaces and their consequent asynchrony, and the openness and consequent synchrony of the visitor space is fundamental to the genotype.

For the visitor even the inhabitants he sees have this marginal asynchrony. But behind them are layer upon layer of inhabitants he does not see. In the nearest spaces on the deep side of the interface there may well be further synchronised or semi-synchronised inhabitants; but beyond them, in spaces with higher relative asymmetry reflecting stronger and stronger categoric control, are higher- and higher-level inhabitants, until in all likelihood in the space with the highest relative asymmetry there are the inhabitants whose preoccupation is, at least relative to the others, with principles rather than cases. Thus the genotype is one of a shallow nondistributed space in which visitors are synchronised, an interface that is closed for inhabitants but open for visitors, and beyond the interface an asymmetric structure of space mapping in its relative asymmetry the differential statuses of inhabitants. In its basic structure this is a transformation of the elementary building hardly more complex than the shrine.

It may seem a large step from a social security office to a doctor's surgery, but the difference in size reflects a fundamental difference in the way in which professional, as opposed to bureaucratic interfaces imply a spatial configuration. In the ideal model, a professional, being a person rather than an organisation, is dispersed with respect to his peers. Only the minimal organisation is required to construct his direct interface with the cases with which he must deal. The small size of the lowest-level professional interface is thus itself a function of the underlying genotype of relations. The spatial form is related to the bureaucratic building, but subtly different in almost all respects. There is a shallow space which synchronises visitors while they are waiting to see the doctor. But this space is never as shallow in the building as possible; there is always some minimal extra structure which increases the relative asymmetry of the space. There may possibly be a kiosk-type arrangement, but still this will only be for managing bureaucratic matters. The interface of doctor and patient itself will be deeper in the building, often with its depth emphasised by a chicane or some other mechanism which increases the relative asymmetry of the space. The patient disappears from the synchronised visitors' space and never reappears again, In other words, not only are the inhabitants asynchronous with respect to each other – maintaining their high status as individual professional persons – but also the interface is strongly asynchronous. Again the transformation on the elementary building is subtle but pervasive, and it is necessary to realise the abstract model of spatial relations implied by that type of interface. Once again, also, the depth of the doctor in the building as seen by the visitor is eliminated for the doctor himself by an alternative route to the outside, one which renders his space shallow. In this we see again the general phenomenom of the 'stage door' effect.

The genotype of the doctor–patient interface does not entirely disappear in that most complex of institutional buildings, the modern hospital. But the hospital acquires its complexity by not being simply the professional interface writ large and multiplied, but by requiring, in one way or other, all four types of interface we have so far discussed. First, insofar as it interfaces spatially with its surrounding community, the hospital is a kind of ramified elementary building. Its external controls and boundaries are weak, if only because the number of people who have reason to cross its boundaries is a very large. This is particularly true of the older hospitals where the hospital complex is often more like part of the surrounding urban fabric than a separate closed domain. Second, insofar as it selects from its surrounding area a special subset of visitors (in the model sense – that is, in-patients and out-patients) then it interfaces with these through the bureaucratic method, that is, through a shallow and synchronised control space. Third, insofar as it ultimately exists to construct the professional interface on a large scale, then the building constructs direct interfaces which are asynchronous and asymmetric with respect to the rest of the building. And finally, insofar as the interface also requires a spatial control of inhabitants over visitors, then the building becomes reversed, as in the 'ward' structure.

The hospital is, in effect, a nexus of potentially conflicting and contradictory socio-spatial forces, each in itself well defined but each as likely as another to gain a temporary ascendency in the evolution of designs. The hospital is characterised not so much by a single genotype, but by a genotypical conflict, perhaps one whose resolution is largely illusory. This renders the hospital more difficult to describe, but not entirely opaque to analysis – provided that analysis concentrates not so much on universal models for ideal hospitals, but on the spatial relations where conflict between genotypical dimensions can occur, and the ways in which the conflicts are characteristically resolved. For example, the doctor-patient interface is ideally asynchronous, that is, it is realised in space set apart. This is simply realised in the out-patients and casualty department by a simple cubicle system, into which the patient moves from the synchronised visitor space. In the wards, however, the inhabitant–visitor relation becomes reversed and a spatial control over the body of the patient becomes necessary; ideally this requires the synchronisation of the control relation by means of the open ward. This, however, means that the synchronised reversed control interface is in conflict with the non-reversed and asynchronous direct interface of doctor and patient. A simple solution is to 'fine-tune' the spatial structure of the ward by providing easily drawn curtains or screens to turn the bed-space of the patient into an asynchronous space. However, this transformation is only made when definite medical events at the doctor–patient interface are taking place. If the doctor is merely visiting on his rounds no attempt is made to construct the separated space. In this case the doctors participate not so much in the professional interface but in the control interface. The progress of the doctors from one bed to another is a celebration of the fact of reversal in the building, and emphasises the radical inequality of a relation in which one body controls the space of another. It is a declaration of the class relation between doctor and patient. Consequently when the more affluent patients have separate rooms the doctors' rounds are not a celebration of the reversed control dimension but of the professional interface with his client.

But the very essence of these relations is realised in the principal space of the hospital drama: the operating theatre. From the point of view of the model of a building as an interfacing system, this is a special space indeed. First, is it the space in which the reversal effect is maximised, in that it is here that the spatial control of the visitor's (in the model sense) body by the inhabitant is made total. But second, it is the space in which the direct interface of doctor with patient is realised in its most heightened form. The spatial structure of the operating suite genotypically reflects both dimensions. It reflects the first in that the suite is highly distributed, in the sense that it has many exits and entrances, and in this it maximises the control by the inhabitants of the distributed system. It reflects the second in that the interfacing space is deep with respect to the rest of the complex, reflecting the almost 'sacred' category associated with this heightened interface. The operating theatre illustrates the essential social 'meanings' of both dimensions of the syntax model: that symmetry–asymmetry is about the strength of categories and distributedness–nondistributedness is about the control of categories.

These rather abstract considerations of buildings in terms of their species of interface does not, unfortunately, tell us how to design them properly. On the other hand, it does show that what we know already about buildings has a certain underlying logic to it, in spite of the formidable heterogeneity of types that buildings appear to present. The model suggests that our intuitions about what is and is not proper in a particular type of building may be founded in considerations that have more to do with the structure of society than with idiosyncratic prejudices or alleged preferences for certain types of spatial relation. The sense of appropriateness about spatial relations does not arise from some psychological predisposition, but from the socio-spatial model of underlying relations portrayed in the space. This implies that space responds more to macro-social formations than to psychological ones.

However, this does not mean that normative issues of design can be settled simply by reference to genotypical arguments. Leaving aside for a moment too-frequent conflicts between genotypical dimensions (conflicts that may only be spatially solvable by *ad hoc* fine-tuning of solutions), there is one theme that underpins all others in the analysis of buildings as relations between inhabitants and visitors. This is the theme of inequality. By articulating a relation between one who is a privileged adherent of some domain of knowledge ascribed in the spatial structure and social purpose of a building and others who are only petitioners in the building is implied that a building is of its nature about relations of inequality. Almost by definition questions of inequality can only be described, not solved, by analytic means. The pervasive dimension of inequality in building forever puts out of range a solution arrived at by purely analytic means. A building is already a normative statement and it would be wise not to pretend that it is anything else. All we have tried to do here is to show how these normative forms of inequality enter our unconscious by taking on physical form in the real world.

But if it does not permit us to design buildings by pure analysis, a precise description of the spatial interfacing of inequalities by buildings does at least raise the possibility of a pathology of designs and, perhaps more important, a pathology of the fashionable and changing genotypical themes underlying design at every stage of the evolution of real building types. Suppose, for example, an office organisation decides to move from subdivided office to what is euphemistically called 'open-plan'. How is this to be interpreted? The model is very clear. In the elementary building the status of inhabitants is given by occupation of an asynchronous space on the deep side of the main circulation system. The relative asymmetry resulting from such subdivision guarantees the status of inhabitants, if nothing else, however low their status is (unless of course the building is reversed). The effect of abolishing this set of spaces and, in effect, synchronising a subset of the former inhabitants (it is never all of them – status is still mapped into asynchronous spaces with higher relative asymmetry) is clear and simple; it converts inhabitants into visitors. This transformation is then confirmed by a certain reversal effect, which is achieved by the synchronisation of the distributed system of spaces, that is, by the synchronisation of the control dimension. Part of the effect of openness lies in the transformation of the distributed system. Because it is synchronised it is no longer possible for the individuals depending on that system to move freely. This has the effect of converting the distributed system from a permissive circulation system, neutral with respect to categories of inhabitants, into a control system by which those dependent on it become fixed to their places. It is paradoxical perhaps that opening up the system is the means of controlling it. Nevertheless, the logic of the model tells us what direct experience tells us more obscurely: that the open-plan is a means of converting what were status differences between inhabitants into what is virtually a class difference within the inhabitant structure of the building. Of course this will not be the case if all the occupants of the space have equal rights of movement in the distributed system. This will change the nature of the model completely by changing one essential dimension of its logic. Nor will the open-plan model necessarily be realised in a 'semi-open' plan. It depends on the degree of synchronisation of the distributed structure and the degree of closure of the individual spaces. Even so, it remains the case that in its pure forms, the open-plan transformation can act as a means, other things being equal, of virtually 'proletarianising' part of the workforce.

The open-plan movement in school design is more subtle, but again it is not the 'liberalisation of space' that it is often presented to be. A traditional school design, with its separate class-rooms, its separate circulation system, and its special space for assembly and play, has a clearly defined genotype. The visitors, that is, the pupils, are everywhere synchronised, provided they are in inhabitant primary cells deeper than the main circulation system of the building: that is to say, they are everywhere locally synchronised with respect to particular inhabitants. These inhabitants, however, are asynchronous with respect to each other, maintaining their relative categoric statuses by being mapped onto separate spaces with a higher relative asymmetry value than the spaces of the circulation system. Their status as independent professionals is also preserved from the control hierarchy of the organisation in that the head teacher's room is located near the entrance, thus governing the circulation structure of the building, that is, the space of the visitors, more than the deeper space of the inhabitants, that is, the teachers in their class-rooms. This leads to a very characteristic inequality structure in the school as a whole. The relation of inhabitants and visitors is locally elementary, in that the teacher in his class-room is not a guardian of the circulation system, fixing visitors in a specific space, but an inhabitant of space asymmetric with respect to the pupils, from which point he interfaces with them. The separate room guarantees this asymmetric interface with the pupils as well as relative asymmetry with respect to other inhabitants, implying a stronger category and therefore status. Globally, the school has a relatively weak control dimension, in that the relation of distributed circulation system and class-rooms does not map the differential between inhabitants and visitors. Globally, as well as locally, the system is one run by asymmetry rather than control – that is, it is more like a ramified elementary building than a reversed building. Only insofar as the highest status inhabitant occupies shallow space near the circulation system, and that circulation system has few rather than many points of control, is there a global control dimension mapped into the building.

Now if we simply transform this structure by increasing its ringiness – one very typical modern transformation – then the principal effect this will have will be to give individual inhabitants more control of the system than was the case when it was more tree-like and the head teacher was located near the base of the tree. This seems an unambiguously 'progressive' move in something like the sense it is intended to be. But if the transformation to open-plan is made, a much more radical transformation appears in the genotype in all the vital dimensions of the traditional model. First, the status given by the relative asymmetry of the class-room space is eliminated, so that the statuses of teachers with respect to each other are no longer supported by the spatial structure. Second, the open-plan has the effect of synchronising the distributed structure, thus forming it into a unified system of control; this undoubtedly increases the degree of control potential in the system. Finally, the relation of teacher to class is transformed from elementary to reversed, in that the teacher is no longer so much in an asymmetric relation to the class, but in a relation of one who controls the circulation system to those who are fixed into a particular space. In Basil Bernstein's terms, the relations are shifted from those of power to those of control.[8] Once again, space is neither what it seems to be at first sight, nor what it is represented as in the manifestos for spatial change. The result of what appears as a liberation is that, apart from the head teacher, inhabitants lose status and the visitors are subject to a reinforced regime of control, not locally as before, but at the global level of the whole structure of space in the building.

Buildings, it would appear, are rarely what they seem. No individual spatial relationship reveals itself except by reference to the global scheme of the building, and no global scheme reveals itself except through the nuances of its local relationships. There are no principles by which it can be said that in any conditions whatsoever a particular relationship has a certain social reference. Yet buildings are analysable, provided they are approached with a model that looks first for the global genotype, then for the fine-tuning of particular relationships in particular locations. All that can be said at a general level is that being what they are, that is, a means of ordering relations between those who through the building have the status of inhabitants and others who through the building have the status of visitors, buildings always act to reinforce some structure which, locally at least, appears as an inequality.

But this need does not lead us to be pessimistic about the nature of buildings in general. What is locally an inequality is not necessarily an inequality in the global system, in the obvious sense that the fact that everyone in a settlement lives in a separate house, generating everywhere the local inequality of inhabitants and visitors with respect to that domain, does not imply inequality at the level of the whole settlement. The matter is more subtle and often the contrary can be the case: local inequalities can be the means by which global equalities are realised in the form of a describable system. However far we may proceed in analysing buildings in their own terms, their global nature will not reveal itself unless we also relate them to the global socio-spatial system of which they form a part. This means looking beyond the level of the settlement to the level of society itself. Society, it will be argued, is not an abstraction which finds itself a physical location and then defines an arrangement, but an entity with its own internal spatial logic and even its own spatial laws. This 'spatial logic of society' is the subject of the final chapters of this book, and it is the means by which the analysis of the spatial structures inside and outside primary boundaries can be seen in a clear relation to each other to constitute the social logic of space in the fullest sense. But before we can proceed to this, we must first of all return to the formal foundations of the syntactic argument and draw out certain general theoretical principles from our examination of the syntax of space – theoretical principles which will then become foundation stones for a model of the spatial logic of society.

6

•••

The spatial logic of arrangements

SUMMARY

The argument now returns to the foundation of the problem of order and argues that, by using the full framework set out in Chapter 1, it is possible to describe physical arrangements in terms of their abstract ordering principles in such a way as to relate order and randomness in a new way. Randomness emerges, in effect, as a form of necessary order both in spatial arrangements and in social systems. A general framework of relating different kinds of order is then established, dealing with both material and conceptual components of the arrangement in a unified way, and dealing with randomness and order in the same terms. The chapter ends by relating the dimensions of the arrangemental model to notions of ideology, politics and productive base of a society.

From structures to particular realities

In Chapters 2, 3, 4 and 5 the aim has been to show that, in spite of its variety, human spatial organisation has, however imperfect, a certain internal logic. This internal logic accounts, we believe, for the knowability of space. Because it has the property of knowability, space can operate as a morphic language, that is, as one of the means by which society is constituted and understood by its members. By embodying intelligibility in spatial forms, the individuals in a society create an experiential reality through which they can retrieve a description of certain dimensions of their society and the ways in which they are members of it. These descriptions are essentially abstract in nature, although they are drawn from a concrete reality. Descriptions are summaries of the principles of a spatial pattern, not simply an enumeration of its parts. In the fashionable language of structuralism, these descriptions would be called 'deep structures'. However, as far as space is concerned there need be no mystery or imprecision. These abstract structures are what we express and quantify through syntax. Syntactic statements are the abstract genotypes of spatial realities.

In setting out to exhibit the variety of spatial forms that exist as the product of an underlying system of generators we have, within reasonable limits of interpretation, followed the principles of

what might loosely be called the structuralist method. The phenotypical forms of space are seen as the products of abstract rules,
and the different rules underlying different phenotypical forms
themselves form a system of transformations. But structuralism
has always had a philosophic aim as well as a methodology. This
aim is to *objectivise* the concept of structure in such a way as to
show that the sources of social behaviour lie in society itself and
the particular forms it takes, not in the individual. The syntax
model, to some extent perhaps achieves this. It shows that spatial
organisation is not only a means by which collections of individuals can constitute society but, because space has its own laws
and its own logic, it can also act as a system of constraints on the
society. Space, because its laws of pattern are independent of
human wishes, has at least a dialectical relation with society. It
can answer back. It does not obey some set of social determinants
without imposing some of its own autonomous reality.

It could be objected that, in arriving at relatively autonomous
descriptions of the genotypical structures of space organisation,
we may have inadvertently removed some of its most important
dimensions of social content and meaning, in particular those
which have to do with the broad economic and political structure
of society. It may be even worse. In saying that in a morphic
language, like space, formal syntactic patterns and quantifiable
relations are the dominant properties, and that these constitute
society and 'mean themselves' rather than exist to communicate
information about other aspects of society, there is a danger that
space is thereby split off from the main fabric of society. It may be
that, in showing how space can locally be constitutive of social
reality, we have done so only at the expense of showing how
globally it does so.

This difficulty may be inherent in structuralism. It may even be
a paradox in the method as a whole. If structures are to be shown
to be objective and not dependent on individuals, then they must
be shown to follow autonomous laws. Forms and patterns are not
to be explained as the product of different external determina-
tions. Instead, by the very act of describing structures and
demonstrating their existence, it is implied that the laws of
structure are in some sense internal, not external. This is why it
is possible for structuralism to follow the classic scientific procedure of trying to associate a mathematical model of some kind
with the phenomena under study, as both a description and an
explanation.[1] The paradox arises if the exercise is successful. If
the laws of particular structures in society are internal and
autonomous, then what can they have to do with society? It is an
easy step from the idea that structures have autonomous laws to
the conclusion that they are therefore an autonomous reality. It
may even be entailed in the premises.

In the case of the syntactic approach to space the problem is

particularly difficult, because in several instances we have deliberately tried to eliminate the most commonly asked questions
about space. For example, in some cases the question as to why a
particular society adopts a particular settlement form is answered
not in terms of some social or economic function, but by saying
that, given some set of initial conditions and a consistent process
of aggregation, the settlement form is a product of autonomous
spatial laws, not of human determination. If questions of social or
functional determination are then reformulated in terms of those
initial conditions and the consistent process, then there hardly
seems enough matter for any reasonable external determination to
grip onto.

But the paradox only appears if it is assumed that the essence of
society is something other than its structures, that is, in present
terminology, something other than its morphic languages and the
patterns they constitute. Once this assumption is dispensed with,
the problem is transformed. It becomes a matter of showing how
society is constituted by the inter-relations of morphic languages,
all of which are realised, and are therefore observable, in real
space and real time.

The essence of the argument to be put forward in this chapter
follows from this. All social processes, whatever their abstract and
conceptual nature, are realised in space. For example, kinship
systems – a speciality of abstract structuralism – have well-
defined spatial outcomes in terms of who lives with whom, who
shifts residence and when, and what patterns of encounter are
entailed by the formal system of relations. The intention here is to
consider such systems only in terms of their spatial output and
pattern. Having, in the last three chapters, tried to *socialise* the
notion of space, we hope now to show how our conception of
society can be usefully *spatialised*. The convergence on the
notion of a system that is at once social and spatial will suggest,
we believe, certain perfectly natural – and in some cases often
observed – correlations between spatial organisation and fundamental structuring mechanisms in societies – mechanisms that
seem close to what a society essentially is.

First, it will be necessary to bring the syntax model properly
into the conceptual framework of the notion of an arrangement set
out at the end of Chapter 1. This will entail a fairly fundamental
critique of one of the invisible tenets of structuralism as it has
developed so far, one that appears largely responsible for the gulf
that now exists between analysis of generalised structures and the
capacity to analyse particular realities effectively. It will lead on
to a more precise articulation of the dynamics of arrangemental
systems, suggesting how it is possible within this framework to
bridge the gap between a *statistical* view and a *structural* view of
social reality, views which within current habits of thought appear
to be far apart.

Second, we will try to set up a simple – and simplified – model for considering societies as spatial systems, and examine a few examples that illustrate its basic dynamic dimensions. This will, we hope, achieve two objectives, albeit in a rudimentary way: to show that spatial dynamics may have a more fundamental relation to social morphology than has generally been thought since nineteenth-century anthropology first opposed 'territory' to 'kinship' as the two polar bases of society[2]; and – a more philosophical aim – to show that it is possible to build a model of society in which structure does not appear as an abstract global system anterior to, and independent of, social realities, but as a *property of reality itself*. In fact, by spatialising our concept of society, it appears possible to build bridges over the enormous gulf that structuralism has opened up between theory and particular social realities by its pursuit not only of abstractions, but of abstractions that refer only to abstractions in society itself.

Abstract materialism

The fundamental theoretical problem of any sociology is to show what society can be, that it can get inside individuals and come out as behaviour and thought. Sociology by definition reverses the normal concept of scientific reduction: the behaviour of the small entities, individuals, is to be explained in terms of the larger collective entity, society. Of course, there is no necessary reason why such an aim should be pursued. It might be better to explain the larger entity in terms of the small. But in this case we are virtually compelled to abandon sociology, since either there exist no laws at the level of society itself, in which case the subject is reduced to an extended psychology; or there exist laws that have no effect on the individual, in which case they would be pointless. An authentic sociology must therefore somehow accomplish a reversed reductionism: it must show how different forms of society produce different forms of thought and behaviour in the individual.

The programmatic aim of structuralism has always been to solve this problem by objectivising the concept of structure at the level of society itself. Structure always means some unified system of rules possessing an internal logic of their own, which the individual is able to internalise and follow in his own behaviour. Since rule structures do not generate closed systems but can be open-ended, the concept permits the notion of 'rule-governed creativity' whereby the creative and to some extent unpredictable behaviour of individuals is reconciled to the idea that there exists some substructure of rules.

Without doubt this conceptual scheme has yielded useful insights into some aspects of social reality. Yet there remains an underlying scepticism as to whether the underlying problem has

been broached, let alone solved. It appears clear that structures are
involved in the actions of individuals, yet it is not clear that those
structures in any sense represent society. On the contrary, they
appear to emerge from a realm of pure thought, unformed and
even uninfluenced by the processes of a working society. Structuralism pays attention to how structures organise society, but not to
how society organises structures. Any reasonable sociology requires an answer to both questions. Structuralism only interests
itself in the second. Its desire to show the logical form of
structures leads its proponents to found structure in logic itself,
and eventually, by a natural extension of the argument, in the
human brain. Structuralism therefore seems to avoid both the
question of the *origin* of structure, and the question of its *locus*.
Ideally the answer to questions as to where structures originate
and where they are located ought to be: in society itself. Structuralism does not suggest how such an answer could be given. This is
the first of two counts upon which structuralism is commonly
criticised.

The second count again concerns the relations between structures and society. But whereas the first criticism concerned the
problem of society as anterior to structure, the second concerns
the problem of society as a consequence of structure. Structures, it
is said, may help us to understand what society is made of, but
they do not tell us how societies work. If we accept that the
concept of structure is necessary in principle to any real situation
in which socially meaningful events are transacted, the concepts
of structure we possess, with their emphasis on internal logic,
appear too pure. At worst they appear almost to contradict our
intuition of society as an unstable, achieved, continuously re-
negotiated phenomenon. Structures are ideal and abstract. Society
is incongrously imperfect, existing only by virtue of concrete
activity. Structures are algebraic and static. Societies seem subject
to dynamic and statistical laws. Structures have 'on–off' switches.
Societies have thresholds which vary, continuously or catas-
trophically, with the presence or absence of a large number of
variables. Important aspects of pattern and form in society are to
do with the organisation of material production. Structures
appear as a preoccupation with the cognitive and with social
reproduction. Structures, at best, deal with one set of social
phenomena at a time. But society itself is organised by the
conjoint effect of a multiplicity of structures. How can these
conflicts be reconciled without an inconsistency in the method,
and without abandoning a structural approach? Yet if we do
persevere with the structural approach and look for 'meta-struc-
tures' or 'co-ordinating structures' we are in danger of over-
determining society and producing a *reductio ad absurdum*.
Whatever it is, society is not a dance or a ritual. It is, at the very
least, a statistical not a mechanical reality.[3] Structuralism cannot

bridge this gap. It is therefore seen to fail to provide a reasonable solution, even in principle, to another vital aspect of the fundamental problem. It fails to provide an account of the relations between abstract structures and particular realities.[4]

As a result, we are left with structures that inhabit a separate reality. They connect to society neither in their origins nor their consequences. Instead, their ultimate *locus* is said to be outside society altogether in the human brain itself: their order reflects its structure; their logic reflects its logic. The realities made by man express and articulate the elementary structuring mechanisms of the brain. Starting from a sociology that reduced society to individual action, structuralism has, it seems, only presented us with a sociology that reduces individual action to collective thought. No way has, after all, been found out of the fundamental problem.

This is because there is a simple but fatal flaw in the foundations of structuralism. It lies in the concept of 'rule' itself. In the common concept, a rule is anterior to the events it governs. A rule is followed. An event or behaviour obeys a rule. The rule of necessity exists prior to the event. In structuralism the idea of a rule is basic. In it is the foundation of the concept of structure. A structure is a co-ordination of rules. A code is an underlying system of rules by which spatio-temporal events are to be correlated and interpreted. It follows that structures, or codes, are prior to events. Structuralism was predicated on the insight that the variety of surface appearances in society would be expressed as the product of underlying, and therefore anterior rules.

The fatal flaw follows from the original insight. This principle of the 'anteriority of the rule' sounds innocuous enough, but it has hidden consequences. If a rule exists prior to an event, then it must exist somewhere. If there is a programme, there must be a programming organ, some centre where these rules are encoded. What other candidate for such a centre can there be other than the brains of individuals. If behaviour is rule-governed then the rules are prior to the behaviour. And if the rules are prior to the behaviour, then the *locus* of these rules must be the brain itself. The 'brain structure' theory of the *locus* of structure thus follows from the premises of structuralism and, eventually, from its original insights. However, we are now back where we started: with a society in which the principles of order are located in individuals, not in society itself. The main aim of structuralism therefore turns back on itself, and degenerates into what it was trying to escape from.

The discussion of arrangements in Chapter 1 may clarify one reason why this has come to be so. The function of the brain in the structuralist theory is to act as the *description centre* for the social system. In this way, the biological model is re-introduced, not as a proposition, but as an invisible assumption. The 'brain structure'

solution to this problem offered by the structuralist is nothing less
than one more reduction of society to a spatially continuous
biological system in which the unfolding of spatio-temporal
events is pre-programmed. From there, since society is not a
spatially continuous biological system but a system structured
from discrete entities, the degeneration of the theory is inevitable
and immediate. The failure of structuralism to become a sociological theory follows from this degeneration.

The relevance of the idea of arrangement can now be made
properly clear. Arrangements, we may recall, are systems composed of spatially discrete entities, or individuals. The genotypical stability of arrangements arises not from the existence of
description centres, since manifestly there need be none at the
level of the collective system. Instead each individual is equipped
not with a description centre in which its arrangemental instructions are encoded, as genetic instructions are encoded into the
organism, but with a description retrieval mechanism, by which it
can retrieve and internalise a description of its arrangemental
situation. The syntax theory shows how such descriptions can be
abstract, and can be retrieved from complex realities.

In arrangemental systems, the concept of a rule is reversed. The
spatio-temporal event precedes the rule. No spatio-temporal event
in itself necessarily implies a rule. The rule exists only when an
abstract description is retrieved from a spatio-temporal event and
is then re-embodied in another such event. In arrangements
reproduction is the fundamental concept, not that of the abstract
rule. In place of the rule existing prior to the event, we have the
abstract description retrieved from events, and made the model for
the reproduction of that event. The abstract entity is in a kind of
'reality sandwich'. In order to exist it must be abstracted from one
reality and re-embodied in another. If the description is not
re-embodied, then the description is not sustained for that
arrangement. If it is not retrieved in the first place, then it does not
exist. The scheme: reality$_1$ → description → reality$_2$ is the fundamental motor of the arrangement, not the pre-existing rule.
Without it no arrangement exists.

It follows that in an arrangemental system the existence of
structure depends on two kinds of work: on practical activity and
on intellectual activity. Without either, the system is not sustained. Yet either objective reality or the description retrieval
mechanism can be responsible for evolution in the system. As the
syntax theory shows, new spatio-temporal structures can emerge
from a collection of individual activities, where the collective
structure is of a higher order than any of the descriptions that
were followed by individuals in their action. Nevertheless, descriptions of these higher-order realities can be expressed in the
same abstract language as the lower-order descriptions. On the
other hand, the unfolding of the syntax schemes themselves

shows how, given an initial step, aspects of descriptions may be combined with each other to form more complex descriptions which may then be followed. Thus there is no problem at all in distributing the tendency of arrangements to morphogenesis between both the laws of objective spatial reality and the combinatorial powers of the human mind. Yet, in spite of this dialectic between the mind and objective reality, we may still posit the autonomy of the structural laws of space. The practical limits of thought are the limits of what is constructible. In arrangements, practically speaking, the laws of the mind are nothing less than the limits of possibility in particular realities.

In structuralism the principle is that of the primacy of structure, that is the primacy of the rule. In the theory of arrangements we may establish the contrary principle: the *law of the primacy of the phenotype,* that is, the *primacy of particular realities.* It is only through embodiment in spatio-temporal reality that structure exists. It is only through the intellectual activity of man in retrieving descriptions that structure is reproduced and perpetuated. Without reproduction there is no arrangement. Therefore there is no arrangement without structure. The law of the primacy of the phenotype and the law of the necessity of structure are not in contradiction. The one requires the other. This necessity comes from the fact of reproduction. Arrangement is only arrangement by virtue of reproduction. Reproduction only exists by virtue of description retrieval. Description retrieval only exists by virtue of the prior existence of a spatio-temporal reality.

This is why it was so important to found syntax on the concept of a random, ongoing process, that is, a process *without* description retrieval. It is necessary, in order to establish the primacy of the phenotype, to establish the dominance of reality over the rule. At the foundation of an arrangement, there is no predetermined structure: only randomness. For syntax to appear requires not that the rule precedes the event, but that an initial description is retrieved from spatio-temporal reality and then applied consistently in the succeeding events in the process. Syntax is a consistency in description retrieval and re-embodiment from one moment to the next. The process itself is guaranteed by the random underlying system.

As previously argued, the underlying random process is conceptually analogous to the inertia postulate in physics. It allows a formal theory to emerge unencumbered by the metaphysics of ultimate causes and unmoved movers. Without the anteriority of an unordered reality, we would be forced into an Aristotelian stance, assuming as natural that which needs to be explained. The proper question is: how and why do human beings *reproduce* what they do, and how does this unfold through the dialectics of thought and reality into a morphogenetic, unfolding scheme. If we do not place reality before the rule, then by inevitable logical steps we are forced back to the brain structure theory. The brain as originator of structure is none other than the unmoved mover of Aristotelian physics in the guise of a computer.

In effect, the substitution of a description retrieval principle for description centres answers the two intrinsic questions about structures – their formal origin and empirical *locus* – with one and the same answer: reality itself. The mind, and in most cases many minds, is the control mechanism but not the substantive entity. The logical powers of the mind do not account for the well-ordering of structures. The logic is external to the mind and located first in the configurational limitations of space–time itself. The mind reads structure and re-invents it, and learns to think the **language of reality. But it does not originate it unaided, and it does** not sustain it unaided. Without embodiment and re-embodiment in spatio-temporal reality, structure fades away. Even though structures have internal laws, they are only made real as abstractions by the physical and mental activity of many individuals. Thus structure is not a global abstraction, floating in a void and superimposed on reality as an abstract set of determinants; it is both derived from and depends on reality. Moreover, such structures are not systems of rules in the accepted sense: they are – possibly marginal – restrictions on an otherwise random process leading to global outcomes that have a partly structural and partly statistical nature. Because this is so, the extrinsic questions about structure – principally those of the social origins and social consequences of structure – can be brought into a new focus. Abstraction and materalism are not in conflict in sociology any more than they are in natural science. An abstract materialism is possible.

The semantic illusion

The notion of an arrangement with description retrieval permits, in principle, the re-integration of the material and conceptual aspects of order in artificial systems, aspects which the structuralist tradition strongly separates. It does so by introducing a spatio-temporal dimension into the notion of structure itself. A further exploration of the mechanics of spatio-temporal arrangements can take the argument a little further and suggest how the mechanical, or deterministic notions of a rule-governed system that prevail in the structuralist tradition can be assimilated to – in effect be shown to be a limiting case of – the statistical or probabilistic notions of order that have tended to prevail in empirical sociology. One further result of this exploration will be to show that the notion of control of structures is not merely a separate dimension of the system, as it were in an orthogonal relation to structure, but an aspect of the structure itself.

Description retrieval mechanisms in spatio-temporal arrangements can be illustrated in a very direct and practical way by taking the reader back to the discussion of beady ring settlements in Chapter 2. The reader was first presented with a set of small aggregations without any apparent order (Fig. 4(a)–(f)). Then it was shown that all larger settlements in the area, while retaining the local indeterminacy characteristic of the smaller set, had the beady ring structure, subject to local topographical constraints. Once the reader saw this and understood the principles of generating global beady ring structures from a system with purely local rules, then he could look back on the earlier set, and see these formless aggregations in a new way: as settlements *on the way to becoming* a beady ring structure. As might the inhabitants themselves, the reader, as it were, retrieved a description of the abstract global form and with this model in his head saw the world, from which the model was derived, in a new light.

This process is easy to demonstrate and easy to describe in words. What is not clear is how a process that involves both a morphogenetic event in the real world – the appearance of the global beady ring form out of the local rule – and a conceptual event – the mental process by which this morphogenesis is grasped – can be thought of and represented as dimensions of a single system. This is after all not just a problem of pattern recognition, to be circumnavigated by general statements about 'interaction' between the mind and the physical world: it is the central problem of sociology, asked in a slightly more precise way. A society is a very complex set of inter-related physical events in some unknown relation with the structures of the brains of individuals that appear to control events locally. To give a precise account of how the description retrieval mechanism works in this relatively simple case of morphogenesis involving both material and conceptual dimensions might therefore provide some clue about the parallel mechanisms in societies in general.

The first step is to recognise that systems with both material and conceptual dimensions are not at all rare in society. In fact, they are normal and everywhere, used in a perfectly natural way, but not recognised for what they are because our habit is to assume that the mind and physical objects inhabit separate domains. Take for example an everyday system like a pack of cards. This perfectly illustrates the pervasive co-presence of material and conceptual aspects in the same system. A pack of cards is at least a set of material 'individuals', each of which exists to embody an individual in a purely conceptual system: the identity of being the four of hearts or king of clubs. When usage is taken into account the inter-relation is even stronger. Card playing invariably involves material events, such as card distribution and shuffling, whose material randomness continually creates novel situations, without which the game cannot be played. Card games depend as much on these material transactions as much as they depend on a permanent orientation of the mind towards description retrieval in relation to these transactions. It is not enough to see these relations as an interaction. The material and conceptual components of the system interpenetrate each other so completely, that it would seem that there must be a way to capture its dynamics more exactly.

First, consider the abstract logic of the pack of cards. It is clear that the knowability of an individual card, say the four of spades, is dependent on certain well-defined properties of the whole pack through which it constitutes a structured set. The four of spades – although it does not mean anything apart from its own structure – is only intelligible by virtue of being a member of a set governed by a rule system: in this case the rule system that assigns one real card to each possible member of an abstract set generated by four suits and thirteen numbers. This rule system we may think of as the 'master card' of the pack. It does not exist in a physical sense, but its logical existence is indubitable. It is implied by the structured set of real cards and it gives them knowability. The master card may be thought of as something like a genotype of the set, and the individual cards as the complete set of phenotypes generated by the genotype. Each phenotype implies the genotype in order to guarantee intelligibility.

In effect, the act of playing a card really means playing what might be called a bi-card: that is, a card divided into two parts, say an upper and lower half, in the upper half of which is inscribed the genotype, and in the lower half of which is inscribed the phenotype. Of course, it is simpler to assume the genotype, and not to include it in the phenotype. Nevertheless, the fact that it can be omitted from the spatio-temporal aspect of the system we call a set of playing cards does not mean that it can be omitted from the logic of the system. The master card, or genotype, tactit or otherwise, is the precondition of having any real playing cards at all.

But likewise the necessity for the system to be realised through a set of physical individuals, capable of being re-arranged and re-shuffled at will, is omitted from the representation of the logic of the system as contained in the marks made on each card. Seen abstractly these would constitute the same logical system if they were all realised on a single sheet of paper. The existence of individual cards is recorded only in the empirical fact of their separateness. A pack of cards, in effect, embodies a much more subtle interplay of conceptual and physical events than appears at first sight to minds habituated to such systems. But, at least its principles of knowability and usability can be made clear by a careful description.

It may seem initially far-fetched to compare a spatial arrangement, like a settlement, with such a system, but there is a way of seeing them that will make the analogy precise and useful. Take

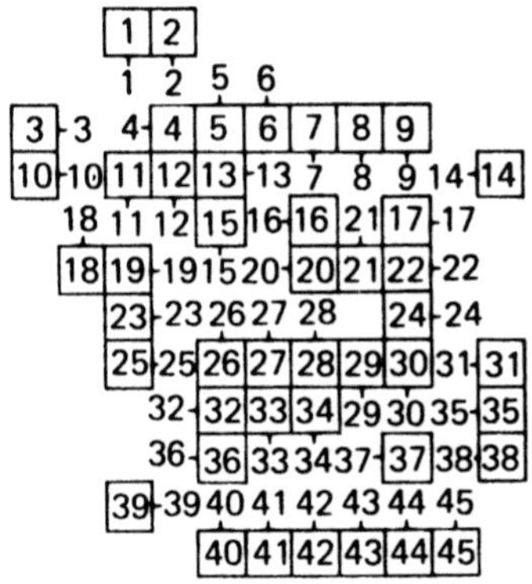

Fig. 118 A computer-
generated 'beady ring'
settlement.

for example a computer-generated beady ring form (Fig. 118). This, or any settlement, is made up at least of a set of individual cells which, even if initially indistinguishable from another, have acquired what we might call a *relational identity* by becoming part of the arrangement. Each cell has, for example, a certain configuration of adjacent spaces. If for example we take each y-space attached to each individual cell as a centre for its neighbours, the arrangement can be represented as a set of local adjacency maps (Fig. 119), which for clarity can then be converted into a parallel set of alpha maps (Fig. 120).

Certain rather obvious statements can be made about this set of local maps. Each one will have certain relations in common with all the others: that is, each open cell will be attached to exactly one closed cell and at least one other open cell. We know this because this is the local rule according to which the arrangement has been generated. This relation can therefore be said to be genotypical for the whole collection of local maps. However, using the same analogy, other relations which are not the same for all the maps can be said to be only phenotypical, in that they are part of an actual local spatial arrangement but not a necessary part.

Seen in terms of its local maps, therefore, the settlement can be seen as a system of similarities and differences, that is, as a system with both a genotypical and a phenotypical dimension. These similarities and differences can be seen both spatially and transpatially. Spatially we are aware of the degree to which adjacent maps are similar to and different from each other. Transpatially we consider the whole system as a set of maps regardless of their adjacency to each other, as we would a pack of cards.

Now to use the biological term phenotype for these local maps could be rather misleading, if for no other reason, because it would be natural to think of a whole settlement as a phenotype and its common structure with others – say, in this case with other beady ring settlements – as the genotype. Here we are dealing with the local relational identity that each individual cell acquires by

Fig. 119 Fig. 118 as a set of
local maps; centred on each
open space.

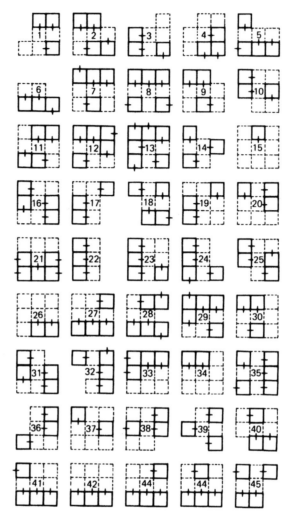

being a part of the whole arrangement, and not with the global properties. We are dealing, in effect with arrangemental individuals, which without their membership of an arrangement would be indistinguishable from each other. To make this distinction clear, we shall therefore use the term *p-model* for local phenotypes, that is, for individual cells seen in terms of their particular configuration of local spatial relations, and the term *g-model* for the genotypical relations that exist in the set of p-models in an arrangement. Thus a p-model refers to all the local spatial relations of a cell, seen from the point of view of that cell; while a g-model refers to the subset of relations that are invariant for the set of p-models making up an arrangement.

The arrangement can now be represented as a bi-card system. Each individual space can be thought of as, or as having a bi-card on which two descriptions are inscribed: on the upper half the

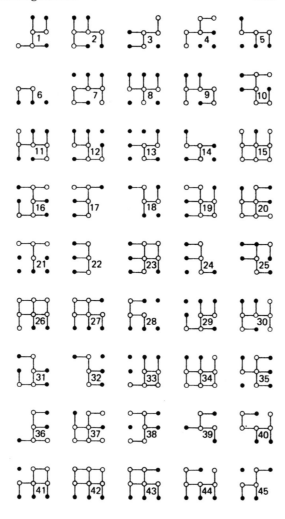

Fig. 120 Fig. 119 as locally centred permeability maps.

g-model of the set of individuals; and on the lower half the phenotypical identity of that individual. The master bi-card of the system, which of course has a logical rather than a physical existence, then has the g-model in its upper half and all the different p-models in the lower half. Now obviously, these p-model descriptions should not contain unnecessary information or unnecessary repetition. They should be as compressed as possible, like all formal descriptions, and g-models will therefore have a certain length, depending on how many of the possible relations of local models are to be specified as necessary rather than contingent. The list of p-models will have a certain variety of types, with repetition of a particular type recorded by some mark indicating repetition, rather than by the reduplication of the p-model itself. Clearly there will be a relation between these two descriptions, since the more relations are specified in the g-model, then the less scope there is for variety in the set of p-models. In the

computer-generated beady ring we have looked at, the g-model is
clearly a relatively short one, in that it specifies only a few of the
possible relations of each cell, and the list of types of p-model is
consequently relatively long. If we required each cell to obey more
necessary rules of contiguity, then it follows that the set of
p-model types will be correspondingly reduced.

Even leaving aside questions of particular syntactic patterns,
the relative length of g-models and p-models is itself one of the
fundamental dimensions of our intuitions of spatial order. For
example, a settlement that appears 'organically grown' rather than
deliberately planned – beady rings are a good example – is likely
to appear so because it has a short g-model and a long p-model,
'long' in the latter case meaning a long list of p-model types. A
'short' g-model means that, as new objects are added to the
scheme, only localised co-ordinations are specified, with the
result that a good deal of the growing global pattern is a consequence of the contingent relations specified by the random process.
Another way of saying this would be that the *generative* aspect of
the process prevails over the *descriptive* aspect. What is in the
g-model is what is already described as holding among the objects
in the arrangement. What is generated is a result of the process
governed by such a description.

But what of the global, emergent structure of the beady ring
settlement – that is, the beady ring itself? The transcription to a
bi-card system has so far only referred to the local structure, and
this is tantamount to ignoring morphogenesis. How can a morphogenetic global event be represented in a bi-card system? The
difficulty seems considerable at first because on the one hand the
beady ring is undoubtedly a structure, but on the other hand it
seems to be exactly and only a higher-order phenotype. A rather
more searching examination of the difference between p-models
and g-models seems to be required.

A p-model is, in fact, by any reasonable definition a 'structure',
in that it is a definite local organisation of relations. The difference
between a p- and a g-model does not lie at all in the nature of
individual structures, but only in their comparability. A structure
only becomes a g-model when it occurs as a *regularity* in a set of
comparable cases. A g-model is properly speaking a g-regularity.
This then makes it easy to characterise a structure that has not yet
acquired regularity status but is a describable structure nevertheless: it is what we might call a *g-singularity*. Every p-model in this
sense can be thought of as a g-singularity. But in the case of the
beady ring there is more occasion to call it that, since from the
point of view of individual cells in the system, it is exactly as a
global singularity that the beady ring will appear. This singularity
will then appear in the system as a g-regularity only when it is
seen to be an invariant structure of a family of comparable spatial
arrangements. Suppose, for example, we have a landscape com-

prising a dispersed set of beady ring settlements, of the same order of similarity and difference as shown in the original examples selected. It is clear that not only is the beady ring now a g-model, but also it is a relatively short g-model at the global level, since it requires only a very basic set of relations to be invariant, and permits a great deal of variety in the actual phenotypical variety of settlements. Thus the system works the same way at both the level of a spatial arrangement and that of a transpatial arrangement. At each level a relatively short g-model produces a large equivalence class of p-models. For convenience, a system with these general properties could be referred to as a p-model system, since it invests more in a large p-model equivalence class than in a strong g-model structure. But it must not be forgotten, of course, that every arrangemental system has a g-model, even if it is a relatively short one.

Now let us turn to another kind of system, one which on the surface, while being comparable in size, appears to have virtually the contrary properties of the beady ring settlement: the Bororo village illustrated in Fig. 30. Initially this appears not only to be a very different type of spatial arrangement, but a different type of system altogether. Apart from its much simpler global form, it has a kind of complexity completely absent in beady ring structures, in that an enorous amount of purely sociological information is embedded in the spatial arrangement: information about clans, moieties, classes, sex relations, and even cosmologies. In short, it is the type of spatial arrangement that leads many to argue that the analysis of space in its own terms is idle, since all depends on the meanings that particular societies assign to particular spaces. The analysis of the arrangement in terms of the bi-card model can, we believe, demonstrate the opposite: that what appears as the domination of the system by nonspatial information is no more than a natural extension of the internal logic of the bi-card model in a particular direction, that is, the direction of a very long g-model. The semantic illusion is, it turns out, a product of the paradigm which views real space and the human mind as separate domains.

The first property of the Bororo village when considered as a bi-card system is very obvious. The maps of local relations of individual cells, that is, the set of p-models, are all the same with the exception of the men's house in the centre. This means that the g-model is of the same length as the p-model, all of whose relations are specified. The g-model is therefore said to be long in comparison to the p-model component of the system, and the system is therefore locally a g-model system. The same appears at the global level. All Bororo villages are based on the same plan, and the global g-model will therefore have a very small equivalence class, just as the local p-models did in the case of the individual cells. However, this is a relatively unimportant property compared to what appears when we try to take into account all the information in the system that appears initially to be not of the nature of the spatial arrangement, but superimposed *upon* it: that is, the complex set of labels assigned to different spaces and the relations that exist between these labels. With the addition of a new concept to the system – or rather the clarification of one already implicit – the system of labels can be shown to be a dimension of the spatial arrangement.

In terms of the bi-card model of a spatial arrangement, the problem with the Bororo village is that the labels appear to be an important part of the genotype, in the sense that in each village certain necessary relations are realised between labels, and these are common to all villages. Thus all villages are divided diametrically – though purely conceptually – on both the east–west axis and the north–south axis, these divisions corresponding to important social divisions in the society. Moreover, individual clan huts have to be in a certain position on the circumference in relation to each other and in relation to the diametric division. Then each hut is subdivided within itself into 'classes' which are again arranged in a certain order. Not only is extra semantic information added to the genotype, but each space in the system appears to feature in several different conceptual dimensions at once, simply by virtue of its position relative to other spaces.

The first step to a proper assimilation of these unfamiliar properties to our model is to give a proper characterisation of the new types of relation that have been added. In the beady ring arrangement, all that had been specified in the g-model was rules specifying relations of spatial contiguity. All inter-object correlations were of a spatial kind, and as such easily representable on a planar graph. In the Bororo system, it is clear that inter-object correlations of a new kind have been added in the form of relations that leap across immediately contiguous spaces and refer to other spaces at some distance away. These are relations that cannot be realised in a planar graph; we require the greater resources of the non-planar graph to represent them. How has this been done? The answer is that a fundamental new spatial property has been introduced, but one that is already implicit in the generative syntax model. This property we can call *noninterchangeability*. To present this clearly we must briefly return to some of the basic arguments in the generative syntax, where the idea of the structure of a system as restrictions on a random process was first introduced.

An important property of processes where a large number of p-models are co-ordinated by an extremely compressed g-model – as in the beady ring – is that all the objects are interchangeable, that is we can switch one with another without affecting the g-model. This is part of what was originally meant by describing relations between the objects as symmetric: since the relation of x_1

to x_2 is genetically the same as the relation of x_2 to x_1, the two may be interchanged. Interchangeability turns out to be a very fundamental property indeed. For example, the reason that large settlements can be generated by comparatively short g-models is that most of the objects are interchangeable. It is this that allows us to add new objects to the complex without specifying any relations between particular objects – that is, we can add them randomly, provided they join onto the complex as a whole in a way that preserves the structure of the elementary relational scheme. Thus symmetry, randomness, and the compressibility of g-model descriptions all seem to be in some way the essential constituents or consequences of one general concept: that of interchangeability.

Now suppose we require a typical process – say the beady ring process – to have the opposite property: namely, that as each new object is added to the scheme it is required to be linked to a particular object already present. In other words, suppose we introduce noninterchangeability for the objects that in the previous case were interchangeable (see pp. 209–12). It is very easy to write down such a process: beginning from $(( )_1( )_2)$ we then bracket each next object with the object in the existing complex with which it is correlated. For example, if we require $( )_3$ to be correlated to $( )_1$, and $( )_4$ to be correlated to $( )_2$, then we should write $((( )_1( )_3)(( )_2( )_4))$, and so on. Now this process has two very significant effects on the bi-card. First, it makes labels on spaces much more important than they were, since previously unlabelled and therefore interchangeable spaces were joined to each other, whereas now specific labels, and relations between labels, feature in the relational scheme; second, while this makes no difference at all to the p-models, *it prevents the compression of the g-model descriptions*; in fact, if all the phenotypical connections in the complex were made noninterchangeable then the length of the g-model description would be the same as that of the sum of p-model descriptions. In other words, the effect of introducing noninterchangeability is to add genetic structure to the complex and to make its g-model description non-compressible.

We may now return immediately to the example of the Bororo village and see that its special characteristic was that it added to the basic spatial structure (involving a large number of apparently interchangeable or symmetric components – that is, all the huts around the periphery) a very large number of inter-object correlations, rendering them highly noninterchangeable. This results in a highly non-compressible g-model description and an increase in the degree of genetic structure in the scheme as represented in the bi-card.

However, this non-compressibility also appears in the p-model. If g-model invariance is extended beyond the relations necessary to realise a particular scheme spatially into possible transpatial inter-relations among objects in the scheme, then each p-model will, to specify the invariants, have to specify more and more of these relations, as seen from one point of view in the scheme. In the limiting case – which the Bororo village approaches – each p-model must specify necessary relations to every other object in the complex; and since a p-model specifies not only the relations of an object to its surrounding objects but also the relations holding among those objects, then it is clear that in the maximal case the p-models and g-models will be as long as each other and as non-compressible. In other words, the genetic structure of the scheme as a whole is reproduced in the p-models of every object. Not only has the global scheme acquired more structure by the addition of noninterchangeability, but also this structure has been reproduced in the individuality of the constituent objects. The local form has become a perfect mirror of the complexity of the global form.

We thus have a formal way of representing that property in aggregates of requiring each constituent object to obey more and more rules in relation to other objects, rules of the same generic kind as we first introduced with the asymmetric relation. In effect, we have applied a logical component of asymmetry – noninterchangeability – to the symmetric parts of relational schemes. Because this type of scheme adds structure over and above the basic spatial configuration represented in the proposition with interchangeability of symmetric objects, we will call this type of formula transpatial: it adds transpatial rules of correlation to a spatial disposition of objects, and co-ordinates labels, or categories, as well as spaces.

A special case of transpatiality is where noninterchangeability is introduced not between any pair of symmetric objects, but between one particular object in the scheme and all other objects. For example, if we take an elementary Z_5 or central space scheme, (see p. 78) and then require each added object to define a segment of y not in association with all the x-objects in the scheme, but specifically in association with the initial object of the scheme, x_1, then the results will be that the added objects will eventually surround the initial object with a continuous y-space between the single x-object at the centre and the set of x-objects at the periphery. This gives the form of the Bororo village, with the men's house playing the role of the noninterchangeable initial x-object. This property can be called *duality*, since its effect is always to select some special object in a scheme, and relate all other objects to it in some way. Duality can exist in all the distributed syntaxes, but will take a different form in each reflecting the specific syntactic conditions. In a Z_1, or cluster syntax, for example, a dual object will be nothing more than some special object in the vicinity of which all subsequent objects are placed. In a Z_3, or clump syntax the dual object will be some initial object which acts as the seed from which the clump grows. In a Z_7, or ring-street syntax, the result will be, as in the Z_5, a single free-standing object, but around it will be not only a space but also an outer ring, as for example in the well-known Trobriand village of Omarakana, illustrated first by Malinowski (and subsequently by numerous other authors).[5] Duality cannot, of course, be applied to asymmetric nondistributed syntaxes since the initial object in the scheme already has the privileged status of a dual object, in that it contains all other objects. In fact, just as transpatiality appears to borrow a logical property of asymmetry and apply it to symmetric cases, so duality appears to borrow a logical property from nondistributed syntaxes and apply it to distributed cases.

Whatever form it takes, noninterchangeability has specific syntactic effects both at the level of the g-model and the p-model: it extends g-model relations beyond those of physical adjacency between objects. It literally makes relations work at a distance. In parallel, it tends also to restrict relations of spatial adjacency. A strong g-model means literally control of local spatial relations. An object with a strong noninterchangeable category will often tend therefore to be associated with a lack of other objects in its immediate vicinity. The typical noninterchangeable building – a church, say, or a major public building – will be free standing and surrounded by an open-space barrier. The classical model of a town perfectly illustrates this principle. The strong g-model public buildings will be located in an area where the spaces appear to surround the buildings, because each is free standing. The strong p-model areas of the town will on the other hand be strongly contiguous and everywhere define the open space by being both adjacent and permeable to it. But this does not of course mean that the g-model buildings have fewer relations. Because there is no limit to the number of transpatial relations that can be added among a set of objects, we have moved from the situation in the beady ring settlement where p-models were much larger than g-models to a situation where g-models are much larger than p-models. Between the two poles we have the system that is strongly descriptive but not transpatial: it specifies all the spatial relations between objects, but leaves it at that.

Now with the bi-card model we can define the differences between a deterministic and a probabilistic structure, and indeed, between a more deterministic and a more probabilistic structure. A more deterministic system is one with a long g-model in relation to the number of p-models in the system, that is, a high proportion of the possible relationships is specified in the genotype as necessary to the description of the system. A more probabilistic system, on the other hand, is one with a short g-model in relation to the number of p-models in the system, that is, a low proportion of possible relationships is specified, and a large number can therefore be randomised. For a growing system this can be approximated by the simple dichotomy: short models are probabilistic, long models are more deterministic. Short models establish systems which work on *principles* of structure; long models establish systems which work on the *realisation* of structures.

Now if stability in an arrangement is defined as the reproduction of the g-model structure by description retrieval from and re-embodiment in the p-model structure, the stabilising mechanisms will vary according to whether the system is more probabilistic or more deterministic. A short model system must continually embody its principles in new events with a large equivalence class: a long model system must ensure that events conform to establish structures with a small equivalence class. This implies that the stability behaviours of the individuals composing the arrangement will also vary. For example, in a system with a long g-model in relation to its set of p-models, each syntactic event must obey many rules, including transpatial rules. The extreme case of such behaviour is what we call ritual. To be stable a strongly g-model system must control events. Events that fall outside the prescriptions of the g-model undermine the stability of the model: they obscure its structure. For a complex g-model to be retrieved as a description, extraneous events must be excluded, since they will confuse the message. Each event and each relation between events must carry as much information as possible. Therefore only the number of events required by the g-model can be allowed to take place. As a prerequisite of its functioning g-stability requires the elimination of the random. The Bororo village form perfectly illustrates the properties and problems of g-stability. In a system with so long a g-model the addition of new syntactic objects can only be carried out through the addition of relations as complex as those already in the system. Random accretion of new objects would quickly destroy the stability of the system, not only in a subjective sense of making it unintelligible, but also in the objective sense of adding objects whose locations as recorded in the bi-cards were more probabilistic than deterministic.

A p-stable, or probabilistic arrangement has the contrary properties. Consider a theoretical surface, an extended version of the Z_3 surface, generated on a computer. The general global form of this surface is shown in Fig. 121, that is, a large number of intersecting beady rings, each as individual in its form as the local configurations immediately adjacent to each primary cell, yet of the same generic type. This type of surface can be called a *polyfocal net*, since although the system taken as a whole lacks any kind of focal point, each point in the y considered as a focus sees, both in its neighbourhood and globally, the same kind of system and therefore retrieves the same kind of description. The set of local p-models for all points on the surface will form a broad equivalence class with a large degree of phenotypical variety, and so will

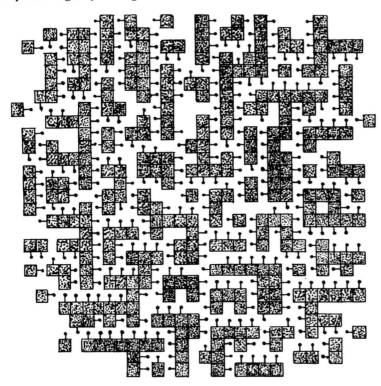

Fig. 121 A large, computer-generated 'beady ring' surface.

the beads and rings considered as the centre of higher order p-models. The description that is retrievable from any point in the system will therefore be of the same probabilistic type, but also with a great deal of local variation.

In such an arrangement each added event has relatively few rules to obey. Provided it respects the rule of local connection, the rest of its spatial relationships will be determined only by whatever local configurations happen to be available. In fact, the stable reproduction of the system will depend on there being a sufficient variety of these local configurations to embody the global descriptions of the system. Additional syntactic events must be randomised aside from the rule, since otherwise the global descriptions will not be realised and reproduced. In other words, while a g-stable system must emphasise structure, a p-stable system must equally emphasise randomness and variety in order to maintain stability in its description. Moreoever, whereas a g-stable system had to control and exclude events in order to clarify its description, a p-stable system must generate and include events in order to clarify its description. A g-stable system will, therefore, of its morphological nature tend to invest more and more order in fewer and fewer, and more and more controlled events, whereas a p-stable system will require more and more relatively uncontrolled events in order to realise its description more and more in the spatio-temporal world.

From points within the two types of system local conditions would also appear very different. A strong g-model system like the Bororo village has the important property that, as we have seen, all its local p-models (with the exception of the one drawn from the men's house') are spatially identical. But they are also transpatially identical, since in spite of each being noninterchangeable with all the others, each local model contains all the transpatial structural information present in the global system, by being required to relate in a certain way to each other object in the system. In contrast, the local models in a p-stable system need only have the minimum common structure to guarantee the consistency of the local syntactic rule, and no transpatial structure at all. Local conditions in the two types of system will therefore appear different from the point of view of control. From a point within a g-stable system boundary control would appear to be strong, whereas in a p-stable system it would appear to be weak. The latter would admit, and even require, a good deal of movement across local boundaries, and these boundaries are likely to be shifting and locally unstable, while retaining the global, statistical pattern. The former would make control of local boundaries one of the primary means by which description control was achieved. Uncontrolled movement across local boundaries would tend to destabilise, whereas in the latter case, it is an important aspect of stability.

The systems will also respond differently to the elimination of syntactic events. Random elimination even of comparatively large numbers of objects from a p-stable system will have relatively little effect on the stability of the description, provided it is large enough in the first place. A p-stable system generates, and can regenerate order simply by continuing to work. A g-stable system, on the other hand, *depends* on order embodied in the system to a greater extent, and tolerance of the random elimination of events is correspondingly low. Loss of events can damage the description of a g-stable system, since far more is invested in each syntactic event and in the spatial and transpatial relations of that event.

These basic dimensions of arrangement dynamics illustrate in principle how *pattern* and the *control of pattern* are inter-related in syntactic processes. At root the differences come down to differences in the degree to which an unfolding process is subject to genetic control. These differences of degree lead to pathways of development which appear more and more as polar opposites, or 'inversions', as the system becomes large and complex. It is as inversions that these dimensions have been frequently observed by anthropologists and sociologists. For example, Durkheim's distinction between 'mechanical' and 'organic' solidarity seems related to the differences between g-stable and p-stable pathways of growth.[6] Mechanical solidarity, predicated on identity of local models, or segments (to use the accepted term) coupled to a principally expressive form of embodiment, encapsulates the main aspects of g-stability; organic solidarity, predicated on local differences in instrumental forms of embodiment, encapsulates the main aspects of p-stability. Durkheim, of course, thought of the two forms of solidarity as inversions, and as empirical properties of societies. As such, the concepts have a heuristic rather than analytic value, since most social systems exhibit at every level both types of solidarity. Conceived of as pathways arising from differential patterns and degrees of restriction on an otherwise random process, and as internal morphological dimensions of the arrangemental model, the concepts acquire a more formal structure and, as we hope to show, analytic potential.

Just how fundamental these different pathways are to the evolution of syntactic arrangements can be even more simply illustrated. It has already been said that the two pathways arise from different kinds and degrees of restriction on the underlying random process, giving rise to radically different relations between p- and g-models. Suppose now we minimise both. First, the minimisation of both implies that p- and g-models are equal to each other. This can therefore be written: $(p = g)_{min}$. It is clear that we have in another form the formula for the least-ordered syntactic process, that is, the random process that provided the minimum set-up for an arrangement, in which each syntactic event is independent of all others that take place on the surface. If we then write $(p = g)_{max}$, then it will refer to the case where the local p-models and the g-model are the same size as each other, but as large as possible. This is exactly what was meant by a descriptive system, that is, one that contained as large a genetic spatial description as possible for that number of syntactic events, but without the addition of transpatial relations. Large village greens, ideal towns and such, all therefore belong to this pole. As many syntactic events as possible, all featuring in each others' local models in the same way, constitute a unified arrangement with a common focus.

The remaining types of surface are described by varying p and g in relation to each other. $(p > g)$ that is, 'p greater than g', implies that the set of p-relations grows larger than the prescribed g-relations, and this is the case with generative arrangements, such as the beady ring or the polyfocal net. $(g > p)$, or 'g greater than p', implies the opposite: that many more genetic relations exist in the system than spatial relations; and this is the case with a transpatial system, such as the Bororo village. It only remains to be said that, in all the elementary schemes in the generative syntax, $(p = g)$ for that number of objects.

These four polar types of system – the random, the generative, the descriptive and the transpatial – all derived from analysis of the relations between p- and g-models, can be tied back to some of the most common concepts currently in use to describe social systems. The random system itself is not, of course, so much a system as the precondition for having any kind of system at all. A generative system, on the other hand, is that least-ordering of the random system, such that a system which some describable syntactic ordering can be said to exist: that is, it characterises the most basic levels of patterning of encounters and relations that ensures that, even in the ways in which individuals ensure their biological survival and reproduce themselves, some structure is perpetuated through time which outlasts those individuals. Generation can therefore be associated with the most basic levels of production in society. Description and transpatiality are then different modes of elaborating the basic system in order to ensure the reproduction of the system. Description means, properly speaking, the *control of descriptions*. All societies have mechanisms, formal or informal, for the conscious control of descriptions. Insofar as they are open-ended and modify descriptions we call them politics; and insofar as they are concerned with the implementation of description control we call them law. In general, description control refers to what is commonly called the 'juridico-political superstructure' of a society. Transpatiality, on the other hand, refers to the other commonly acknowledged dimension: the 'ideological superstructure'. Ideology is not about the conscious control and modification of descriptions, but about the unconscious enactment of descriptions. Transpatiality means building into patterns of space and action complexes of noninterchangeable relations which ensure, through the ritualisation of life, the reproduction of the systems of categories required by that society.

The arrangemental model thus ends by reiterating commonly held views about the fundamental structuring mechanisms in societies. But it does not reiterate them in the same form. It does not, for example, require us to believe that the metaphor of base and superstructure refers to definite and separate entities. It shows them to be only different modalities for handling the reproduction of society, hardly more, in fact, than different forms of emphasis inherent in the need for the most elementary relations of the discrete system to reproduce themselves.

7

●●

The spatial logic of encounters: a computer-aided thought experiment

SUMMARY

The argument then proceeds by showing that, using this framework, a naive computer experiment can generate a system with not only some of the most elementary properties of a society, but also requiring some of its reproductive logic. These simple initial ideas are then extended to show how certain fundamental social ideas, especially that of class, may be given a kind of spatial interpretation through the notion of differential solidarity – it being argued that spatial form can only be understood in relation to social solidarities. Furthermore it must first be understood that societies are never one single form of solidarity but relations between different forms of solidarity. Space is always a function of these differential solidarities.

A naive experiment

Considered as an arrangement, then, spatial order can begin to acquire some markedly sociological and semantic properties. Aspects of what we might be tempted to call the social meaning of space can be shown to be, after all, a matter of how relational patterns are produced, controlled and reproduced. The word meaning seems inadequate to describe such cases. It seems to be not merely a reflection of society that appears in space, but society itself.

But what is it about society that can require complexity and subtlety in its spatial order? The answer seems to require the proposition that society is of its nature in some sense a physical system. We may have already assumed as much in arguing that the physical arrangement of space by societies is a function of the forms of social solidarity. This could only be the case if social solidarities already possessed, in themselves, intrinsic spatial attributes that required a particular type of unfolding in space.

In what sense, then, could this be the case? One answer is obvious. What are visible and therefore obviously spatial about societies are the encounters and interactions of people. These are the spatio-temporal realisations of the more complex and abstract artefact that we call society. Now encounters and interactions seem to exist in some more or less well-defined relation to physically ordered space. The observation that this is so provides, in effect, the principal starting point for an enquiry into the relations of society and space.

Now if the spatial realisations of society are well ordered in some way, then obviously the sources of that order must be a part of whatever it is that we call society. Two definitions therefore suggest themselves: solidarities are the organising principles of encounters and interactions; and encounters and interactions are the space–time embodiment of solidarities. In other words, encounters and interactions can also be seen as a morphic language, capable of forming arrangements, and taking on their dynamic properties.

This immediately presents a serious problem for our present efforts to establish a theory of space and society. It means that, properly speaking, we need to be able to analyse the principles of different forms of social solidarity in such a way as to understand how and why they require different unfoldings in space. This is not only beyond the scope of the present work, but also beyond the capability of authors who lack the skills and concepts that anthropologists and sociologists would bring to bear on such a project. What is proposed here, however, is a little more modest and more tractable. As with space, we propose to turn the problem round and begin, not by examining solidarities and asking about how they might determine space, but by addressing ourselves once again direct to the spatio-temporal world, in this case encounter systems as we see them, and asking in theory what organising principles *could* give rise to the kinds of difference that are commonly observable. We have in mind such manifest and general differences as differences between the organisation of informal and formal encounters, differences in encounters and avoidances within and between sexes and classes, and the differences between encounter patterns in urban and non-urban societies.

Even with these more limited aims, what follows may appear a little strange, and should not be misunderstood. Because there is relatively little data available of the kind that would be needed to make a proper investigation of encounters as morphic languages, we are forced to proceed in a largely deductive way. Our aim is therefore less to establish what is the case, but what in principle can be the case. How could encounter systems acquire differential properties, such that they would have different manifestations in space? Because our aims are so limited, we may begin by a very simple, though possibly bizarre experiment, the intention of which is simply to show that even in an arbitrary and oversimplified physical representation of systems of encounters, properties may arise which in some ways are strikingly like some of those possessed by real societies. The experiment – really a computer-aided thought experiment – is therefore carried out without any regard whatsoever for the historical or evolutionary origins of human societies. We are only interested in how properties which appear to us as being social in some sense can arise in a physical system.

Suppose, for example, we interpret the 'clump' generative process for encounters by the simple procedure of substituting points and lines for spaces and contiguities as the basis for our morphic language, with points standing for individuals and lines connecting them for relations of encounter. As before, let there be two types of object: dots representing men and circles representing women; and let a line joining two objects stand for something like 'repeated encounters requiring spatial proximity'. In other words, we are interested not just in any encounters, which are assumed to be happening randomly in any case, but in encounters which are durably reproduced between individuals as a result of spatial proximity. Lines, in effect, represent encounters of which a description has been retrieved and embedded in the system.

Let the basic unit of aggregation be a man–woman dyad represented by a dot joined to a circle placed unit distance apart on a regular grid, with the line joining the dyad representing repeated encounters, perhaps of a sexual nature. (The regular grid enables the system to be represented clearly and simply, although, as with settlement generators, the outcomes do not depend on the grid – they do, however, depend on some reasonable interpretation of regular spacing, which has the effect of keeping men towards the outside of groups.) Let the rule of aggregation be that circles in dyads are joined to other circles, again placed unit distance apart, but that dots are not joined together. Instead, the positions of the dots are randomised, apart from being attached to a circle as a member of a dyad. In other words, we have completely reproduced the structure of the beady ring process, with the exception of the rule forbidding vertex joins. It might, in fact, be best to visualise the process as a spatial process, with the spaces defined by the presence of an individual.

Now let some initial dyad be labelled generation 1, then let the dyads generated immediately adjacent to generation 1 be generation 2, and so on, meaning that the lines joining circles together represent repeated encounters requiring spatial proximity between mothers and daughters. In effect, therefore, we are experimenting with a system with two kinds of relation of repeated encounters requiring spatial proximity: those between men and women, and those between mothers and daughters – but not between mothers and sons or fathers and sons.

We now have a kind of clump syntax system in which the circles behave like open cells and the dots like the closed cells. The initial stages of a typical computer experiment are shown in Fig. 122, and a much later stage in Fig. 123. One of the effects of this system is that a whole new family of potential relations of

Fig. 122 The initial stages of a computer experiment in aggregating dyads.

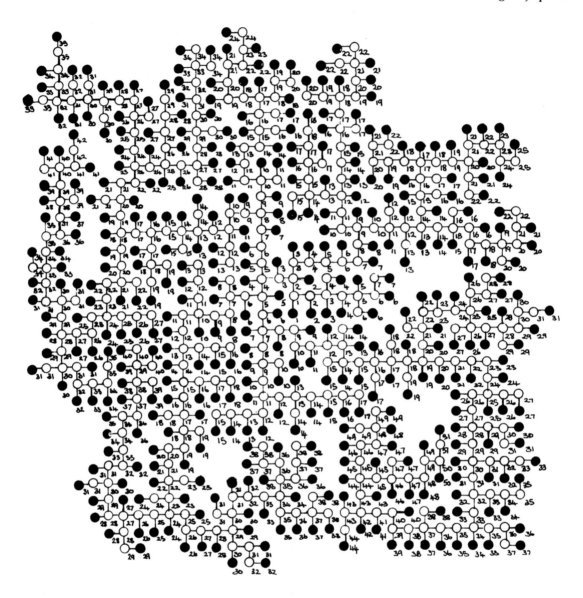

Fig, 123 A later stage of the experiment of Fig. 122.

spatial proximity has been generated, relations for which there is a perfectly normal term: *neighbours*. These proximity relations are over and above those built into the system from the outset as rules relating affinity and descent to encounter frequency; they have arisen as a spatial by-product of the physical realisation of the system – that is, they are a product of the arrangemental nature of the system. Now as we all know, relations of neighbours that arise in this way can also be the basis for repeated encounters of a durable kind, and we may therefore reasonably think of adding to the system lines representing such links if we wish to represent the whole thing as an encounter system. The arrangement ac-

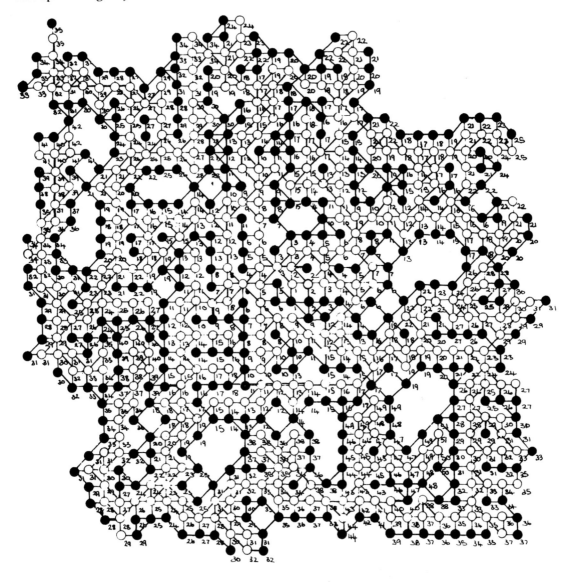

Fig. 124 Fig. 122 with neighbour relations added.

quires interesting properties as soon as we bias the selection of these neighbours in favour of contacts within the sexes rather than between the sexes – you might say that we have allowed sexual jealousy to play a role in restricting the durability of neighbour contacts between the sexes but not those within the sexes. If we add to the system all lines joining immediately within-sex neighbours for both men and women then the result is Fig. 124.

If we then disentangle the male and female components of the system and print them out first separately, then together, but without 'marriages', certain interesting morphological trends appear, in particular, that both locally and globally women's

Fig. 125 The women's
network of Fig. 124.

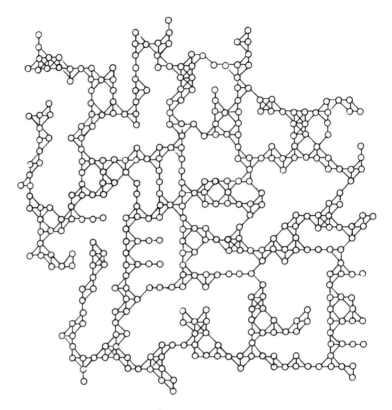

Fig. 126 The men's
network of Fig. 124.

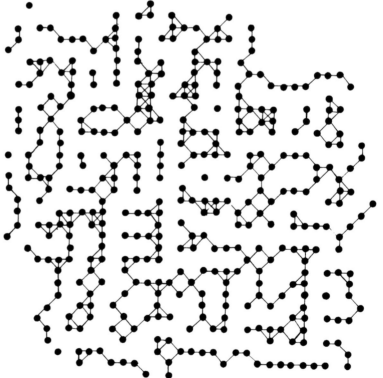

networks are, as we would expect, denser, ringier, and more symmetric than men's, while men's networks are both sparser and tend to form isolated, or near-isolated islands. (Fig. 125, 126 and 127). In other words, a uniform underlying generative process can produce, quite systematically, *differential encounter patterns* for the two label groups constituting our initial dyads. If we then refer these differences back to the analysis of p- and g-models, then a significant possibility appears: that differential encounter patterns would, if the system was to reproduce itself, have to be associated with differential principles of behaviour to reproduce the different sets of relations in the system. In other words, even at this level, we can generate the possibility of differential solidarities for men and women as part of the same system.

Of course there is an obvious objection to all this: we have forgotten about mortality. We have been dealing with a system tens of generations deep, which is of course absurd. However, it is a simple matter to reduce the total model to succesive generation bands, and when we do so some more interesting properties of the system are revealed. Fig. 128 takes four generation bands for each generation up to generations 6–9, showing three maps for each: women only, men only, and women and men with 'marriages', the last being the full system at that point. Fig. 129(a)–(f) then extends this in larger jumps up to generations 21–4. Fig. 130 summarises certain numerical data for this series.

Fig. 128 The growth of
men's and women's
networks, separately and
together, in four-generation
bands.

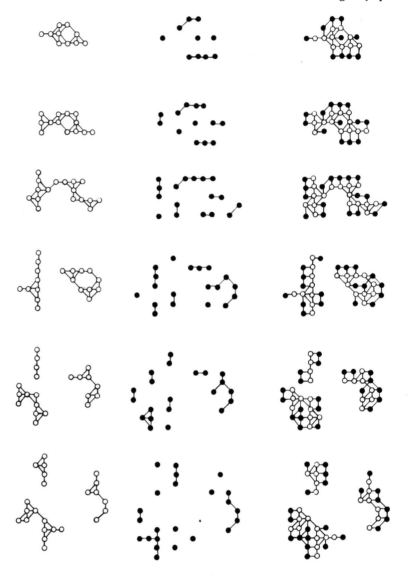

The series shows certain very marked trends. First, spatial
groups form at an early stage, divide and re-form of their own
accord. Second, women's groups are larger, fewer, and internally
denser, while men's groups are smaller, more numerous, and
internally sparser. This means that, insofar as men and women
form conjoint groups, women are 'stronger' in them, in the sense
that their encounter densities are much greater. For example, the
percentage of women who are members of at least one 'triangle'
remains above 70%, whereas that for men dwindles rapidly to
single figures. Third, the size of the women's groups tends to
decline rather than increase as they diffuse to cover a larger area,
while the size of the men's groups stays more or less the same.

These are interesting properties, but they are still purely spatial. We have yet to add a transpatial dimension by allowing points in the system to have labels. In fact, each point is already labelled: with a generation number. Suppose descriptions are retrieved of these. It can easily be seen that relatively few generation-mates are also neighbours. From any point in the system, male or female, retrieving a description of a generation set means recognising a group that is locally represented by a few members but which is constituted largely across space. Without adding anything at all to the system, the objective conditions exist to retrieve descriptions of generation sets as transpatial groupings with representatives in each local complex. In other words, we have already an arrangement with both spatial and transpatial groups.

Suppose we then extend the scope of description retrieval in the system by allowing it to apply to another property: the lines of descent from some particular ancestor. Suppose, for example, that each of the circles of generation 4 is given a different label, and these labels are transmitted to descendents as part of their local descriptions. Note that in adding labels nothing new and extraneous has been introduced into the system. Lines of descent are perfectly objective properties of the system. But strangely enough, in spite of their 'objectivity' they become of morphological interest chiefly because they appear differently in the descriptions of different components of the system when considered as a self-reproducing arrangement. By this we mean, very simply, that for the circles, that is the women, the description of the descent label is automatically correlated with at least some repeated encounters in the local group, and the label can therefore be said to be embedded in and re-affirmed by normal encounters; whereas for the dots, or men, the descent label is not correlated with encounters, and will therefore only be reproduced if some extra description is added to the system. If such a label is introduced for the men then two further points of interest arise. First, it will be a matrilineal label – that is, it will label men according to their line of descent through their mothers – in spite of being a mechanism for reinforcing the male component of the system; and second, it will be a transpatial label, in that the members of the label group are more likely to be dispersed in a number of spatial groups than to be densely present in a few. In other words, we have a system in which not only would encounter patterns differ between men and women, but so also would the principles of within-sex solidarity. Men would require more transpatial encounters and a stronger local g-model in order to reproduce a level of description which for women arose through a relatively localised p-model system.

Now this might appear to put women in a relatively weaker – because more localised – position than the men, given the same amount of description in the system for both sexes, were it not for certain other features of the system that can arise equally objec-

Fig. 129 The growth
process of Fig. 128 taken at
3 points up to generations
21–4.

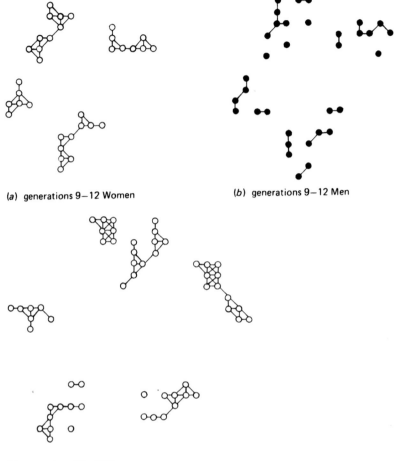

(a) generations 9–12 Women   (b) generations 9–12 Men

(c) generations 15–18 Women

(d) generations 15–18 Men

Fig. 129 (cont.)

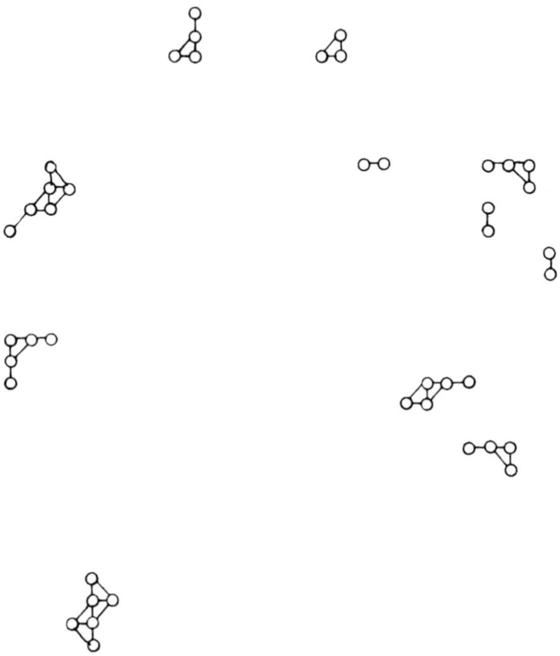

(e) generations 21–24 Women

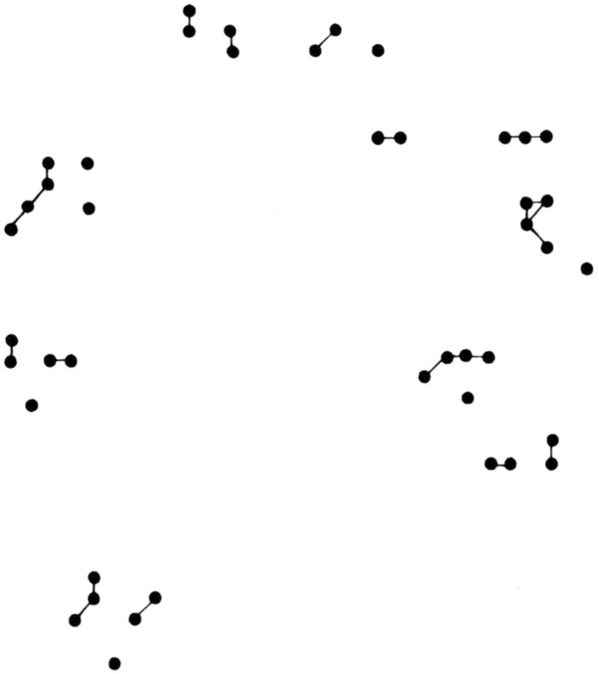

(f) generations 21–24 Men

Genera-tion band	No. of dyads	No. of clumps			Average clump sizes			Mean RA of points		Mean RR of points		
								●	○	○—●	●	○
1–4	10	1	1	5	10	10	2	0.244	0.160	0.371	0	0.467
2–5	13	1	1	6	13	13	2.2	0.161	0.225	0.312	0	0.381
3–6	17	1	1	7	17	17	2.4	0.234	0.184	0.302	0	0.310
4–7	19	2	2	8	9.5	9.5	2.4	0.274	0.197	0.288	0	0.283
5–8	21	3	3	8	7	7	2.6	0.306	0.218	0.341	0.126	0.271
6–9	23	3	3	11	7.7	7.7	2.1	0.295	0.216	0.271	0.075	0.294
9–12	34	4	4	14	8.5	8.5	2.4	0.272	0.201	0.328	0.059	0.336
12–15	5	7	7	19	7.3	7.3	2.7	0.287	0.204	0.326	0.036	0.336
15–18	58	7	9	22	8.3	8.3	2.6	0.241	0.193	0.280	0.057	0.324
18–21	53	9	11	24	4.8	4.8	2.2	0.347	0.227	0.263	0	0.346
21–4	43	9	11	21	4.8	4.8	2.0	0.363	0.240	0.271	0.019	0.372

Fig. 130 Numerical data for the experiment shown in Figs 122–9.

tively. Take for example the three women's groups in generations 5–8. The two groups on the left side both share a common ancestor in that both are immediately descendant from the same generation 4 circle. In other words, these two groups have a transpatial identity as groups, which can only be reinforced by the internal spatial and transpatial solidarity of the groups. The right-hand group, on the other hand, has the contrary property: it is descended from two ancestors, the merging having been produced by the tendency of the women's transgenerational networks to form rings. In other words, we have a local system that reproduces locally the description of two lines of descent, both of which are also likely to be reproduced elsewhere. The effect of both of these phenomena will be to shift the women's system in the direction of a noncorrespondence system in which p-model solidarity is naturally extended across space from one local group to another by linking categories together. The polyfocal net effect is, as it were, created at two levels not one: not only will the internal relations within the local group tend to take that form, but so also will the more global relation across space between local groups and sub-groups.

Societies as encounter probabilities

All these arguments, however, are purely formalistic and clearly depend on physical conditions that are unlikely to be realised. All we have shown is that social-type structures can in principle arise naturally in an arrangemental system. To explore this approach to modelling solidarities further and make it more lifelike, let us assume not that well-defined networks and spatial groups exist, but only that on a surface composed of a number of individuals there is a certain probability that subsets of individuals tend to group their encounters more with each other than with others. This will have the effect of dividing the surface up into a series of what might be called *semi-islands* with denser relations within the semi-islands than between them. The degree to which differential rates of encounter occur within, as opposed to between islands may be assigned as a probability attached to the restriction that produces the semi-island in the first place. Semi-islands will approach full islands, entirely separated from other islands, when the probability of within-island encounters approaches 1. 'Semi-islandness' will disappear altogether as the within and between probabilities converge.

If in this system we take the point of view of any individual, the field of encounters will be divisible into two kinds: first, intra-semi-island encounters, which occur with relatively high frequency and in a dense way, in that there is likely to be not only an encounter between a and b and between b and c, but also between a and c within a reasonable time-span; and second, inter-semi-island encounters, which are less frequent and sparser in that, if the individual a of A semi-island encounters b of B, and b of B encounters c of C, then the probability of an encounter between a of A and c of C within a reasonable time-span is much lower due to the relative infrequency of inter-island encounters.

Considered from the point of view of the arrangemental dynamics, and particularly from the point of view of the stability of the arrangement, some interesting consequences follow from the very nature of this arrangement. As has already been suggested, the intra-semi-island encounter set will not require a strong g-model since the local field of encounters is, by the arguments already advanced, dense and rich enough to work on p-model stability, provided it is big enough and provided the encounter rate is maintained. But the inter-semi-island encounter system, being sparser, is less likely to be workable on the basis of p-model stability. It would follow from this that there might well be a general tendency for intra- and inter-semi-island encounter sets to tend to different poles: the intra-set would be maintainable on the basis of p-model stability and would not therefore, other things being equal, need to introduce strong g-model ordering; whereas to the extent that the system as a whole, that is, as a set of semi-islands, retained a stable description across space, the inter-semi-island encounter set would tend towards more structure, that is, towards extending the scope of the g-model.

This is, of course, really an elaborate way of saying that there are formal reasons for expecting social relations to become more formal as they become less frequent; and this has again, other things being equal, an obvious spatial reference, in that the high frequency and density of encounters within the semi-island could follow only from spatial compression unless there were restrictions or rules preventing it; and likewise the relative infrequency and sparseness of encounters in the inter-semi-island set could follow from spatial distance. It might even be reasonable to think of dense encounter sets as spatial groups and the sparse encounter set as a transpatial group, regardless of the degree to which they form a separate group. We can expect that spatially organised encounter sets, wherever we find them, will tend to be p-model, that is, lacking in strong formal order and relatively unrestricted, and that transpatially organised encounter sets, wherever we find them, will tend to be g-model, that is, more selective, more formal and more structured.

This suggests that one of the principal dimensions of variability of social existence may be founded on considerations that are at once formal and spatial. On the one hand, there is a natural correlation between the spatial and p-stability, giving rise to the concept of intimacy, and behaviour that is normal in an everyday, practical sense, rather than 'normative' in the sense of being concerned to re-affirm global categories of the society; on the other hand, there is the natural correlation between the transpatial and g-stability, giving rise to the concept of ceremony, and behaviour that is normative rather than merely normal. This duality need be founded on nothing more metaphysical than the relative encounter rates at different physical distances, given also the need to maintain the social system at both a local and a more global level. It is a consequence of the fact that societies are, after all, special kinds of physical systems: more precisely, perhaps, strategies to overcome their physical nature. If societies by their very existence have overcome space, in that a coherent object is constructed out of entities that remain spatially discrete, then they also acquire structure through the means available to overcome space at different levels. Fundamental properties of societies can in this way be seen as products of the underlying model of what a society is, rather than in terms of some hypothetical set of psychological predispositions.

This basic relation between space and society has often been observed by anthropologists. One of the most explicit versions is that of Elman R. Service in his introductory text to the study of the evolution of primitive societies. Speaking of the central Australian Aborigines he writes:

Those very central Australians who have such a formalised and explicit social organisation in all aspects are those whose demographic arrangements of residential groups is the most variable by season and year, whose membership is ordinarily the most scattered and whose association is the most fortuitous . . . A further interesting characteristic is that a regular progression from the rich, rainy, coastal areas with their large and

relatively sedentary social groups to the desert interior with its widely
scattered, small, wandering population is equally a progression from
least formality and complication in the former to the *greatest* in the latter
area . . . When subsistence factors cause band members to be widely
scattered so that the residental factor is weak then the band comes to be
more like a sodality with insignia, mythology, emphasis on kinship
statuses and so on, which make the band a more coherent and cohesive
unity.[1]

An economic basis for the duality is suggested by Wolf, among
others, through his distinction between the 'caloric minimum',
that is, the extent to which the products of human labour are
directed to the biological survival of the individual, and the
'ceremonial fund', that is the proportion of the labour product that
is given to the intensification of relationships that ensure the
continuation of society at a more global level than the basic
economic groups:

Even where men are largely self sufficient in food and goods, they must
entertain social relations with their fellows. They must, for example,
marry outside the household into which they were born and this
requirement means that they have relations with people who are their
potential or actual in-laws . . . a marriage does not involve merely the
passage of a spouse from one household to another. It also involves
gaining the goodwill of the spouse to be and of her kinfolk; it involves a
public performance in which the participants act out, for all to see, both
the coming of age of the marriage partners and the social realignments
that the marriage involves; and it involves the public exhibition of what
marriages – all marriages – ought to do for people and how people ought
to behave once they have been married. All social relations are surrounded by such ceremonial, and ceremonies must be paid for in labor, in
goods, or in money. If men are to participate in social relations, therefore,
they must also work to establish a fund against which these expenditures
may be charged. We shall call this the *ceremonial fund*.[2]

However, it is not difficult to point to cases where the simple
association of ceremony and formality – g-model intensification –
with transpatial relations does not seem to hold; for example,
cases where transpatial relations are relatively informal, and cases
where local spatial relations are highly formalised. But all is not
lost. The underlying model has further resources. To draw these
out it is best to return once again to the foundations.

The basic distinction between spatial and transpatial integration linked the two concepts together, in that spatial integration
was the pre-condition for transpatial integration – that is to say,
some means of identifying objects is prior to their formation into a
class – but also every spatial integration creates the possibility of a
transpatial integration. Thus when we form an arrangement,
creating out of what was an unarranged set of individuals a
quasi-spatially integrated complex (that is, a spatial arrangement),
then this also can be the subject of transpatial integration. Unless
the arrangement is a singularity there will be other such g-similar

(i.e. sharing the same g-model) arrangements, together with which the arrangement itself forms a comparable, though as yet un-arranged set. However, it is already the case that the constituent objects of the arrangement – the individuals – are still themselves capable of transpatial integration with individuals in other arrangements since they will still be similar to other individuals in different spatial regions, whether these individuals are likewise arranged or not. In other words, out of any arrangement we create two levels of transpatial integration: the big level of the arrange-ment itself, and the small level of the individual constituents. The formation of the larger scale set implies the formation of the smaller scale set.

However, in any such system, in addition to forming a transpa-tial unarranged set across arrangements, the individuals are also locally arranged; and since the arrangements are of a comparable type (this enables us to form them into a set in the first place), then individuals in different local arrangements will be comparable to each other by sharing comparable positions within their local arrangements. This will give rise to a form of transpatial integra-tion based not simply on membership of comparable arrange-ments, but also on comparability of local models within the arrangement. This is a transpatial integration of an altogether higher order. If transpatial integration has cognitive significance for individuals, then the more complex transpatial integrations possible by transpatially linking individuals similarly located within arrangements must be a more potent example of the same phenomenon. It is transpatial integration plus arrangement. If we allow that transpatial integration is a means by which human beings identify with each other – not yet arrangementally, but conceptually – then the more such individuals are locally arranged, and the more there is correspondence of arrangemental positions, then the stronger we may expect this transpatial in-tegration to be from a psychological point of view. Being a patriarch, for example, with its strong local model, is a more potent basis for transpatial integration with others than simply being a father.

If arrangement potentially strengthens transpatial integration from a description retrieval point of view, then this in turn potentially strengthens spatial integration within the local arrangement. Transpatial integration implies that each member of a local system will have, in addition to his local p-model, a transpatial label derived from the transpatial set. This label reinforces the local description and makes the local system work in a two-level way. Each set of local relations is, as it were, reinforced at the conceptual level by the transpatial labels in-volved. As transpatial models become stronger, local individuals and encounters become more recognisable.

Now suppose we complicate the matter a little by combining the two previous ideas, and imagine an arrangemental set-up in which the initial collection of individual men and women have higher rates of within-sex encounters than between-sex encounters. This could result, for example, from a system in which men formed co-operative hunting parties while women stayed in relatively less-mobile groups. This would have an immediate consequence according to the theory: within-group relations, that is, relations among men or relations among women, would tend to be more informal and p-model than relations between the sexes, which being sparser would tend to become more formal and more g-model.

Let us add the complication that the encounter rates within the sexes also differ on the spatial–transpatial dimension. Suppose, for example, that as a result of greater mobility, the bias in favour of intra-semi-island encounters, as opposed to the inter-semi-island encounters, was less for men than women, even allowing that both were still biased in the same direction. The implication of this would be that the relative solidarities of each of the sub-groups, within the semi-island would follow a different dynamic. Women's solidarity would become more p-model, men's less so; the former because women's encounter sets would be realised to a higher degree within the domain of the semi-island, the latter because men's would be realised more outside it, and would therefore be more diffused and sparser. In this case, differential encounter ratios on the spatial–transpatial dimensions for different sub-groups of individuals would be expected to lead to divergent principles of description retrieval for the two groups.

The control and nature of descriptions in arrangements has already been associated with what we normally call politics. Here we have differential descriptions and differential principles of embodiment and retrieval for the two sub-groups of individuals in the society. In our hypothetical society the solidarity of women is achieved initially within the spatial group through encounters that are dense and normal rather than sparse and normative, and its stability arises in a p-model way. Women's solidarity then diffuses across space through the polyfocal net of category relations, creating a two-level system that will work homogeneously provided the category relations across space are also realised in a p-model way – that is, provided women are reasonably mobile.

Men's more 'clubby' solidarity, in contrast, is founded initially more in the transpatial domain, through encounters that are sparser and normative, and it stabilises in a g-model way. It will then generate as a two-level system to the extent that the transpatial solidarities are allowed to diffuse locally, by forming local collections or 'clubs'. Women's solidarity, therefore, by its very formal nature would emphasise non-exclusiveness, growth, and easy access and egress, whereas men's solidarity would, of its very nature, emphasise exclusiveness, restriction, symbolic ordering, and controls on access and egress.

It is then the basic dialectics of the process that the penetration of 'normativeness' and the g-model ordering into the spatial domain, that is, in this case into the domain of women's p-model solidarity and normalness, will weaken women politically and strengthen men; whereas the extension of p-model ordering and normality into the transpatial domain will strenthen women politically and weaken men. Likewise the reduction of the size of the spatial group will make g-model penetration into the spatial domain more likely; whereas expansion of the spatial group will make p-model penetration into the transpatial domain more likely.

Thus by considering encounter systems as arrangements, we can in a fairly natural way arrive at a system with *differential solidarities* for men and women, that is with women being members of a local-to-global system in which kin and neighbourhood relations are used both to create strong local groups and also to project wider networks across space; and men being members of more contrived associations or clubs that are realised to a greater or lesser extent in the local system. The degree to which either system succeeds in being a two-level system is likely to be an index of the strength of the solidarity. For women, localisation is weakness; for men the failure to find a local realisation is weakness. Inequalities will exist to the extent that one is a more powerful two-level solidarity than the other.

Differential solidarities seem to us to be a very general property of societies. It is also a property that is of fundamental importance for the understanding of space, since space is likely to be ordered in the image of a relation between solidarities, whether this is a relation of inequality or equality. This is no less true of contemporary societies, and other class societies, than it is of simpler societies, where the relation between male and female solidarities is perhaps the dominant force shaping space.

This is because class relations can themselves be seen, for the purpose of spatial and arrangemental analysis, as to do with differential solidarities. From the point of view of spatial arrangement, a class society might be held to exist when subsets of individuals dependent on the same productive basis have differential forms of solidarity, and these different solidarities are realised to a radically different degree through the expropriation of the ceremonial fund in the interests of description of one solidarity rather than the other. In other words, a dominant class will realise the description of its forms of solidarity to a greater degree than a dominated class, and this superior description will inevitably involve a larger spatial scale, and a stronger local model. The technique of ascendancy will then be to maximise one description and minimise the other, thus involving space pervasively in the dialectics of inter-class relations.

Spatially this will mean that a dominating class will always seek to use space to reduce the degree of arrangement of the dominated class, principally by fragmenting it into as small groups as possible, while maximising the spatial scope of its own network. Thus under some circumstances the relation of men and women could itself be seen as a class relation. Differential solidarities, it would seem, are at once part of the means by which groupings of individuals form themselves into that larger system that we call society, and also the means by which that global system is unbalanced by the formation of those global inequalities that we call social classes. However, whatever form they take, differential solidarities are a crucial component of spatial order: the form this relation takes is a major clue to the spatial nature of real societies.

8

••

Societies as spatial systems

SUMMARY

These concepts are then applied to certain societies whose spatial form is well documented, following which a general theory of the different spatial pathways required by different types of social morphology is sketched. The aim of this theory is to try to relate the existing, well-known evidence into a coherent framework as a basis for further research, rather than to establish a definitive theory.

Some societies

With these concepts in mind, we may now look briefly at a number of societies that differ strongly both in terms of the way they order space, and in terms of their spatial logic as social systems. Obviously, within the scope of this book, this cannot be an exhaustive exercise. All we can do at this stage is to take a number of well-known cases where authors have described spatial properties of societies in such a way that they can be transcribed into the concepts we have used. In doing so we are, of course, adding nothing to the findings of these authors. We are merely using their work to show that the arrangemental model can provide a means for moving from social commentaries to analysis of spatial form. We may begin with the two well-known ethnographies: Fortes[1,2] on the Tallensi of Northern Ghana, who live in dispersed compounds; and Turner[3] on the Ndembu of Northern Zambia, who live in small circular villages.

Tallensi compounds differ considerably in size and complexity, but always are based on a strong underlying model, which can be seen in the gamma map of the simpler of the two compounds shown in Fig. 131.

Globally the compound is governed by a sequence of spaces from the carrier to the heart of the compound. The first of these is a space immediately outside the entrance, marked by a shade tree and ancestor fetishes. The second, immediately inside the entrance, is a cattle yard, with but one dwelling giving onto it, that of the headman. This is the headman's personal space, although he rarely uses it other than to keep possessions in. More important, the hut is also said to be the dwelling of the headman's ancestor

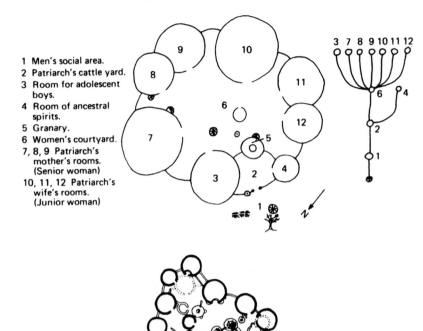

1 Men's social area.
2 Patriarch's cattle yard.
3 Room for adolescent boys.
4 Room of ancestral spirits.
5 Granary.
6 Women's courtyard.
7, 8, 9 Patriarch's mother's rooms. (Senior woman)
10, 11, 12 Patriarch's wife's rooms. (Junior woman)

Fig. 131 Simple and complex Tallensi compounds, after Fortes and Prussin.

spirits. Both the space outside and the space inside the compound entrance are strongly identified with males, and this identification is in both cases supported by strong transpatial categories, in one case the ancestor fetishes, in the other the ancestor spirits. Only by passing through this sequence of spaces can one arrive at the first space identified with women, and this is invariably the sub-compound of the senior wife. Just as the male courtyard is the most powerful space governing inside to outside relations, so the senior wife's sub-compound is the most powerful space governing inside to inside relations, in that at this point the compound changes from a unipermeable sequence form to a tree form. In effect then, relations of men to women are governed by the outside to inside sequence form, and relations among women are governed by the internal tree form. Noninterchangeability is added to this asymmetric nondistributed tree structure in that, as the compound expands towards the more complex form, the domains of individual wives have a specific location in the compound according to seniority. Various hierarchical social practices – one must greet the senior wife first on entering the women's domain – are associated with this noninterchangeability in the space, just as others – the women cook and eat as separate nuclear groups rather than co-operatively – are associated with the segregative tree syntax itself. The granary is the focal point of the compound, coming between the men's and women's domains. Powerful sanctions govern the dispensing of grain, however, and women may not do it independently of the headman. The word for compound and for the people in it are the same word in the Tale language, and strong rituals and beliefs govern the location of houses in relation to the ancestors of the headman. When sons set up their own households – the Tallensi are both strongly patrilineal and patrilocal – the same basic spatial pattern is followed, initially by adding a new section with its own entrance to the parental compound, but later, marking full independence, independent of the parental compound, though probably still in the same vicinity. The cultural investment in the compound, and also in the locality, is aided by strongly developed beliefs and ritual practices attaching individual lineages to specific locations.

However, in spite of the strong spatiality of the Tallensi culture and religion, there is little spatial organisation visible above the level of the compound. On the contrary, the compounds appear to be spread across the landscape in a completely random array, as Fig. 132 shows. Two factors mitigate this, both difficult to perceive in a purely visual way. First, although the compounds are randomly clustered in a particular region, sub-groups of compounds are identified as settlements and distinguishable from each other, just as the compounds are, by intervening no man's land; and there is also a similar sub-clustering of small groups of

Fig. 132 Tallensi landscape, after Prussin.

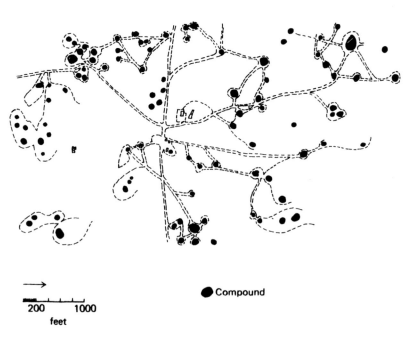

200   1000
feet

● Compound

compounds within this on a close kinship basis. In syntactic terms, this is of course a 'cluster of clusters of clusters'. Second, there are also cluster-type dual spaces located somewhere in the landscape with respect to each cluster, for at least two, and possibly all three cluster levels. These dual objects are shrines, and indicate a strong tendency to project major ritual practices and congregations 'into the landscape' and away from living areas.

Socially speaking, the Tallensi form a hierarchical lineage system, and 'every minimal lineage is a segment of a more inclusive lineage defined by reference to a common grandfather, and this in turn is a segment of a still wider lineage, defined by reference to a common great-grandfather'.[4] This formal principle for organisation is represented in ancestor rituals, where: 'sacrifices to the shrine of his ancestor require the presence of representatives of every segment of the next lower order; and this rule applies to all corporate action of a ceremonial or jural kind of any lineage'.[5] This elaborate lineage system, with its strongly asymmetric (though distributed) structure is mapped strongly onto the landscape, giving a conceptual ordering of space that is highly developed, and in complete contrast to the apparent random scatter of the settlement form.

Among the Ndembu the most prominent spatial unit is the village, not the compound; in fact below the level of the village itself, there is no physical ordering of space to speak of, only single cell huts (Fig. 133).

With the open-sided men's hut in the centre of a group of rather casually placed huts the village is, like the Bororo village (Fig. 30), a dual Z_5 form, and this is invariant in spite of considerable geometric variation in the placing of huts, and in their numbers. In addition to the concentric structure, articulating an opposition between men and women, there is also a diametric division separating and opposing adjacent generations, though also joining alternate generations, in that the great-nephews of the founders build their huts in the gaps between the senior generation's huts, rather than adjacent to their mother's brothers on the other side. There are a number of hunting shrines near the periphery of the central space, mostly concentrated in front of the headman's house. Ritual sanctions warn women not to approach too closely to these shrines. The men eat in the central hut; women and children on the periphery.

Superficially the Ndembu village appears to be a case where the ideal of a correspondence between social and spatial structure is achieved. In fact, according to Turner, nothing could be further from the case. Ndembu society generally, and its dominant spatial manifestation, the village, in particular, is characterised by high instability. So far as their personnel are concerned, most villages are relatively temporary affairs. Admittedly the Ndembu ideal is a

Fig. 133 Ndembu village,   Plan of Mukanza village
                after Turner.

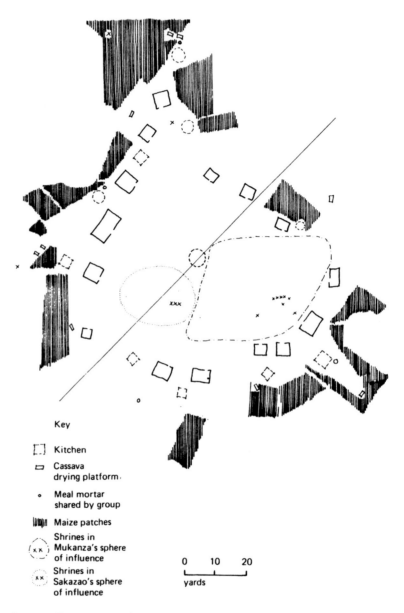

Key

⟦⟧ Kitchen

⌂ Cassava
      drying platform,

o Meal mortar
      shared by group

⟦⟧ Maize patches

Shrines in
(ₓ ₓ) Mukanza's sphere
      of influence

Shrines in
(ₓ ₓ) Sakazao's sphere
      of influence

0   10   20

yards

large village, several generations deep, but in practice this hardly
ever occurs. There are structural reasons for this. Ndembu society
is matrilineal – maternal decent, traced from mother's brother to
sister's son, giving prior right to residence, succession to office
and inheritance of property – but also avunculocal – women go to
live with their husbands, who themselves have moved at puberty
from their natal village to that of their mother's brothers. However, in spite of avunculocal residence, the matrilineal principle

ensures that the strongest grouping in the society tends to be the uterine sibling group. It is this group that normally founds a village, and it is the same group that often fissions from an existing village. There is a very high divorce rate among the Ndembu: women go back to their brothers, taking their children with them. Since descent is matrilineal, the ties of mother and child, and of that group back to the mother's sibling group in another village, are stronger than the ties of father to child, and stronger also than the residential ties that group the family together in the paternal village. The result is a society with a high degree of mobility of personnel among villages.

Socially speaking, this mobility and tendency to break up is the dominant principle, in total contrast to the Tallensi with their elaborate lineage system erected on a strongly territorial basis. The Ndembu do have a level of spatial organisation above that of the village, the vicinage, but it is as unstable and as variable in its composition and personnel as the village itself. However, Turner's conclusion regarding the relation between the local and global level of the society is clear, and repeated several times throughout his text: 'Conflicts which split sub-systems tend to be absorbed by the widest social system and even to assist in its cohesion by a wide geographic spreading of ties of kinship and affinity.)[6] Or: (We have also noticed how the unity of the widest political unit, the Ndembu people, gains at the expense of its significant local unit, the village . . . fission and mobility, while they break up villages interlock the nation.'[7] On the mechanics of fission Turner is even more explicit: 'After the feelings of animosity associated with the initial breach have died down, each has a special claim on the hospitality of the other, the members of both exchange long visits, and each may serve in turn as the basis of the other's hunting expedition.)[8]

The contrast we hope to draw is now becoming clear. The Ndembu represent the type of case where the social mechanisms ensure that the transpatial encounter rate is maximised in a p-model way. The high degree of mobility in the population ensures a high rate of direct, relatively improvised contact between individuals and sub-groups living in different semi-islands. The semi-island effect is therefore minimised; and as the formal theory predicts, the strength of the transpatial g-model is correspondingly reduced. This is a case, therefore, where the p-model stability penetrates outwards from the spatial group and eats into the g-model at the inter-semi-island, or transpatial level. This is the opposite of the Tallensi where the extreme 'staticness' of the population is associated with a very high level of local development of a g-model, coupled to a strongly noninterchangeable ritual (that is ritual with a large g-model), which requires the presence of specific sets of persons to carry out specific series of actions without which the ritual will be ineffective.

Among the Ndembu, in contrast, ritual is in the main characterised by its relative openness: at least for part of most rituals
anyone may attend. Very large numbers often do, and it is made
the occasion for general eating and drinking. There is very little
relation between ritual and the lineage system; that is, the ritual
does not carry a great deal of exogenous information as it does
among the Tallensi. On the contrary: 'Ritual performed by these
cults is conspicuous for its content of dominant symbols *which
represent principles of organisation and not corporate groups.*'
(Our emphasis.)[9] This, very precisely, is what is meant by a short
g-model. The fact that Ndembu ritual normally takes place within
the village, that is, within the domain of the spatial group, while
Tallensi ritual is for the most part separated from the everyday
domain by being projected into the landscape, lends a further
spatial dimension to the contrast.

Thus ritual, as well as mobility, confirm the basic formal
tendency for Ndembu social morphology to spread p-models
outwards from the spatial to the transpatial, reducing the need for
strong g-models at the transpatial level. This was the trend that, it
was argued, would favour women more than men; and indeed in
Ndembu society, in spite of initial appearances, we find a greater
degree of equality between the sexes than among the Tallensi.
Tallensi society exhibits the inverse tendency: the g-model at the
transpatial level penetrates down into the spatial group, both
reducing its size and importing to it a strong degree of internal
ordering. This is the trend that will disadvantage women; and we
find accordingly relations between the sexes that are much more
asymmetric.

These arguments have correlates in the social system of a
syntactic kind. With the Ndembu the contradition between the
descent rule and the residence rule results in a principle of
p-model interchangeability at the transpatial level, run on a
minimal g-model, that is, the principle of matriliny. This is
associated with a lack of asymmetric ordering of the kinship
system at the transpatial level. On the contrary, the transpatial
syntax of relations between uterine sibling groups (who might
almost be seen as temporarily living apart while the women of the
group are having their children in their husband's village) is both
symmetric and distributed. If we imagine the contiguity relations
of the clump syntax being drawn out into imaginary filaments
running across the landscape, then a syntactic homology can be
seen; the syntax of matrilineal groups is a kind of highly extendible
polyfocal net, with the uterine sibling groups providing the
foci of the system. In being of the form of a polyfocal net it needs
only a short g-model, provided it tends to grow rather than shrink,
and provided a dense but informally structured encounter rate at
the transpatial level is maintained. In this sense the dominant
syntax of Ndembu society is at the inter-semi-island level. Hence

the political and ritual weakness of the superficially more-ordered village as compared to the transpatial polyfocal net.

If the Ndembu system projects a symmetric and distributed syntax into the transpatial level, the Tallensi does the opposite: it projects an asymmetric and nondistributed syntax into the local spatial group, tending to keep this small in order to keep the structure clear and controlled. There are two aspects to the argument. First, with the Tallensi the dominant political level is the largest spatially continuous group, in this case the compound itself. If this group were other than strongly ordered, then a multi-layered system could not be erected on it, since hierarchy implies noninterchangeability. The small, strongly ordered, relatively isolated group is the natural corollary of a multi-layered system. At every level, it must segregate and render its component individuals noninterchangeable in order to preserve the principles of the system. Second, the predominantly territorial nature of the lineage and clan system can be seen in a similar way, as the domination of the spatial by the transpatial. Whereas clans and solidarities are often highly spatially dispersed, thus providing a cross-cutting network of transpatial relations finding its realisation within each spatial group, with the Tallensi the system is reversed, and space at the higher level is made to serve the hierarchical, transpatial lineage system. There is a strong correspondence between transpatial category and spatial group. This then finds its expression in the dispersed clusters of the Tallensi landscape. Dispersion preserves the local g-model as the dominant morphological principle.

It might not be too far-fetched to suggest a relation between this polarity and the fundamental structure of biological kinship. In the basic biological system necessary for reproduction there are both symmetric and asymmetric relations in a precise syntactic sense: the relation of siblings is symmetric in that, other things being equal, the relation of a-sibling to b-sibling is the same as the relation of b-sibling to a-sibling; the same is true of the relation of spouses (of course we can introduce asymmetry into either, but in the pure state this is not the case), whereas the relation of parent and offspring is syntactically asymmetric: the relation of a-parent to a a-offspring is not the same, but the inverse of the relation of a-offspring to a-parent. It seems unsurprising, therefore, that the Ndembu system with its symmetric and distributed syntax is built on the basis of the symmetric sibling relation, whereas the hierarchical lineage system of the Tallensi is constructed from the asymmetric parent–child relation.

It has already been suggested that the relation of men to women can, and often does take the form of a class relation, depending on the degree to which the different principles of solidarity within each of the sexes are differentially realised by the global arrangement of the society. The Tallensi appear to be such a case. The elaborate transpatial ritual structure erected on the basis of the patriarchial homestead is almost exclusively a male domain. By means of its elaborate system of roles and offices, which penetrates every aspect of culture and much of daily life, men achieve a degree of arrangement, or solidarity, for which there is no counterpart for women. On the contrary, women remain isolated within the homestead, subject to innumerable rules and restrictions in their daily lives. To drive the point home, the wives of a given patriarch do not even form a cohesive group within the compound, in the sense perhaps of a day to day co-operation in household tasks. Instead there is rivalry, and spatial subdivision, reinforced by a hierarchical scheme of relations among them realised through noninterchangeability and correspondence. The tendency among Tallensi women is to become unarranged as a group, and by contrast arranged only with respect to their local menfolk, and then in a clearly subordinate role.

With the Ndembu, the situation differs in two critical ways. First, the ritual structure, while elaborate, is not exclusive to men. Women also participate strongly. And as would follow ritual is spatialised, strongly tends to p-models, and occurs in the village, not in some corner of the landscape. Second, the high degree of female mobility between spatial groups clearly compensates for the men's attempts to dominate the spatial group through the dominance of the hunting ideology within the village space. In this case, the basis for women's solidarity is much more closely comparable to the men's. The relation between the sexes does not therefore tend to become a class relation in the sense in which we have defined it.

Now let us consider a third, again very different example: the segment of the Hopi society living in the pueblo of Oraibi at the time of the map made by Mindeleff (Fig. 134).[10] The map shows the physical layout of the settlement (though without the tiered structure rising from the ground-plan) and the physical distribution of the clans (localisation of *gentes*). At the level of the clan (as also at the level of the 'phratry' which groups clans together, mainly for ceremonial purposes) the arrangement is a singularly clear instance of the principle of noncorrespondence, in that each clan occupies a series of sites dispersed without discernible order throughout the settlement. Now from the point of view of the encounter system, clans have three important attributes. First, they are often the official holders of land and various important practical and ceremonial rights; second they are an important medium through which the extensive ceremonial life of the pueblo is conducted; and third, a principle of classifactory kinship applies within a clan, so that any individual will have mothers, brothers, and so on in all parts of the settlement. This has the effect that the transpatial system is constantly generating a larger network of encounters and reinforcing them with affective

Fig. 134 The pueblo of
Oraibi, after Mindeleff.

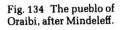

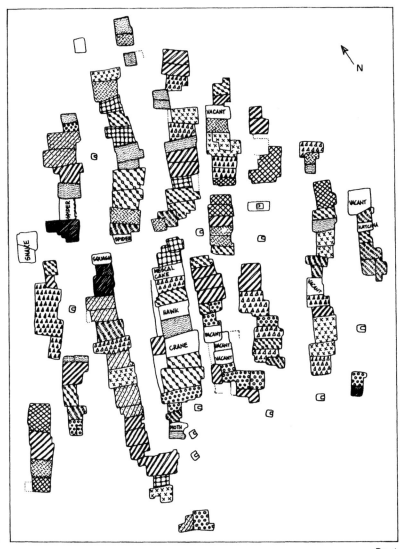

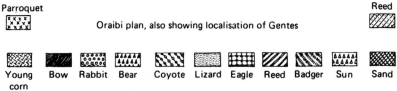

ties and practical constraints. The relations of the spatial and
transpatial system in effect tend to globalise the encounter system,
and create encounter density at the level of the settlement as a
whole. The same of course applies to relations between settlements, since each clan is represented in at least two and usually
several villages.

The local clan groups shown on the map are matrilineages,

usually made up of three or four households, each consisting of six or seven persons. The household is defined by the presence of a husband – obviously from another matrilineage, and indeed from another phratry – and the core membership of the matrilineage is a group of women descended from a single immediate ancestress. The principle of classifactory kinship also applies locally, and it may be expected that it will be reinforced by the frequency of contact within the local encounter space. The local encounter space of the matrilineage women is therefore very durable, but there is *not* a fixed association between a matrilineage and a position in the settlement. On the contrary, the local configuration constantly changes as matrilineages grow and shrink.

Since space and category are also interchangeable at the local level, then the transpatial category is not part of the g-model for the settlement. At both spatial and transpatial levels, therefore, the socio-spatial system constituted by Oraibi is distributed (each group is constituted equally by several different but equal sites), symmetric (the principle of classificatory kinship is the addition of symmetric components without the addition of rules of structure), noncorresponding between spatial groups and transpatial categories, and p-model at both levels, in that the system works in a dense rather than controlled way at both levels. The system is in fact a very clear version of the two-level polyfocal net postulated earlier as the elementary form of global arrangement.

Two important aspects of the encounter system of Hopi society can, we believe, be clarified as necessary consequences of these morphological principles. The first is the relative equality between men and women; and the second, the prevalence at every level of *mixing mechanisms* outside the relatively short g-model for the two-level polyfocal net. The two are interconnected. Mixing mechanisms are social practices that have the effect of multiplying the number and range of encounters generated by a particular arrangement. For example, classificatory kinship is a mixing mechanism, but so also is the habit of male clan dancers to dance in all the kivas of the other clans; and so also is the Hopi habit of eating household meals close to the open doorway of the house so that people passing can also take part in the meal. Even the fact that much of Hopi ceremony is carried out within the system of public spaces of the pueblo can be seen as a mixing mechanism. There are are also ceremonies and aspects of ceremonies which are segregated and hidden from the more general view, but we may associate this smaller range with the g-model component of the system, and the public ceremonies with the – even more important – p-model dimension. The presence of mixing mechanisms in a society always has the same morphological principle behind it: to maximise the system of encounters at both the spatial and transpatial levels, in order to make the system work on p-stability rather than g-stability.

The relative equality of the sexes results from the workings of this principle at both the spatial and transpatial levels. Women dominate the solidarity of the spatial group, while men dominate the transpatial groups. However, the fact that the system runs by the expansion of the dense encounter zone from the local to the global level – this is what a p-model system essentially is – means that the spatial solidarity and the transpatial solidarity are of comparable strength. Although there is differential solidarity between men and women (men are strangers in their spatial groups, but associate with each other in clan kivas), the two domains are closely tied together by the general p-model principle, which is the principle of a spatial group. Thus the women's form of solidarity prevails throughout the system, even though men do have a strong hold on ceremonial life. It would seem natural, within this framework to see the extraordinary intensity of collective ceremonial life among the Hopi as a means of making the p-stability effective at the global level, by maximising the global encounter system within and between individual villages.

Thus, in almost every respect, the Hopi are unlike the Tallensi, and morphologically the most basic of these differences is that the Tallensi are a correspondence society while the Hopi are a noncorrespondence society. The contrast with the Ndembu is more subtle. In both there is a relative equality of the sexes because the differential principles of solidarity between men and women are more or less equalised. But with the Ndembu the women have the advantage at the transpatial level, through a women-centred density in the global network realised through the high divorce rate and the matrilineal principle. Among the Hopi the women have the advantage at the local level, primarily through the matrilocal principle and the extension of the women-based spatial group as the foundation of the global system. Thus the Ndembu men order their space in a rather strong local g-model, with local sanctions against women; but these are rather ineffective, since the women's transpatial solidarities enable them to be relatively free of local sanctions from the men. In contrast the Hopi order a settlement which is highly distributed and highly open, with minimally complex dwellings, this being the ideal form for maximising p-model probabilistic local encounter networks and realising p-stability. Thus Ndembu women are weak locally and strong globally, and are matrilineal, meaning that the women's focus is transpatial rather than spatial; whereas the Hopi women are strong locally but are weaker globally, through the spatial matrilocal principle.

These examples suggest that it is useful to make a clear distinction between the *morphological*, or *arrangemental*, principles of a society and the actual *social and spatial mechanisms* by which these principles are realised. This permits a form of comparison, and a means of identifying similarities and differences that is at once more concrete than the customary method, and more abstract, since it deals with the dynamic principles behind particular structures, not simply the comparison of the structures themselves. Take, for example, the forms of community reported in the East End of London by Wilmott and Young and others.[11] Although the relationship between mothers and daughters is crucial in the construction of social networks in these communities, there is no question of rules of matrilocality or matriliny, any more than there are formal clans or phratries. Using the arrangemental method, however, it can be shown that even without these strong rules, nevertheless the system resembles the type of two-level polyfocal net, with its characteristic p-stability, that characterises the Hopi. The encounter space of an individual in this system has a very dense local network, which includes some kin, but also a large number of others who are familiar only through proximity and frequent contact. The kinship system, comparable in its scope to the local matrilineage in the Hopi community, in this instance works transpatially, rather in the manner of the clans in Oraibi, although of course much less formally and much less strongly. Nevertheless, the essential function of the kin network is to create encounters at a larger scale than the immediate locality, where the mix of kin and neighbours prevail equally. As a result, an individual will encounter the local network of kin at a relatively greater distance. The system is therefore always tending to grow towards the larger system, as with the Hopi, rather than to consolidate the local group.

The two systems can also be compared on the ceremonial dimension, and on the man–woman dimension. The characteristic ceremonial forms are the 'party' of all available kin, which is a transpatial event, drawing in even remote kin from outlying areas; and, on very special occasions, the 'street party', which is a spatial event linking together a local network of streets, although in a focal rather than bounding way. On the man–woman dimension again there is relative equality resulting from the more or less equal development of the women-based spatial solidarity of the local networks, spreading, using the extended kin network, to the transpatial level, and the male solidarity based on the pubs and clubs, with equally well-developed arrangements for the circulation of members through different pubs in the locality and even further through sporting encounters, and so on. The pubs are analogous to the kivas of Hopi society, in the sense that they operate not only in a localised way, but as a means of generating a higher order system.

The same type of morphological principles, though with a very different social mechanism, is illustrated by the relation between the division of labour and the wider social system in a European medieval town. Guilds are transpatial categories functioning first and foremost in a dense encounter zone in which they are necessarily mixed. In this sense they are analogous to 'dispersed clans', but more powerfully so, since the dispersion in most cases goes down to the level of the individual, rather than the local group. The transpatial categories themselves are strong systems, with rules for entry and rules for conduct. Even so, their primary function is one of making a transpatial level for the two-level polyfocal net created by the intense and spatially inter-dependent working patterns of the medieval town. The important thing is that the transpatial system is, first, defined by what happens in the primary encounter zone; and second, it is fully dispersed in the primary encounter zone. In an important, if limited sense, therefore, the medieval town also has aspects of the noncorresponding two-level polyfocal net.

According to Nakane, virtually the contrary principles appear to be the case in Japanese society.[12] Here the categoric identification is always with what she calls the 'frame' group of an individual rather than the 'attribute' group; that is, with the spatial, functionally inter-dependent group, rather than with the transpatial, or dispersed group:

A man is employed in a particular occupation and is also a member of a village community. In theory he belongs to two kinds of groups: the one, of his occupation (attribute) and the other of the village (frame). When the function of the former is the stronger an effective occupational group is formed which cuts across several villages . . . where the coherence of the village community is unusually strong, the links between members of the occupational group are weakened and, in extreme cases, the village unit may create deep divisions among members of the occupational group. This is a prominent and persistent tendency in Japanese society . . . throughout Japanese history, occupational groups such as a guild, cross-cutting various local groups and institutions have been much less developed in comparison with those of China, India and the West. It should also be remembered that a trade union in Japan is always formed primarily by the institution, such as a company, and includes members of various kinds of qualifications and specialities, such as factory workers, office clerks and engineers.[13]

This seems to be another specification of a system based on the principle of correspondence between spatial group and transpatial category, and in such cases we have come to expect that groups will be hierarchically organised, that the internal structure of groups will be hierarchical, that boundaries will be strongly maintained and that the encounter space will be penetrated by strong g-model rules of an asymmetric and nondistributed kind. According to Nakane, this is precisely the case at all levels of organisation in Japanese society. Japanese society is, she argues, based on a 'vertical principle' both at the level of the internal structure of the (relatively closed) group, or at the level of relations between groups. The vertical principle is illustrated by diagrams on the lines of Fig. 135, showing that Nakane means an asymmetric and nondistributed generator. This principle is so pervasive that,

Fig. 135

In everyday affairs a man who has no awareness of relative rank is not able to speak or even sit and eat[14]

and

a group which has neither internal hierarchical order nor the superior–inferior type of human relations still demands that its members give unilineal participation and develop their own closed community . . . if a homogeneous group adds members from outside itself or experiences external influences internal differentiation is the normal outcome. In the case of a group based on individual specialisation the addition of members with identical or similar specialisations will result in the development of vertical relationships, since . . . no two persons can occupy the same rank.[15]

The correspondence principle which, so we believe, underlies the vertical principle applies all the way through Japanese society, and even constructs the relation of household group and kinship group in a way that is virtually the opposite of the East End case:

the human relationships within this household group are thought of as more important than all other human relationships. Thus the wife and daughter-in-law who have come from outside have incomparably greater importance than one's own sisters and daughters, who have married and gone into other households.[16]

Notes towards a general theory

These pairs of contrasting examples could be multiplied, but the detailed enumeration of ethnographic cases is beyond the scope of this primarily theoretical exposition. Even so, it seems possible to suggest a limited number of generalisations linking the social logic of space to the spatial logic of society, arising partly from the evidence but also perhaps partly from the logic of the arrangemental model. One fundamental morphological generator appears, as we have said, to be the correspondence or noncorrespondence of spatial group and transpatial category. If the transpatial category corresponds to the spatial group, then the members of that group will not be arranged with others across the landscape by virtue of the existence of categories, but must be combined with others as a whole, by some kind of superordinate logic existing over and above the system of spatial groups. In such cases the boundaries of the spatial group must be strong, as must the internal structure of the group, and this implies a strong local g-model, consequently strong boundary controls, a more deterministic rather than probabalistic local encounter space, and probably a controlled and relatively exclusivist ceremonial space.

If the transpatial category and the spatial group are in a noncorresponding relation, the logic of the system works in the opposite way. Members of spatial groups are already linked across the landscape by categoric mechanisms which also ensure recognisability in the local encounter space, that is, by a logic that is already embedded in the system. The local group cannot be either strongly structured or maintain strong boundary controls, since either would work against the natural tendency of the system to be stable through the density of events in the encounter space, both at the local and ceremonial level. The p-model logic of both levels of the system requires a probabilistic, rather than a deterministic local encounter space, and a form of ceremonial that maximises the density of transpatial encounter events, and therefore tends to be inclusive rather than exclusive.

Under what circumstances do these two different pathways appear? The answer would appear to lie in the problem of *inequality* and, in particular, the form of inequality that was identified broadly as class inequality, that is, where different sub-groups — say men and women — had differential forms of solidarity and different degrees of access to the means of reproducing descriptions of the principles of solidarity. But it is not simply that the correspondence model tends to prevail in societies with such inequality and the noncorrespondence model in societies without it. It is more that the correspondence model is the means by which the inequality of groups is institutionalised, by being incorporated in a strongly controlled local g-model, such that the less privileged of the unequal partners appear to reproduce and even to desire the conditions of their own inequality. The correspondence principle, in effect, is a way of making inequality disappear, while at the same time giving it institutional form. Thus in a Tallensi compound the norms of wifely behaviour within the deterministic spatial order of the compound will in effect be a primary means by which the inequality of men and women is realised. Perhaps in a way we have uttered no more than a truism: the strategy of domination is to isolate and separate the dominated, and to establish local behavioural forms through which the system reproduces itself effortlessly.

The distinction between correspondence and noncorrespondence systems tells us something of what the system is like locally, and how it is experienced as an encounter system. But it does not offer any account of the global structure of the system, that is of the relation between social and spatial form in the fullest sense of the word. To sketch a possible way in which this relation might be made, we must take into account two more factors: first, the question of growth — how systems produce, control, and reproduce structure as they become larger; and second, the tri-partite distinction between generation, description and transpatiality, which was suggested as an approximate arrangemental counterpart of *production, politics* and *ideology*.

In brief, the argument is that if all arrangements have both discrete spatial groups and transpatial groups, then it follows that they must have both local and global types of order. As arrangements grow in size, then the global order will come to be more and more important, since there is more to be held together by that order. But there are different pathways of growth, and the different pathways require different degrees of emphasis in different dimensions of the model. The lawfulness of the relation between society and space considered globally will then be something like the lawfulness of these different pathways.

In principle, we may conceive of two fundamentally different types of growth in an arrangement. In the first type, objects – whether cells or individuals does not matter – are added to the system without increasing the size of the spatial groups; in the second, objects are added by increasing the size of the spatial groups. The first leads to a dispersed landscape; the second to a clumpy landscape. The first we might call the pathway of *transpatial growth*, since any arrangement will be concerned principally with making links across intervening space; the second, the pathway of *spatial growth*, since the links of added objects will, in the first place, be with more or less continuous aggregates. Neither will, of course, ever be free of the other. There will always be spatial groups of some size, even in the most transpatial system; and there will always be transpatial links of some kind, even in the largest spatial clump. Each type of system will, therefore, be a two-level system, with both spatial and transpatial components. Moreover, as the systems grow larger, then they can also begin to look more like each other, in that a dispersed landscape can become denser under the effects of aggregation, while a clumpy landscape will need to invest more in links between clumps as it becomes larger. The differences between the two pathways will always be differences in the degree of emphasis given to different structural principles.

According to the elementary logic of arrangements, a system on the transpatial pathway ought to tend locally to a more g-model mode of operation, implying groups that are small and structured, and a system on the spatial pathway, to a more p-model mode of operation, implying groups that are less controlled for growth and less internally structured. Expansion of the two types of system will then present different kinds of problems if the principles of each system are to be preserved. The transpatial system must have mechanisms to add new members to the structure of the local groups as they appear, and it must have mechanisms to segment, in order to prevent the local groups from becoming too large. The spatial system must increase the amount of description in the system as it grows – that is, it must ensure that the spatial aggregate has some global structure, as well as a local one – and it requires mixing mechanisms to ensure that the system does not degenerate into local g-model groups. All of these requirements, of course, assume that the system is both growing and relatively fixed to certain locations. A system that is small and mobile could operate in a more or less p-model kind of a way, in spite of relative dispersion, with mixing mechanisms and the periodic formation of larger groups.

It is, of course, the structuring of fixed space that allows both sets of requirements to be realised in the two types of expanding system. The need for strong categoric control and the need for segmentation can both be realised by using the *inside* of the boundary or, if needs be, the inside of a system of boundaries, which construct, as the system expands, a system of related and controlled categories. The need for integrating or mixing mechanisms and increased description can be realised *outside* the boundary, through the elaboration of the system of continuous external space, into a system with more axial and convex organisation as it grows. To the extent that spaces inside boundaries have categoric order, they will be more deterministic than exteriors, carrying information about who can be where, and what can occur in different locations. In contrast, insofar as an external domain is ordered, it will be a more probabilistic domain, generating more spaces and encounters than it describes. The latter is therefore a space of description retrieval, whereas the former is a space of description embodiment and enactment. The latter is akin, therefore, to the integrated space of Durkheimian organic solidarity, while the former is akin to the segmented space of Durkheimian mechanical solidarity.

The logic of the boundary is therefore to construct a different mode of arrangemental integration of its two sides: on the inside, there is the space of relations of categories, that is, of ideology: while on the outside, there is the space of generation and negotiation, or, as one might say, of politics. The latter is the space in which social relations are produced: the former, the space in which they are reproduced. Something like the 'central paradox' of space follows from this: each type of arrangemental integration, or solidarity, depends on the realisation of principles which would put the other at risk. The appearance of large numbers of unstructured events (space or encounters) in a strongly structured, or g-model system will undermine its form of stability; lack of sufficient numbers of the same types of event in a less structured, or p-model system will undermine its stability. Likewise, too much structure will undermine a p-model system, while too little will undermine a g-model system.

This socio-spatial duality is fundamental, but it is not all that exists. The system needs to operate at two levels, not one. The duality we have described so far is a property of a socio-spatial system *insofar as it constructs a global order based on its local elements*; that is, from the domains controlled by individuals. The two pathways are those of a system considered as a local-to-global phenomenon. But there will also be a global-to-local system, which exists over and above the domains of individuals, and which expresses itself in some system of boundaries and spaces which have a more collective or public nature. The men's hut in the Ndembu village, the earth shrines in the Tallensi landscape, and the kivas in the Hopi town, are all examples of such structures, as are the public buildings and churches of the more familiar urban landscape, or the 'totemic landscape' of the Australian Aborigines.[17]   Now the essence of the global-to-local system is that, in comparison with the local-to-global system, its logic is reversed. The external relations of buildings are used to construct an ideological or conceptual landscape, a space whose relation to description is one of representation, but *not* of control; while the interiors are used to define a domain in which descriptions *are* controlled. The former are, in the first instance, shrines; the latter, in the first instance, meeting places. In all the cases we have looked at, the distinction between local-to-global structures and global-to-local structures has been the means whereby differential solidarities are articulated and related to each other.

These two principles can be summarised in a more abstract version of the diagram drawn in the Introduction (see below) and

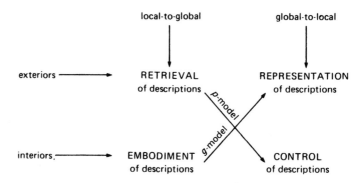

from this, a more general and comprehensive principle may be sketched: the more the system grows both spatially and transpatially, then the more the logic of the system will tend to run from global-to-local, rather than from local-to-global, and the more the logic of the system will follow the reversed form. The 'state' can be seen, in these arrangemental terms, as existing not when an ideological landscape is defined by conceptual relations between spatial groups, but when the control of descriptions, which under more primitive conditions ceases at the limits of the spatial group, is projected across the landscape and forms discrete spatial aggregates into a continuous political territory.

The more this is the case, that is, the more the global-to-local prevails over the local-to-global, then the more we can expect the landscape to be dominated by a system of ideologically related structures, and the more there will be interiors which exist to control transactions. Under these conditions, the distinction between exterior and interior space becomes the distinction between power and control: that is, between an abstractly defined set of power categories which prior to their projection into a unified symbolic landscape have no form of spatial integration; and systems of arrangements for the control and reproduction of social categories and their relations, realised in more and more specialised interiors.[18] The external space in the global-to-local logic is the space of structured and immutable categories, the opposite to what it is in the local-to-global logic; while the interior space is the space of personal negotiation and transaction, which will be negotiation of inequalities to the degree that the global-to-local system prevails in the system as a whole.

To say that space is a function of social solidarity is, then, perhaps a little too simple. Differential solidarities, whether in the form of classes or not, exist in all societies, and the two kinds of logic that the socio-spatial system possesses are the means by which these differences can be related, or come into conflict. They can even be the means by which one group achieves domination over another. But they can also be the means by which an equality of solidarities can be realised – an equality from which the logic of space today, with its preoccupation with an external landscape of representations and closed internal domains of control, is moving steadily away.

Postscript

SUMMARY

The theory, however, sketchy as it is, does permit an outline of a theory of contemporary space which is sketched here and related to basic differences in social formations in the advanced industrial countries. The principal aim of this argument, again, is not to establish a definitive account, but to provide a coherent model for linking together and making sense of the 'obvious' phenomena of contemporary space, phenomena which are normally given a simple functionalist or economic explanation. However, modern space is, it is argued, while different in kind, a further instance of the principle that spatial organisation in society is a function of differentiation principles of social solidarities in relation to one another, whether this is a complementary relation or, as now, a class relation.

The social logic of space today

It has been said that the art of mathematical proof lies in finding a framework within which what one wants to say becomes nearly obvious. The same might be said of theories. A good theory should render 'nearly obvious' interconnections between observable facts that had previously appeared puzzling or anomalous. What is puzzling about the situation today is why we should have undertaken such extensive revisions to urban and locality structures, when the effects of the new forms of spatial arrangement appear, at best, as no improvement and, at worst, as socially damaging. It is often said that changes in the urban surface were the result of the invention and spread of the motor car. This is untenable for one very simple reason: the morphological prototypes of the new urban surface were developed fifty years before the invention of the motor car, and by the time when the motor car was only beginning to penetrate the more affluent regions of society, the diffusion of the new prototypes was already under way. What is interesting about the motor car explanation is that it is yet another instance of our pervasive tendency to give technological and functional explanations for processes that are essentially sociological.

If we were able to take a bird's-eye view of recent physical changes in the urban surface with the principles of syntactic analysis in mind, then a number of pervasive themes would readily identify themselves. At the most general level, there appears to be a fundamental shift from a system that is continuous, through the operation of the everywhere ringy, open, and distributed street system, to one that is discontinuous, that is, divided into a number of relatively closed local domains. The essence of this change is encapsulated in a change in habitual terminology: a street is an open and distributed local event in a larger open and distributed system, whereas the generic term that has replaced it, the estate, refers to a discrete, probably closed local domain with some degree of segregation from surrounding estates. This linguistic shift records a basic alteration in the way in which our society thinks itself out in spatial terms, from an open, distributed concept, to one that is closed and nondistributed. The change is deeply ingrained: it is a concept we think *with* rather than a concept we think *of*.

Within this overall shift, however, we find a family of variations. In some cases we find a strong tendency to use physical boundaries as the segregating medium; in others, open space plays a similar function, by flowing all round the buildings rather than being constituted by them. Again, in some cases we find that these closed domains are relatively shallow and lacking internal hierarchy; in others, we find a marked tendency to hierarchical – that is asymmetric – development within the closed local domain. Why should our society produce such a pattern of similarities and differences? And why should comparable patterns of similarities and differences appear to exist both in the West and the East, and transcend social systems?

The first step might be to recognise that, in spite of the very fundamental differences that exist between the Western and Eastern social systems, nevertheless there is a certain common core to both types of society. Both systems might be bracketed together as 'industrial bureaucracies', in that both are strongly orientated towards increasing industrial production, and both support classes of non-productive workers whose responsibilities include both the organisation of production and the organisation of social reproduction. These two functions of the non-productive classes may be strongly integrated, as they are in the East, or appear to be segregated and in conflict as in the West, but in both cases the proportion of production that goes to the development and reproduction of the society passes through their hands.

The essence of the industrial bureaucratic system, however its variants originated and whatever its explicit social values, lies in two principal morphological features. First, there is a fundamental inequality in the system between those who have some kind of control over the forms of production and social reproduction, and those who do not. This creates the precondition for the formation of classes, since the different relations of groups to the basic social processes means that differential forms of solidarity are likely to come into existence, linking those in the same relation to the basic social processes and separating them from those in a dissimilar relation. Second, there is an expanding, state-sponsored apparatus of intervention in the social relations of the society, whose principal function is to mitigate or eliminate the worst effects of this inequality by redistributing a certain proportion of the productive surplus (the old 'ceremonial fund') to those who do not have access to it through the elementary structure of the system. In a literal sense, therefore, the orientation of the state interventionist apparatus towards the mitigation of the effects of inequality is in fact an intrinsic and necessary part of the means by which that inequality is institutionalised and perpetuated.

The central task of the interventionist apparatus is simple: to reproduce a viable social order, in spite of the fact that the orientation of the society as a whole to the increase of production is likely to rupture existing social bonds and undermine the forms of social reproduction that prevailed in the traditional antecedents of that society. How this social reproductive function can be carried out, however, varies a great deal. The Western version of industrial bureaucracy, which we call capitalism, is not a static system: its very stability is a dynamic one. It depends essentially on the appropriation of surplus in order to increase the rate of production, whether by improving technology or intensifying work, and thus arriving at a higher relative level of wealth. In the growth phases of capitalism, the goods produced themselves play a significant role in social reproduction, since an essential feature of the system is that goods of certain kinds acquire social meaning. To participate in the consumption of goods is to participate in society. It is not simply a distinction between use and exchange value: there is a distinction between the use value of goods and the value of goods in articulating the social relations and the status of the consumer concerned. It is this ascription of social signification to products that helps capitalism to generate its own stability, but only while it is able to increase the production of goods at a rate that ensures that sufficient numbers of people take part in the social game of consumption.

However, when growth slows down this tendency of the system of production to provide a naturally available means of social reproduction slows down with it. This generates a tug-of-war between the two aspects of the system. The system of production requires to maximise its share of the surplus in order to re-invest and restore the dynamic to the system, and thereby restore its stability; whereas the system of social reproduction, that is the state apparatus, requires a larger and larger share, in order to build an alternative basis of stability by an apparent redistribution of the surplus in favour of those most disadvantaged by the system. The conflict between the needs of the productive sector and those of the reproductive sector is one of the principal foundations of the spatial dialectics of Western society.

We may now come back to the same point by a slightly different route. In comparison with classic urban society, a major structural change in the productive sector effected by industrial bureaucracy is the separation of the worker from his tools. The tools, the physical means of production, move into the possession of capital, and in fact acquire a new name: fixed capital. A second mutation is implied by this. When the worker is a specialist who owns his tools he utilises this speciality to make relations with his fellow men that are essentially symmetric and distributed. The basic form of an instrumental division of labour is symmetric and distributed, in that inter-dependence guarantees that asymmetry and hierarchy have no productive basis for development. Relations between specialists are essentially lateral ones, and do not tend to the formation of asymmetric structures. Under capitalism the principle is changed. Workers do not make relationships with each other. Each individual makes a relation with a factory owner who employs him. These are vertical relations. The elaboration of this principle naturally and necessarily tends to be a system in which asymmetric and nondistributed relations are the syntactic principles of the system.

Now the asymmetrical nondistributed systems – think, for example, of a simple tree diagram as in Fig. 71 on p. 132 – have certain formal properties. First, there are no lateral connections at all in the system. At each level all relations between symmetric units exist only by virtue of the unit which controls both. Second, the system is extremely fragile. Removing any single relationship in the system partitions the whole system into at least two disconnected segments. Thus in any such system there is a threat of structural risk attached to each asymmetric relationship. But at the same time the integrity of the system depends on these asymmetric relationships. This is one basic reason why asymmetric nondistributed relationships tend to be reinforced with g-model apparatus: noninterchangeable statuses, insignia, hierarchical rules, and so on. These are a means of shoring-up the system against the natural tendency to fragment. By contrast a p-stable symmetrical and distributed system does not require such embellishments. Its relative stability against fragmentation is guaranteed by the size of the system, its openness to new additions, its number of linkages, and its tolerance of loss.

Now of course the entire logic of workers' movements is based on remedying this lack of symmetric and lateral relations in the system, since while the asymmetric nondistributed system remains, each is alone and each is powerless; but by establishing symmetric relations and acting corporately, the logic of the system is overthrown, and the control of the many below by the fewer above is re-established. However, the whole bias in the system of production, which after all creates the everyday reality in which we all live and which is therefore very hard to question, is against this development. It can only result, therefore, from the deliberate and artificial fostering of a solidarity consciousness that overcomes the divisive effects of the system. These mechanisms for solidarity consciousness are what we call trade unions.

However, although the social logic of the system naturally tends to reproduce itself in everyday life, there is a major paradox. The exigencies of production require not only the social separation of worker from worker, but also the spatial aggregation of those same workers. In terms of the model, this is already a danger to the system, since the dense spatial aggregation of people tends naturally to the p-model system in which symmetric and distributed relations predominate, and these threaten the syntactic principles of the system. They also threaten it politically. The system only works well if there is no large scale symmetric solidarity at the lower, and especially at the lowest, levels. Space is in this sense the paradox of capitalism. Fundamentally, this is why the nineteenth-century dreams of a social order, in which the benefits of capitalism are retained through the creation of a quisecent working class, are dreamed in a strongly spatial form. From the factory communities of Robert Owen and the phalansteries of Fourier, to the garden cities of Howard and the technological romances of Le Corbusier, the fundamental form of the dream is identical: the design of peaceful industrial production by the redesign of the spatial form of communities using a new urban genotype.

The dream has two principal forms, which we might call the hard and soft forms. The hard form, which is that arising from the system of production itself, simply aims to reproduce in space the essential syntax of relations of the social system: that is, to reproduce the social separation of workers from each other by the creation of forms of space that similarly separate at each level of hierarchical system. The hard form emphasises asymmetric and nondistributed syntaxes: by imposing a strong descriptive regime on the community, it can at the same time keep it large. It depends on the power of space to separate, and to physically prevent too high and dense a rate of p-model encounters, by using the 'no neighbours' principle. It is wrong to say that high-rise estates are unsuccessful. For their unmanifest purposes of community reduction they are extremely successful. Unfortunately for their creators, this 'success' does not include the stable reproduction of society.

The fundamental shift in the urban surface from symmetric distributed syntaxes to asymmetric nondistributed syntaxes is the physical manifestation of these principles. The classic form of the modern estate, with its outer boundary, open-space barriers, few entrances, separate blocks, and separate staircases, is the very paradigm of this solution. Its morphological origins still stand for all to see: the philanthropic housing of London from the 1840s onwards provides the master models for a spatial form which was, under the guise of a new technology, to sweep the world in the mid-twentieth century, becoming as universal a form of space as distributed street systems were in the previous society.

The essence of the hard solution is to impose strong descriptive physical control on the large aggregate, thus permitting it to remain large in the vicinity of production. The essence of the soft solution has the reverse principles: it works by meaning rather than by syntax, by building up an ideological order, or g-model in the small aggregate. The principle of this form of production requires formally that the basic group remains small, since the system is likely to be untenable with overlarge spatial aggregations. The two principles of this solution reflect these two aspects of g-model stability: the concept of the small community; and the concept of dispersion. Howard's garden cities are the paradigm ideological statement of the soft solution. He proposes nothing less than the disaggregation of cities, and their internal fragmentation into noninterchangeable zones, ordered by a strong exogenous model expressing a conception of social order. The softness of the solution is built up through the imagery of trees and other natural phenomena which, in the service of the social logic of space, can be brought to serve the cause of social stability. The surburban ideal, with its strong emphasis on forms of housing characteristic of immediately previous societies – the cottage in England, the ranch in America, the hacienda in Spain, and so on – and on the dwelling as a primarily *symbolic* entity, are essentially the same thing. The community is ideally small. It has few encounters. Those which occur are non-random and even strongly controlled. And everyday life is strongly conformist to g-models of behaviour, including spatial behaviours, like the maintenance of a certain type of order in the front garden, and a certain standard symbolic configuration within the household.

Behaviour in different regions of the industrial bureaucratic system corresponds more or less to the following simplified model: the more the system of production dominates over reproduction, as for example in France or Brazil, then the more the hard solution will dominate over the soft; the more the system of reproduction dominates over the system of production, as for example in England, then the more the soft solution will predominate over the hard. And when the productive and reproductive sectors of the system are fused together, as in the Soviet Union, then the more the policy of urban dispersion and the hard spatial solution are unified.

Both hard and soft solutions, however, share a common ideological base. The hard solution aggregates large numbers of individuals together, but it separates them strongly into smaller and smaller units by the use of nondistributed syntaxes. The soft solution disperses, more naturally yielding the small and separate community as its primary ideal. The ideological basis for both is the correspondence theory of social and spatial groups, in the guise of the 'ethologically' derived theory of human territoriality. But because the hard and soft solutions are different, in spite of their common foundations, the reformist debate in architecture and planning is always carried out within the confines of the correspondence theory. More social fragmentation, more spatial hierarchy, and more separation of groups is held to be the answer to the crisis created by those very policies. It is virtually impossible to argue in favour of urban communities as they in fact were: large, noncorresponding, encounter-rich and generating p-stability of a curiously pleasurable and durable kind, by a very open and very distributed urban spatial syntax.

It was argued in the Introduction that the essence of the man–environment paradigm, and the source of its conceptual closedness, lay in the fact that it constructed not one single intelligible position, but two apparently opposed positions, seemingly independent but in reality generated by the same underlying paradox. This is true also of space. The soft solution appears progressive because it has been tried less often, because it is the brainchild of the interventionist bureaucracy in its role of creating means for the reproduction of social relations, and **because it more obviously articulates the underlying ideals of** small, separated communities that the system of bureaucratic industrialism generated as its mirror image. But it is not more progressive. It divides, and orders more powerfully because it uses all the resources of space most effectively, not just the syntactic ones, as the hard solution does. Even so, it exists for the same purposes as the hard solution, and will ultimately fail in the same way, perhaps even sooner, since the hard solution at least generates dense concentrations of people with a community crisis which they may eventually begin to resolve by their own efforts. Nevertheless, if there is to be a society that is democratically deployed in space, then it will have to be on the basis of large not small communities, dense not sparse local encounter spaces, noncorresponding rather than corresponding social labels, and above all on the basis of an urban surface locally and globally open, distributed, and unhierarchical. To begin to build such a system – as we already are, in a series of faltering experiments – would not imply a return to the past: only that the laws relating society to its spatial forms are unchanging, and there is no other long-term pathway.

Notes

Preface

1 William H. Michelson, *Man and His Urban Environment: A Sociological Approach*, Addison-Wesley Publishing Company, Reading, Massachusetts, 1976 edition with revisions.

2 Claude Lévi-Strauss, *Structural Anthopology*, Basic Books, New York, 1963; Pierre Bourdieu, 'The Berber House', in Mary Douglas (ed.), *Rules and Meanings*, Penguin, Harmondsworth, Middlesex, 1973; Pierre Bourdieu, *Outline of a Theory of Practice*, Cambridge University Press, 1977; Anthony Giddens, *A Contemporary Critique of Historical Materialism*, vol. 1, 'Power, property and state', Macmillan Press, London and Basingstoke, 1981; Peter J. Ucko, Ruth Tringham and G. W. Dimbleby, *Man, Settlement and Urbanism*, Duckworth, London, 1972; David L. Clarke, *Spatial Archaeology*, Academic Press, London, 1977; Colin Renfrew, 'Space, time and polity', in J. Friedman and M. J. Rowlands (eds.), *The Evolution of Social Systems*, Duckworth, London, 1978; Ian Hodder, *The Spatial Organisation of Culture*, Duckworth, London, 1978.

3 Christopher Alexander, Sara Ishikawa and Murray Silverstein with Max Jacobson, Ingrid Fiksdahi-King and Shlomo Angel, *A Pattern Language*, Oxford University Press, New York, 1977.

4 Christopher Alexander, 'A city is not a tree', *Design Magazine*, no. 206, 1966, 46–55.

5 G. Stiny and J. Gips, *Algorithmic Aesthetics*, University of California Press, Berkeley, 1978.

6 J. H. von Thunen, *Von Thunen's Isolated State*, Pergamon, London, 1966 (edited by P. Hall from the original German edition of 1826); W. Christaller, *Central Places in Southern Germany*, Englewood Cliffs, New Jersey, 1966 (translated by C. W. Baskin from the original German edition of 1933); A. Lösch, *The Economics of Location*, New Haven, Connecticut, 1954.

Introduction

1 Labelle Prussin, *Architecture in Northern Ghana*, University of California Press, Berkeley, 1969.

2 Stuart Piggott, *Ancient Europe*, Edinburgh University Press, 1965.

3 Claude Lévi-Strauss, *Structural Anthropology*, vol. 1, Anchor Books, Garden City, New York, 1967, p. 285.

4 *Ibid.*, p. 285.

5 Oscar Newman, *Defensible Space*, Architectural Press, London, 1973.

6 Elman R. Service, *Primitive Social Organisation*, Random House, New York, 1962, pp. 62–4.

7 Stanford Anderson (ed.), *On Streets*, MIT Press, Cambridge, Massachusetts, 1978.

8 B. Hillier and A. Leaman, 'The man–environment paradigm and its paradoxes', *Architectural Design*, August 1973.

9 Babar Mumtaz, 'Villages on the Black Volta', in P. Oliver (ed.), *Shelter and Society*, Barrie and Rockcliffe, London, 1969.

10 Emile Durkheim, *The Division of Labour in Society*, The Free Press, New York, 1964; originally in French, 1893.

11 Basil Bernstein, *Codes, Modalities and the Process of Cultural Reproduction: a model*, Department of Education, University of Lund Pedagogical Bulletins, no. 7, 1980.

1. The problem of space

1 Hermann Weyl, *The Philosophy of Mathematics and Natural Science*, Atheneum Publishers, New York, 1949; originally published in German as part of 'Handbuch der Philosophie', R. Oldenburg, 1927.

2 G. W. von Leibnitz, in a letter to the Abbé Conti, 1715; given in Alexander Koyré, *Newtonian Studies*, Chapman and Hall, London, 1965, p. 144.

3 G. W. von Leibnitz, in *Nouveaux Essais*, 1703; given in Koyré, *Newtonian Studies*, p. 140.

4 Broadly speaking, these two positions correspond with the distinction between Weber's philosophical individualism and Durkheim's metaphoric organicism. A more extreme example of the former is to be found in the recent rise and fall of phenomenological sociology, together with its late offspring, ethnomethodology; while the latter is exemplified best, perhaps, not so much by a school of thought, so much as by the largely imaginary school of thought so fervently attacked by the phenomenologists – the positivists. Both schools of thought can, however, be traced back to the earliest social scientific formulations in Thomas Hobbes's organicism and John Locke's individualism – in both cases clearly related to a conservative or liberal political viewpoint. However, it is also possible to trace a line of sociological thought which, while not formulating a clear scientific answer to the problem of the discrete system, nevertheless avoids the philosophical traps of the two positions. Such a line might begin with Ibn Khaldun, go through Karl Marx and the Durkheim of the *Elementary Forms of the Religious Life* and the latter parts of *The Division of Labour in Society*, and end today with such theorists as Anthony Giddens, especially his recent *A Contemporary Critique of Historical Materialism*.

5 René Thom, *Structural Stability and Morphogenesis*; first English edition published by W. A. Benjamin Inc., Reading, Massachusetts, 1975, translated by D. Fowler, p. 319. Originally published in French in 1972.

6 This expression is borrowed from Claude Lévi-Strauss, *The Savage Mind*, Weidenfeld and Nicholson, London, 1966, p. 17. Originally published in French as *La Pensée Sauvage*, Plon, 1962. The notion is developed as part of a theory of design in Hillier, Musgrove and O'Sullivan, 'Knowledge and design', in H. M. Proshansky, W. H.

Ittleson and L. G. Rivlin (eds.), *Environmental Psychology*, Holt, Rinehart and Winston, New York, 2nd edition, 1972.

7 W. van O. Quine, 'Identity, ostention and hypostasis', in *From a Logical Point of View*, Harvard University Press, Cambridge, Massachusetts, 1953. This section owes a great deal to Professor Quine's views, although he may well object to our spatial interpretation of them.

8 As suggested, for example, Michael Arbib: 'Self reproducing automata; some implications for theoretical biology', in C. H. Waddington (ed.), *Towards a Theoretical Biology*, vol. 2, Essays, Edinburgh University Press, 1969.

9 This reversal of the relation between information and spatio-temporal events was originally suggested by Adrian Leaman (personal communication).

10 Emil Durkheim, *The Elementary Forms of the Religious Life*, George Allen and Unwin, London, 1915. Originally in French. See for example the excellent introduction.

11 D Michie, *On Machine Intelligence*, Edinburgh University Press, 1974, p. 117.

12 *Ibid.*, p. 141.

13 J. von Neuman, *The Computer and the Brain*, Yale University Press, New Haven, Connecticut, 1958, p. 82.

14 W. McCulloch, *Embodiments of Mind*, MIT Press, Cambridge, Massachusetts, 1965, p. 274.

15 March Kac and Stainislaw Ulam, *Mathematics and Logic*, Penguin, Harmondsworth, Middlesex, 1971, p. 193. Originally in *Encyclopaedia Britannica*, 1968.

16 Jean Piaget, *The Child's Conception of Space*, Routledge and Kegan Paul, London, 1956. Originally in French, 1948. See also S. E. T. Holloway, *An Introduction to the Child's Conception of Space*, Routledge and Kegan Paul, London, 1967.

17 Suzanne Langer, *Feeling and Form*, Routledge and Kegan Paul, London, 1953, p. 95.

18 Basil Bernstein, *Class, Codes and Control*, vol. 1: *Theoretical Studies: Towards a Sociology of Language*, Routledge and Kegan Paul, London, 1971, p. 128.

2. The logic of space

1 Douglas Fraser, *Village Planning in the Primitive World*, Brazillier, New York, 1968.

2 This type of process raises a number of interesting theoretical issues. First and foremost it introduces an extra dimension into questions about the 'causes' of settlement forms. Normally these questions are answered in terms of historical, economic, and social factors, but in this case it is clear that something akin to an internally lawful process of morphological development plays a more important part. In a pure sense, the 'cause' of the beady ring genotype lies in the laws of spatial combination, irrespective of any particular historical events or social process that may have given rise to it. On the other hand, had not a historical or social process given rise to the process, then equally clearly the form would not exist. The matter is confused further by the fact that it is easy to conceive of different social processes that could activate the same process of morphological development, in this case

for example, different patterns of kinship or inheritance could equally well activate the beady ring development.

The proper solution to this might be to make a clear distinction between the lawfulness of the morphological process and the contingent external historical and social factors. The internal morphological rule might be called the 'formal independent variable'; and the external social agency which constructs the rule in this particular instance the 'cause', following the normal usage of the term. This implies a research strategy: when faced with the problem of explaining a settlement form one would always be looking in two directions, not one – at the lawful *internal* process of spatial combination which accounts for the morphology in a formal sense; and at the particular social and ecological circumstances which gave rise to the process.

Another issue of theoretical interest lies in the implication for the study of evolutionary processes. Normally when studying evolution one would be studying the real historical development of a single settlement, or a group of settlements over a protracted time period. Very few such studies have been done, for the simple reason that reliable evolutionary data on settlement forms is exceedingly hard to come by. In the process described, a different possibility has emerged by implication: that of using synchronous sets of data as a kind of evolutionary sample. The procedure appears reasonable, given that there is in some region a more or less well-ordered process of settlement growth of some kind. Where growth appears to be well ordered, it seems reasonable to try the possibility that a sample of settlements of different sizes existing contemporaneously can be used as though they represented various stages of evolution of the same genetic pathway. Where this proved unfruitful it would be reasonable to argue that no single rule-given process prevailed in the area.

3 The argument about basic generators is conducted in two dimensions because, perhaps contrary to appearances, human spatial organisation is not three-dimensional in the same sense that it is two-dimensional – for the simple reason that human beings do not fly and buildings do not float in the air. Human space is in fact full of strategies – stairs, lifts, etc. – to reduce three-dimensional structures to the two dimensions in which human beings move and order space. This is not to say that the third dimension is unimportant; only that it is not comparable with the two-dimensional structure. Buildings of more than one storey are two-dimensional structures laid one on top of the other and connected in a two-dimensional way. Human spatial organisation is, in effect, rooted in two dimensions and elaborated in three. The fundamental structuring mechanisms of the 'social logic' of space are, however, best represented in two dimensions.

4 Even so, the fact that they can be written will in due course appear as a property of considerable importance.

3. The analysis of settlement layouts

1 W. Elsasser, 'The role of individuality in biological theory', in C. H. Waddington (ed.) *Towards a Theoretical Biology*, vol. 3. Drafts, Edinburgh University Press, 1970.

2 J. McCluskey, *Road Form and Townscape*, Architectural Press, London, 1979.

3 Similarly, geographical approaches to the analysis of space, H. Carter 'The Geographical Approach', in M. W. Barley (ed.), *The Plans and Topography of Mediaeval Towns in England and Wales*, CBA Research Report no. 14, 1976; M. R. G. Conzen, *Alnwick, Northumberland, a study in town plan analysis*; Institute of British Geographers, 27, 1960; M. T. Krüger, 'An Approach to Built-form Connectivity at the Urban Scale', *Environment and Planning B*, 6, No. 1 1979, pp. 67–88, fail in principle to deal with this problem of the continuity of the open space of settlement systems.

4 Although only a limited number of cases will be referred to here, it should be stressed that this methodology of analysis is by no means untested. On the contrary, it has been used over several years by M.Sc. students at the Bartlett School of Architecture and Planning to explore a wide variety of settlement forms from all parts of the world. These studies will be the subject of a further volume, but represent a substantial background, against which the cases presented here are set.

5 Lévi-Strauss, *Structural Anthropology*, 1963.

6 All mathematical formulae are original, as far as we know, with the exception of the formula for ringiness which is well known.

7 Note that 'trivial rings', i.e. rings which simply result from axial lines intersecting in the open space, should not be counted.

8 These routes constitute what we call the local supergrid, i.e. the ring of axial lines with E values greater than 1 – or whatever is specified for a 'higher control' supergrid.

9 O. Newman, *Defensible Space*.

10 O. Newman, *Community of Interest*, Anchor and Doubleday, New York, 1980.

11 C. Alexander et al., *A Pattern Language*.

12 Newman, *Defensible Space*, p. 6.

13 C. Turnbull, *The Mountain People*, Jonathan Cape, London, 1973.

14 J. Jacobs, *The Death and Life of Great American Cities*, Penguin, Harmondsworth, Middlesex, 1961.

4. Buildings and their genotypes

1 See for example O. Newman, *Defensible Space*; C. Alexander, et al., *A Pattern Language*. The most common form in which these ideas appear, however, is as assumptions, as for example in: HMSO, *Housing the Family*, MTP Construction, Lancaster, 1974.

2 J. Burnett, *A Social History of Housing*, David & Charles, 1978, pp. 169 and 194.

3 D. Chapman, *The Home and Social Status*, Routledge and Kegan Paul, London, 1955, pp. 112–13.

4 Bernstein, 'Social class, language and socialisation', in *Class, Codes and Control*, pp. 184–5.

5 J. Walton, *African Villages*, van Shaik, Pretoria, 1956.

6 R. S. Rattray, *Ashanti Law and Constitution*, Oxford University Press, 1929, p. 56.

5. The elementary building and its transformation

1 T. Faegre, *Tents: architecture of the nomads*, Anchor Books, Garden City, New York, 1979, p. 24.

2 *Ibid.*, p. 92.

3 Ibid., p. 70.
4 Ibid., p. 92.
5 V. Turner, The Ritual Process, Routledge and Kegan Paul, London, 1969, p. 96.
6 J. D. Thompson and G. Goldin, The Hospital: a Social and Architectural History, Yale University Press, New Haven, Connecticut, 1975, p. 7.
7 H. Jamous and B. Peloille, 'Changes in the French University–Hospital System', in J. A. Jackson (ed.), Professions and Professionalization, Cambridge University Press, 1970.
8 Bernstein, Codes, Modalities and the Process of Cultural Reproduction: a model.

6. The spatial logic of 'arrangements'

1 See for example R. Thom, 'Structuralism and biology' in C. Waddington (ed.), Towards a Theoretical Biology, vol. 4, Essays, Edinburgh University Press, 1972, pp. 68–82.
2 L. Morgan, Ancient Society, London, 1870; pp. 13–14 in 1977 edition from Harvard University Press, Reading, Massachusetts.
3 Lévi-Strauss, 'Social structure' in Structural Anthropology, 1967, pp. 269–319, especially p. 275–6.
4 For a parallel critique, but with a different answer, see Bourdieu, Outline of a Theory of Practice.
5 B. Malinowski, The Sexual Life of Savages in Northwestern Melanesia, Routledge and Kegan Paul, London, 1929.
6 Durkheim, The Division of Labour in Society, chaps. 2 and 3.

7. The spatial logic of encounters: a computer-aided thought experiment

1 Service, Primitive Social Organisation, pp. 62–4.
2 E. Wolf, Peasants, Prentice Hall, Englewood Cliffs, New Jersey, 1966, p. 7.

8. Societies as spatial systems

1 M. Fortes, The Dynamics of Clanship amongst the Tallensi, Oxford University Press, 1945.
2 M. Fortes, The Web of Kinship among the Tallensi, Oxford University Press, 1959.
3 V. Turner, Schism and Continuity in an African Society, Manchester University Press, 1957.
4 Fortes, Dynamics of Clanship, p. 31.
5 Ibid.
6 Turner, Schism and Continuity, p. xxiii.
7 Ibid., p. 289.
8 Ibid., p. 176.
9 Ibid., p. 330.
10 V. Mindeleff, A Study of Pueblo Architecture: Tusayan and Cibola, Smithsonian Institute, Bureau of American Ethnology, 8th Annual Report, 1891.
11 P. Willmott and M. Young, Family and Kinship in East London, Routledge and Kegan Paul, 1957; also Penguin, Harmondsworth, Middlesex, 1962; especially chaps. 2 and 3, pp. 31–61; and chap. 7, pp. 104–17.

12 C. Nakane, *Japanese Society*, Weidenfeld and Nicholson, London, 1970; also Penguin, Harmondsworth, Middlesex, 1973, p. 1.
13 *Ibid.*, pp. 25–6.
14 *Ibid.*, p. 31.
15 *Ibid.*, p. 65.
16 *Ibid.*, p. 5.
17 T. G. H. Strehlow, 'Geography and the Totemic landscape in Central Australia: a functional study', in R. M. Berndt (ed.), *Australian Aborginal Anthropology*, Australian Institute of Aboriginal Studies, Canberra, 1970.
18 Bernstein, *Codes, Modalities and the Process of Cultural Reproduction: a model*.

Index